Contracting Masculinity:

Gender, Class, and Race in
a White-Collar Union, 1944–1994

Gillian Creese

OXFORD

UNIVERSITY PRESS

OXFORD
UNIVERSITY PRESS

70 Wynford Drive, Don Mills, Ontario M3C 1J9
http://www.oupcan.com

Oxford   New York
Athens   Auckland   Bangkok   Bogotá   Buenos Aires   Calcutta
Cape Town   Chennai   Dar es Salaam   Delhi   Florence   Hong Kong
Istanbul   Karachi   Kuala Lumpur   Madrid   Melbourne   Mexico City
Mumbai   Nairobi   Paris   São Paulo   Singapore   Taipei   Tokyo
Toronto   Warsaw

and associated companies in
Berlin   Ibadan

Oxford is a trademark of Oxford University Press

Canadian Cataloguing in Publication Data

Creese, Gillian Laura, 1955–
Contracting masculinity : gender, class, and race in a white-collar union,
1944–1994

(The Canadian social history series)
Includes bibliographical references and index.
ISBN 0–19–541454–3

1. Office and Professional Employees International Union. Local 378
(B.C. Hydro).   2. B.C. Hydro — Officials and employees.
3. Trade unions — White collar workers — British Columbia — Case studies.
4. Discrimination in employment — British Columbia — Case studies.
I. Title.   II. Series.

HD6528.M392O33 1999   331.88'041'09711   C98–933029–X

Contents

Acknowledgements

The support of many people made this book possible. First and fore-most, I wish to thank the members of the Office and Professional Employees' International Union (OPEIU) Local 378, past and present, who shared their views and insights about their activities. I am indebted to Paula Stromberg, Local 378's communications officer, who has been a source of support and encouragement throughout this project. I owe a very special thanks to the president of the local, Ron Tuckwood, without whose support this research would have remained with the union's first 35 years. The union's archives up to 1979 are publicly accessible through the Special Collections at the University of British Columbia, and this material formed the basis of my original research project. Without the generous access I was given to search freely through contemporary union materials, much of this research would have been impossible. Although he has often disagreed with the questions I chose to ask, and sometimes with my interpretation of specific events around sensitive political issues, Ron Tuckwood has continued to support union participation in this research, for which I will always be grateful. I would also like to thank the many union staff who made research at the union office much easier. Over several years and a number of different office filing systems, staff patiently explained the intricacies of the latest system and suggested strategies to track down missing files. Union staff also provided unlimited access to photocopiers and acted as troubleshooters with sometimes temperamental office machines.

Although this study does not attempt to document fully negotiations from the company's point of view—relying primarily on union archives and records that include many company documents—I am

grateful to BC Hydro for providing information about its successive
job evaluation systems and the distribution of employees in the early
1990s. Thanks are also extended to managers and former managers
who agreed to be interviewed.

This research would not have been possible without generous funding from the Social Sciences and Humanities Research Council of
Canada. I received an SSHRC Strategic Research Grant (882–91–006)
for Women and Work for the years 1991–4 to conduct archival
research and interviews, and an SSHRC Research Grant (410–94–0673)
for the period 1994–7, which allowed me to complete the contemporary research and write a general history for the union. Thanks also to
the Centre for Research in Women's Studies and Gender Relations,
which provided me with a term as a UBC Centre Scholar in 1996. During this term I finally found time to begin to write the present work.
The Centre has long provided me, and many others at UBC, with a
supportive community that fosters friendship, collegiality, and
scholarly exchange and I greatly enjoyed my time there. I would also
like to thank the University of British Columbia for awarding me the
Izaak Walton Killam Memorial Faculty Research Fellowship that
allowed me to take a sabbatical without economic hardship, and
thereby find the time to complete this book.

I would like to thank all the graduate students who worked as
research assistants on various stages of this project. For their consci-
entious attention to detail, I thank Francis Adu-Febiri, Anna
Ambrosini, Fiona Angus, Sousan Arafeh, Dawn Farough, Loraine
Littlefield, and Sativa Quinn. Special thanks to Uli Rauch, who
helped to organize a more chronological and thematic history that
was first written for the OPEIU and revised here as Chapter 2. I would
also like to thank the staff at the UBC Library Special Collections for
their help in negotiating the union's archives, and in particular the
help of the Labour Manuscripts Curator, George Brandak.

I am indebted to Greg Kealey, General Editor of the Canadian
Social History Series. Greg provided ongoing moral support and
encouragement, as well as critical insights that helped me to improve
the manuscript. I would like to thank the external reviewer for
Oxford, whose careful review and useful comments helped me to
strengthen the final text. And I am grateful to Ric Kitowski and
Phyllis Wilson at Oxford University Press for their help in getting this
book into press. I would also like to thank Richard Tallman for his
skilful copy-editing.

Parts of this book, in earlier and preliminary form, have appeared
in journal articles. These include 'Power and Pay: The Union and

Equal Pay at B.C. Electric/Hydro', *Labour/Le Travail* 32 (Fall 1993): 225–45; 'Gender Equity or Masculine Privilege? Union Strategies and Economic Restructuring in a White Collar Union', *Canadian Journal of Sociology* 20, 2 (1995): 143–66; and 'Gendering Collective Bargaining: From Men's Rights to Women's Issues', *Canadian Review of Sociology and Anthropology* 33, 4 (1996): 437–56.

I am grateful to friends and colleagues who shared discussions about this research over the years: Fiona Angus, Sousan Arafeh, Don Black, Jane Gaskell, Melody Hessing, Uli Rauch, Becki Ross, and Nikki Strong-Boag. With Nikki, Jo Hinchliffe, Kristin Schopp, and the visiting Centre Scholars, I have also shared a great deal of laughter, and much tea and chocolate, that sustained and nurtured me during my years as the chair of the Women's Studies Program and beyond. Rosemary Pringle also offered her support for this project, and I would like to thank her and the other members of the Australian Institute for Women's Research and Policy and the Centre for Research on Employment and Work at Griffith University for arranging to provide what would no doubt have been a rewarding research environment if fate had not intervened and forced me to cancel plans for an extended visit to Brisbane.

As always, my greatest appreciation is to my partner, Don Black, who shared unpublished research on engineers at BC Hydro, and who took time out from his own busy schedule to provide valuable comments on the first draft of this manuscript. Don has put up with many long hours preoccupied with this project, and has always shown the greatest support for everything I do. Thanks for being there.

Finally, I would like to thank my parents, Ernest and Edna Creese, to whom this book is dedicated. It was from my parents that I first learned to appreciate the struggles for equality and social justice waged by working men and women, and with whose support I dared to pursue my own dreams.

Introduction:

Gender, Race, and Clerical Work

Anyone who has ever worked in an office can attest to the high degree of gender segregation in most office environments. The first job I had after graduating from high school in the early 1970s was as an accounts payable clerk in a large heavy equipment company. I was surrounded by hundreds of other women, at that time mostly young women like myself; some of the women I worked with remained in the same company more than two decades later. We worked in a huge open space, with desks arranged by departments, and separated by rows of filing cabinets and open corridors for walking through the office. Around the walls of the office were rows of private offices, each of which housed a manager. All the managers were men; all but one were White men. A few departments in the office, like purchasing and the mailroom, were largely male, but these were few in number. The office was a feminine environment. Office workers were physically segregated from other types of workers in the company; we were located 'upstairs'. Hundreds of men worked 'downstairs'; these were the warehouse *men*, the machinists, and the sales*men*, and we knew little of what they did.

My partner worked downstairs in the warehouse. He earned more than twice what I did and, unlike the office staff, belonged to a union. I was particularly envious of his union status. Coming from a union family, I understood well that union environments were better paid than non-union environments and provide some protection from managerial whims. I had not yet understood that my partner earned twice my wage largely because he was male, or that a gendered work and wage gap would remain within a unionized environment. Indeed, I did not question how it came to pass that the men's jobs downstairs were unionized while women's jobs upstairs were not. Nor did I appreciate that our racialized White identities played any role in our suitability for clerical and warehouse work, respectively, in what was considered a 'good company' with stable employment. I can only recall two women of colour[1] in the office over a four-year period, a fact that did not seem strange to me at the time. Looking back, of course, the normalization of this racialized-gendered office environment, replicated in companies across North America, requires explanation.

The experience of other office workers may vary somewhat from my own, and certainly the last two decades have brought improvements in job prospects for women and workers of colour, but the following questions still arise: How do some jobs get constructed as male and others as female? How is this process of gendering also racialized, so that women and men of different race and ethnicity are differentially privileged at work? And most important for this study, what is the role of workers and their trade unions in a process that is often seen as the outcome solely of management decisions? This book addresses these questions through a study of the activities of unionized office workers at BC Hydro, focusing on how women and men *actively participate* in structuring the office in which they work and on how these practices help to generate *systemic* structures of power and privilege that shape later patterns of resistance.

If it is true that we do not make the social world just as we please, it is equally true that we do not take it just as we find it. Social life is actively constituted through negotiation, resistance, and accommodation, with experiences mediated through historically situated cultural forms of understanding. Economic institutions are only one site where such negotiations occur, and trade unions one form embodying workplace resistance and accommodation. Yet workplaces remain important sites of negotiation in societies dominated by a capitalist market economy. As collective forms of organized contestation, unions tend to present one-dimensional self-images that tell a binary tale of class-based opposition and solidarity. The complex multivocal nature of working-class experiences is obscured by this characterization of solidarity. On the contrary, class relations never exist in isolation from other determinants of power and privilege. The dichotomies suggested between work/home, public/private, and economy/civil society mask the seamless interconnections in individual lives and the gendered nature of these analytic distinctions. Individual experiences are shaped by complex interconnections among class, gender, race, ethnicity, sexuality, and so on. As others have pointed out, class experiences are gendered and racialized in ways that are often contradictory, and they are never fixed or static.[2]

Gender and race are both socially constructed, not innate or primordial human essences. As we negotiate the social world we construct gender out of physical differences linked to reproduction. In this sense we 'do gender' everywhere, all the time, including within the workplace, a culturally defined accomplishment as much as a set of relations of power that systematically privileges men over women.[3] Race, too, is constructed through ideology, practice, and power, differentiating the 'other' from the self marked through cultural or physical characteristics in a process of racialization.[4] In the North American context racialization is bound up with the history of European colonization, slavery, and the subsequent politics of immigration. All subjects are racialized but those identified as White, a historically contextual and changing term,[5] are often treated as normative and 'un-raced' rather than simply as dominant.[6] Though analytically separable, in practice class, gender, and race interact in complex and diverse ways.

In light of the contingent nature of historical processes, careful attention should be paid to time and place when we consider how relations of class, gender, and race are played out in different sites.[7] This study provides a contextual analysis of workers' negotiating conditions in one workplace, highlighting their role in negotiating racialized-gendered relations in the five decades since World War II.[8] The main focus is on processes of gendering practised by office workers; the term 'racialized gendering' is used to underline that gendering is simultaneously racialized. As the cultural, social, and economic milieu changed during the time period of this study (1944–94) and union membership in the office grew from 1,200 to nearly 3,000, so, too, did union members change their practices of gendering. In important ways, however, past practices shaped later possibilities in ways that union members, without a sense of their own history, were most often unaware.

In most respects the office environment in this study, a public-sector utility company of several thousand employees located in western Canada, is not unlike other offices. Women's jobs and men's jobs in the office were very clearly segregated in the past and remain largely segregated today. Office workers were entirely White in the past and remain disproportionately White at the higher levels. Management positions, while employing more women than even a few years ago, including one high-profile woman of colour,[9] remain a White male enclave, as do most company jobs outside of the office. In particular, a large number of trades*men* are employed in the same company and organized in a separate blue-collar union. The company is generally considered a 'good employer', until recently offering its employees secure employment and, as a unionized environment, better wages and benefits than many other large companies.

The office workers at the centre of this study are probably not unlike other North American office workers in most respects. Yet they are exceptional for forming a union in 1944, at a time when few white-collar workers were organized. In the North American context the unionization of white-collar work was limited until public-sector workers began to organize across Canada and the United States in the 1960s and 1970s. These office workers are also somewhat atypical in terms of gender composition. Throughout the last half-century the union local was more or less half male and half female. The union negotiated a single contract, readily allowing members to compare the situations of men and women and facilitating an early conscious-ness of gender inequality. Union organizing in Canada occurs in a system of closed-shop unions where, after a majority vote by prospective members, a union is certified by the Labour Relations Board to represent everyone within its jurisdiction. In this closed-shop context, the office union challenged and reproduced gendered practices *as part and parcel of bargaining working conditions and rates of pay* for everyone in the office.

As a pioneering white-collar union, then, it has arguably been more sensitive to gender issues in the workplace than have blue-collar unions with typically few female members. Still, distinctions between men's and women's jobs were actively structured by the union, particularly in the decades immediately following World War II. In turn, practices that privileged men in the early postwar years became part of unquestioned union traditions; the taken-for-granted normalized parts of union and workplace culture reproduced masculine privilege even in the 1990s when equity policies were actively pursued. In a postwar culture in which North American workers shared middle-class suburban dreams, union strategies focused on attempts to win breadwinner wages capable of fulfilling such dreams. In postwar Canada, moreover, breadwinners were clearly presumed to be White men. Once established within work-place structures and union traditions, White masculine privilege con-tinued to shape union politics in the office long after any explicit notion of breadwinner rights had been discarded.

Though time and place are critical for exploring the negotiation of racialized-gender relations in the office, this study provides more than insight into the history of one workplace; it provides a basis for better understanding the processes of racialized gendering. For all the attention to the historical details of this case study, then, another purpose is to provide an empirical basis for theorizing about racialized gendering as a social process. A gender-balanced union membership over half a century makes this study unusual because this workplace is neither predominantly feminized or masculinized, nor undergoing re-gendering from one to the other, contexts that form the basis for most contemporary studies of gendering.[10] Tracing how racialized-gendered hierarchies became part of institutional structures, this study illustrates how *inequality became systemic*. Embedded in social relations in ways most participants remained completely unaware of, this inequality did not depend on the beliefs or motives of individual workers or union leaders and, indeed, at times occurred in spite of commitments to equity.

Contracting Masculinity is written with attention to both historical locality and more general processes at work. My intent is to focus less on the individuals and more on the processes of racialized gendering at work.[11] Both the union and the company changed their names during the period of this study. The company began as the British Columbia Electric Railway Company in 1897; it was 'nationalized' by the provincial government and became the core of the British Columbia Hydro and Power Authority in the 1960s. The office union began existence as the Office Employees' Association, affiliating with the Office and Professional Employees' International Union, as Local 378, in the 1950s. The union adopted the name Office Employees' International Union in 1960, and the Office and Technical Employees' Union (OTEU) in 1964. In 1996 the local adopted the same name as its international affiliate, the Office and Professional Employees' International Union.

The chapters that follow explore the origins, continuity, change, and challenges to masculine privilege within the office. Chapter 1 begins with the current situation for women and men in the office. The job segregation, mobility patterns, career paths, and wage structures in the 1990s are placed in the context of general patterns in the labour force and theoretical explanations for how we 'do gender'. Particular attention is paid to how masculinity is enacted at work. The current job hierarchy at the office raises the following questions: how did this come about, and what role did the union play in constructing this hierarchy of work? The rest of the book is concerned with answering these questions.

Chapter 2 provides a historical overview of the origins of Local 378, which began as an association of office employees in the early 1920s, and its accomplishments over its first 50 years of existence (1944–94). The remaining chapters then peel back some of the more opaque layers of the union's history to explore how union practices, traditions, and bargaining agendas were shaped by broader power relations of gender and racialization.

Chapter 3 examines the creation of masculinist culture and practices after World War II and the role of the union in establishing the boundaries between men's work/breadwinner wages and jobs appropriate for women. At the same time, the creation by management of a 'female differential' (a 20 per cent wage gap between equivalent male and female job scales) was an object of union resistance for more than three decades, beginning in 1949. This struggle points to the contradictory processes of gendering, whereby gender inequality can be resisted and reinforced at the same time. Racialized hiring practices that only considered White women and men eligible office employees were embraced by union and management in the postwar decades.

Chapter 4 looks at the construction of masculinity and femininity in the office as women began to adopt more sustained commitments to the labour force in the 1950s and 1960s. During this time some office work was redefined as more technical and masculine than other clerical work, and some men's work came to be excluded from the office job evaluation system as 'non-office' work. Bargaining was enmeshed in conflicts over working-class masculinity, competition with blue-collar workers at the company, and aspirations towards professional middle-class status. At the same time, the language of gender and racial neutrality displaced references to the rights of breadwinners. The shift to neutral language helped to make ongoing processes of racialized-gendering invisible, while technical and clerical streams of office work maintained White men's access to higher positions.

Chapter 5 considers the politicization of gender issues in the 1980s, beginning with the organization of the Women's Committee in the late 1970s. The role of the Women's Committee in re-gendering union issues, the climate for women in the union, and the achievements and limitations of feminizing union leadership are seen in the context of explicit challenges to masculinist union culture. In this process, 'women's issues' came to be seen as the only issues with gender-specific consequences, leaving much of male privilege undisturbed.

Chapter 6 examines change during a climate of economic restructuring in the 1980s and 1990s. Union policies tended to become more protectionist as corporate policies more aggressively constructed a flexible workplace. The union reasserted White male dominance in the office through its emphasis on seniority rights, resistance to employment equity policies, and the limitations of its pay equity initiatives.

These trends illustrate the legacy of racialized-gender hierarchies and the contradictory character of equity struggles in the union today.

Chapter 7 endeavours to draw out what we might learn about racialized-gendering processes and to provide some direction for rethinking union practices that might challenge these workplace hierarchies while still resisting corporate movements towards greater job insecurity. In the context of declining union membership in recent years, more inclusive union strategies are essential for unions to remain effective in the next century. Feminist unionism has much to contribute to this process of redefining concepts of equality, solidarity, and democracy within the labour movement.

Finally, an appendix on methodology is included for those who are interested in a detailed discussion of research methods and sources. This study is based on analysis of the union's archives (1944–78), current union records (1979–94), and interviews with union activists and leaders, non-activist members, business representatives, and company managers.

This study of the production, reproduction, and transformation of systemic inequities embedded in the organization of work and collective bargaining is not intended to be an exposé of forms of union discrimination—as the reader has no doubt recognized, the author is sympathetic to unions and to the progressive role unions continue to play in Canada. Moreover, there is no desire to downplay the considerable accomplishments that Local 378 of the OPEIU has achieved over the last 50 years. In *Contracting Masculinity*, however, my aim is to understand how class, gender, and race are negotiated as part of bargaining conditions of work. To do so requires unpacking the multiple and contradictory ways in which privilege or lack of privilege are differentially produced, reproduced, and challenged, often at the same time. This study contributes to our understanding of how trade unions play an active role in structuring racialized, masculine privilege in the workplace, in the spirit of developing alternative strategies that may more successfully challenge ongoing inequities.

1

Who Gets Ahead at the Office?

Men usually start where women finish. Women finish at
about Group 7 after 25 or 30 years. Men start there.[1]

Ordinary Men: Climbing the Office Ladder

John worked in a large public-sector utility company in western
Canada for more than 35 years. When he first started with British
Columbia Electric in 1952 it was privately owned. In the early 1960s
it was nationalized by the provincial government and expanded
province-wide to become British Columbia Hydro and Power
Authority. John's career was fairly typical of men in the fifties and
sixties. His first job was as a meter reader, the most common entry-
level job for men. As a meter reader John was a member of the
Office Employees' Association (later renamed the Office and Professional Employees' International Union, OPEIU Local 378). His was
one of a number of union jobs classified as 'non-office' jobs, a designation that usually coincided with outside work and with higher
pay than office jobs warranted. Meter reading was paid at a Group
4/5 salary level, a mid-level salary in a 12-group classification
system. For men, and all meter readers were men, it was a stepping-
stone to other jobs as they worked their way up one of the various
hierarchies into more technical positions. In John's case, after a few
years he moved to the sales division and ultimately became a
marketing sales representative (Group 10), a senior union job from
which he retired in the late 1980s. His career was entirely based on
training he received on the job, as was typical for most men of
his generation.

8

Michael started with the company not long after John, in 1955. Like John, Michael applied to become a meter reader, but at the interview he was asked whether he would like to go into data processing in the newly emerging computer division. Michael had no experience with computers but he had scored well on a general aptitude test. He accepted what he described as 'a very junior job' in computing, a Group 5 position. Two years later he moved into the accounting department and worked his way up to become a work leader in the pay department (Group 12), where he stayed until 1975. In 1975 Michael was promoted to management, his background on the union bargaining committee considered an asset for a new manager in the field of labour relations. Michael took CGA (chartered general accounting) courses at night school in the 1960s as he moved up the job ladder. But in the end he believes this training had little to do with his promotion to management; experience and fairness in contract negotiations were more important.

John's career was more typical than Michael's since most men could expect to move into jobs in Groups 9 to 12 but few were promoted to management. In this company virtually all managers were recruited from the ranks of the professional engineers, not from among office workers. These mobility patterns did not change much until fairly recently. Men hired in the 1960s and 1970s, while the company was expanding, could still expect this systematic rise up the office career ladder, and most still began in non-office jobs, though not always as meter readers.

Robert was hired in 1966 in construction, a temporary job digging holes and driving a truck. His first job was not in the office union but under the company's rival blue-collar union, the International Brotherhood of Electrical Workers. His next job as a production clerk (Group 5) made him a regular employee and a member of the Office and Technical Employees' Union (later OPEIU Local 378). Over the next decade or so Robert moved from town to town throughout the province as he climbed the career ladder to become a service planner (Group 11), one of the 'premium jobs' in the office. Robert had no formal training, learning the technical skills required on the job.

Like Robert, Martin also began in construction, hired as an instrument layout man (Group 4/5) in 1969, a non-office job that was part of the office union. He moved into the office as a civil inspector and received on-the-job training to become a designer and then a service planner (Group 10). Peter started in another non-office union job in 1969 as a cashier emptying fare boxes (Group 3/4) and moved up the ranks to become a planning technologist (Group 10). Training for this 'specialized technical work' was also on the job, though he did take some night school computer courses to learn software applications.

Like most of their male colleagues, John, Robert, Martin, and Peter were married and raising children during their journeys up the office career ladder, relocating their families as promotions required.[2] However, they all agree that although they learned their skills on the job, anyone applying for these jobs in the 1990s would have to have a technology degree even to be considered.

All of these men illustrate features common to male career paths at the utility company. The bulk of current male employees were hired in the 1960s and 1970s. Massive lay-offs in the mid-1980s wiped out more than one in four office workers, including most of those recently hired. Subsequent downsizing and restructuring restricted new hiring, stalled the career mobility of others, and coincided with demands for ever-increasing educational credentials. Career prospects for men in the office have therefore contracted during the last decade, and men can no longer automatically expect promotions. Still, a sense of men's entitlement to a steady stream of upward promotions lingers. In contrast to men, career mobility for women became possible for the first time in the mid-1970s. As we shall see, however, for women such opportunities are still rare.

Exceptional Women and Pink-Collar Ghettos

June was hired in 1966 in a Group 1 clerical position in accounts payable. Over the next seven years she was promoted to a Group 2, a Group 3, and then three different jobs at a Group 4, all in the same department. By 1973 June wanted badly to get out of accounts pay-able since there were no more promotion opportunities available. A single woman, June sought a challenging career. She began to take night courses towards a CGA degree at the technical institute and already had completed a year's courses. So June applied for a Group 6 job in cash accounting that required an accounting background. Overlooked in favour of someone with lower qualifications, she filed a union grievance and won.[3] She recalls many people were unhappy with her winning that Group 6 position, an 'entry-level job for men', because they feared her presence would block up the career ladder. June continued to take CGA courses and moved her way up the ranks to a Group 8 in plant accounting. It took another union grievance in 1980 to get beyond Group 8, filed over a Group 10 accounting posi-tion in the budget department. By this time she had finished three and a half years towards her CGA degree and had 14 years' seniority, but the job went to a man with much less seniority. Again, she grieved through the union and won the position. The original incumbent was promoted to a Group 11 job, freeing the Group 10 for June to reapply. In 1981 she was promoted to a Group 11 in the same department. Not unlike Michael, June believes that many of the CGA requirements are not necessary to do the work she does, but they are important to get into the competition.

June's unusual work history was affected by a number of factors beyond her obvious talents. These included her determination to get out of a female job ghetto by taking night school courses, her willingness to assert her rights through the union, her status as a single woman without children, and, not least of all, fortuitous timing. The company was still expanding in the 1970s and management was just beginning to accept the idea of promoting exceptional women.

Karen's experience was similar to June's. She was hired in 1969 as a Group 2 file clerk in cost accounting. She already had two years of university training but it 'counted for nothing' because it was not considered specialized education. By 1972 Karen was a Group 4 and, like June, taking CGA courses at night. Eight years later, in 1980, she became a Group 10 financial studies accountant. Like June, Karen came close but never finished her CGA degree. She married and had two children, but only after she was already a Group 10. Karen credits her 'unusual job mobility for a woman' with starting in the right department—accounting—where mobility for women was possible in the mid-1970s because there were specific specialized courses available. Karen considers herself fortunate that her career did not (as June's did) begin in one of the female job ghettos that are so much more difficult to escape.

May's situation is more typical of women in the office. She was hired in 1977 as a data entry clerk (Group 4). Within a year she took a job at a lower level (Group 3), as a switchboard operator, to be nearer to home. May was then a single mother with one child, but later remarried. It took her five years to achieve a Group 5 job as a customer billing clerk, where she stayed for eight years. When that division of the company was privatized in 1989, she took another pay cut to transfer to a position as a Group 4 marketing clerk. She took on additional responsibilities on her own initiative and by 1992 managed to get her job upgraded to a Group 6. In order to advance further May has been told she needs a two-year accounting certificate, and she plans to return to night school as soon as her daughter graduates from high school.

Like May and Karen, Diane had to juggle her career between the demands of children and partners. She was hired in 1977 as a 'girl

Friday' in the construction division, a temporary position at a Group 4. A year and a half later she got a full-time regular position as a clerk typist in engineering (Group 4). The following year, moving to another city to follow her husband, she took a pay cut for a Group 3 meter transformer clerk. By 1981 she had worked her way up to a Group 5 as a vehicle clerk. Through the union, she successfully fought against an attempt to reclassify her position as a Group 4. More than a decade later, with the workload increased due to downsizing and new skills required by more sophisticated computer software, Diane remained at the same Group 5 job.

Susan, like May and Diane, has experienced limited career mobility over more than a decade and a half. She was hired in 1977 as a temporary district officer (Group 4) in customer service. From this 'typical clerical job' she moved to a regular position as a steno-clerk (Group 4). By 1992, after relocating, she moved up to a Group 6 district office clerk. Susan is married without children and has chosen to put her energies into union activism, believing that there are no further opportunities for promotion at work.

May, Diane, and Susan experienced careers in the office that are typical for most women at the utility company, certainly much more typical than the careers of June and Karen. The lack of job ladders or training hierarchies in most areas in which women are concentrated, the lack of formal educational courses relevant for most of these jobs, the lack of any attempt to create bridges from one division to the next, and family responsibilities that make night school or relocation for promotions difficult for most women have created a glass ceiling. The glass ceiling has inched upward since the 1940s, from Group 4 to Group 6, but it none the less remains a ceiling that few women are able to breach.

A handful of 'non-traditional' women who eschewed the traditional female entry-level clerical positions altogether did breach the glass ceiling by entering male technical hierarchies. An early example is Helga, who worked as a drafter from 1964 until early retirement in 1985. She was trained in engineering and architecture in Eastern Europe. Before starting at the utility company she worked for nine years in a structural engineering firm in Toronto. Clearly, Helga had extensive technical training and experience that set her apart from other Canadian women of her generation. She was divorced, without children, when recruited by the company as a 'draftswoman' at a Group 8 (the highest pay group for women in 1964). Anxious to move to the west coast, Helga took a pay cut from her former position. Although all the men she worked with over the years were at least a

Group 9, and most enjoyed promotions up the technical ladder, Helga remained a Group 8 until she retired 21 years later. Her situation is particularly instructive when compared to that of Robert, Martin, and Peter, men with no formal technical training who were also hired in the mid- to late 1960s, yet they all surpassed Helga's position in the job hierarchy.

As Megan's more recent experience illustrates, even in the 1980s and 1990s the few women with non-traditional formal education have found it difficult to climb male technical ladders. Megan was hired in 1974 as a surveyor's assistant (a non-office Group 5). Prior to her employment at BC Hydro she had completed a year of sciences at university and one year of drafting courses at a technical institute, which she continued to attend in the evenings for several years. In addition, she had experience as an engineering technician with the railway. Still, it took Megan two years to get promoted to 'draftsman' (Group 6). Invariably the first woman and often the only woman in these jobs, she suffered sexual harassment from some of her co-workers. Instead of complaining to management or union she sought a transfer, accepting a pay cut in 1979 to become a support clerk (Group 5) in a technical department for which she was taking specialized night courses. By 1984 Megan was a Group 8, at which point she was laid off as part of corporate downsizing.

Without enough seniority (only 10 years) to compete for sought-after technical jobs and with no desire or training to enter the female clerical field, Megan applied to be a meter reader (Group 4/5). She had difficulty getting hired as a meter reader and threatened to file a union grievance. In the end she was hired in a temporary position. From meter reading she worked her way up another male job hierarchy to customer accounts representative (Group 6) in a small town. According to Megan she was able to accept this promotion at least in part because she is single and childless. In 1989, after another relocation, Megan finally became a Group 8 again, this time as a service technician. To achieve this last promotion, for which she was initially overlooked in favour of a man with less experience and lower qualifications, Megan wrote to the company president and threatened a union grievance. She chose this course of action because the president had just launched a high-profile equal opportunity drive to promote women, and she was a qualified woman being denied promotion. Megan is convinced that men with less training and experience have an easier time being promoted, and she is not alone in her convictions.[4]

The careers of these women illustrate the more diverse paths they have followed in the office, from a few exceptional women who breached the glass ceiling through formal educational qualifications, including two in non-traditional male technical fields, to those more commonly mired in the pink-collar ghetto from which there appear few avenues of escape. What is common for all of these women, however, and in contrast to their male counterparts, is that promotions have not come easily when they have come at all. And unlike their male colleagues, the women who breached the glass ceiling were single and/or childless and pursuing advanced educational training during their journeys up the office ladder. This, too, is typical of exceptional women in the office. While many of the new generation of women hired subsequent to corporate downsizing and restructuring arrive already highly educated, and whose career prospects are therefore more favourable, most female employees, including many of those hired more recently, experience career frustrations similar to those of May, Diane, and Susan and remain a world apart from the way John, Michael, Robert, Martin, and Peter experienced the same office. Indeed, on one level it is not really the same office at all, but two different, interlocking gender-bounded work environments sharing the same physical space. On another level, however, all these long-term office workers shared the privileges associated with 'Whiteness', without which many might not have been hired when they first began employment at the utility company.

The Organizational Hierarchy

Gender divisions are a marked organizational feature of BC Hydro (Table 1). Nearly 6,000 employees in the company are divided into three large employee units. The smallest unit (1,253 employees) consists of management, professional, and confidential staff. These are the only non-union employees at the company and 80 per cent are men. Managerial positions, particularly those at senior levels, remain disproportionately in the hands of White men with professional degrees in engineering. Only 8 per cent of senior management positions were held by women in 1991 and far fewer were held by women or men of colour.[5] Professional staff, mostly engineers with university degrees, form another male enclave. A smaller group of confidential employees, the majority of the women in this group, are secretaries and other clerical workers with access to sensitive information who are thereby excluded from union jurisdiction. All other employees belong to one of two unions, forming closed-shop union environments under Canadian labour laws. The smaller of the union groups (2,026 employees), but historically the more powerful and still higher

Table 1
Distribution of Men and Women at BC Hydro,
by Employee Unit, 1991

Employee Unit	Number of Women	% Women	Number of Men	% Men
MPC*	249	20%	1,004	80%
OTEU**	1,434	55%	1,177	45%
IBEW***	12	0.6%	2,014	99.4%
Total	1,695	29%	4,195	71%

*Managers, professional, and confidential employees. Most of the women in this category are confidential clerical staff such as secretaries. Most of the men are managers and professional engineers.
**Office workers in the Office and Technical Employees' Union.
***Blue-collar workers who belong to the International Brotherhood of Electrical Workers, including truck drivers, janitors, linemen, and electricians.

SOURCE: Employee Counts, 10 July 1991. Supplied by BC Hydro.

paid, consists of blue-collar workers. These workers belong to the International Brotherhood of Electrical Workers (IBEW) and fill a range of jobs, from janitors and truck drivers to linemen and electricians. More than 99 per cent of IBEW members employed by BC Hydro are men.

The third and largest (2,611) employee group is comprised of white-collar workers who belong to the office union. As the above career profiles illustrate, these workers perform a broad range of office work, including some work outside the office that has been linked historically to the job ladders in the office hierarchy. Here, women constitute a majority (55 per cent), but even so they remain concentrated at the bottom of the office hierarchy. Nearly 80 per cent of women are found in jobs in the bottom half of the office job classification system, while more than 60 per cent of men are in the top half (Table 2). The average female office worker in 1991 was in a Group 5 job while the average male was in a Group 8; as a consequence, women's average wage was 77 per cent of their male counterparts in the union.[6]

The office is more ethnically diverse than are management ranks, but here, too, senior positions are dominated by White men. In the past, considerations of both gender and race have shaped job opportunities at the company. In the immediate postwar decades racialized

Table 2
Distribution of Office Workers by Job Group and Sex, 1991

Job Group	Women	Men	All Employees	% Women
Non-office*	34	153	187	18%
Group 2	9	0	9	100%
Group 3	29	8	37	78%
Group 4	383	29	412	93%
Group 5	372	130	502	74%
Group 6	337	139	476	71%
Subtotal	1,130	306	1,436	79%
Group 7	147	112	259	57%
Group 8	55	144	199	28%
Group 9	24	139	163	15%
Group 10	19	157	176	11%
Group 11	19	111	130	15%
Group 12	6	55	61	10%
Subtotal	270	718	988	27%
Total	1,434	1,177	2,611	55%

*Non-office is a designation for some jobs organized within the OTEU but not subject to job evaluation.

SOURCE: Employee Counts, 10 July 1991. Supplied by BC Hydro.

minorities were not hired for office work at all. Due to changes in immigration trends (with the introduction of the universal point system in 1967) and economic cycles (with major recessions in the early 1970s and early 1980s), significant employment opportunities for women and men of colour only opened fairly recently. The concentration of minorities among those with the least seniority remains a structural residue of past hiring practices in spite of recent concerns with employment equity. How contemporary hiring practices might be shaped by racialization is beyond the scope of this study; but 'Whiteness' is not central to employment prospects in the way it was in the past.[7] In contrast, gendered hiring and promotion patterns remain pervasive in the 1990s and the concentration of women in pink-collar ghettos cannot be understood as a product of less seniority. As the above career profiles illustrate, gender is a central organizing principle in the office. Rather than an isolated set of social relations, however, gender is embodied in racialized subjects and power relations and the same structural legacy privileges White women relative to other women in the office. As a result racialized-gender divisions remain an important feature of work at BC Hydro in the 1990s.

Unpacking the Division of Labour: Doing Gender

Within particular workplaces the racialized-gendered division of labour appears as the end result of hundreds of management decisions about who will or will not be hired or promoted for particular types of jobs. In reality, management practices are located within a broader social context. Patterns found among office workers at BC Hydro—resulting in the concentration of women and people of colour at the bottom of the office job hierarchy—are not unique to this industry or this occupation. The racialized-gendered division of labour remains central to labour markets across the globe, albeit in diverse forms tied to local cultural and historical patterns.[8]

The gendered division of labour may be an important feature of contemporary labour markets but its form is highly variable. Even within a particular national context it is not unusual for similar, even identical, jobs to be considered 'men's work' in one place and 'women's work' in another.[9] Indeed, there are many instances of jobs switching gender, so to speak, usually a transition from male-dominated to female-dominated labour, a process referred to as feminization. Jobs as diverse as pharmacy, real estate sales, baking, book editing, and public relations have undergone pronounced feminization over the last 20 years. There is nothing predetermined about this. As Barbara Reskin and Patricia Roos suggest, 'employers gerrymandered the sex labels of jobs that were feminizing for other reasons, selectively invoking sex stereotypes after they decided to hire more women.'[10] Hiring patterns may change when an occupation expands quickly and outstrips the usual supply of workers; when the content or technology of work changes; if those involved in hiring decisions change over time; or if the cost of hiring women changes, through changes either in legislation affecting the costs of exclusion or in workers' resistance affecting the costs of inclusion.[11]

Clerical work is an early example of an occupation that has re-gendered. A century ago office work was a decidedly masculine domain.[12] Office work began to be feminized around the turn of the twentieth century as an 'administrative revolution' rapidly expanded clerical work and women entered a previously masculine environment.[13] As administrative bureaucracies grew two things occurred:

women began to enter clerical work in large numbers and office work was rationalized. Clerical work was divided into numerous tasks and job positions arranged in hierarchical internal labour markets: 'Modern office tasks became more fragmented, mechanized and routinized in comparison with the almost craft-like general skills and responsibilities of the old-fashioned male bookkeeper.'[14] What had once been a fairly high-status occupation, offering male clerks mobility up the office ladder to manage the office or the chance to start one's own company, soon became a three-tiered system sharply demarcated by gender and class.[15] The middle and upper ranks of management were separated from other clerical workers, with access increasingly restricted to men who attended college or university. Male clerical workers occupied the middle tier in the office, with access to skilled clerical jobs but not to management. Women were confined to the bottom tier, performing the most routinized jobs with no career mobility at all.

As Ileen DeVault argues, popular notions of status and class divisions between blue-collar manual and white-collar non-manual work were muddied in this process. Clerical work retained much of the middle-class patina of earlier associations with management but without the same material rewards. At the same time, as office work became feminized, male clerical workers tended to retain identification with management and to differentiate themselves from blue-collar or manual workers: 'The very presence of women in offices called into question the fitness of such employment for young men. Only the relatively high wages, ethnic homogeneity, and sexual stratification of the office work force could begin to counter balance this questioning of masculinity.'[16] Masculinity was very much at issue. For their part, male blue-collar workers maintained the identification of masculinity with physicality and strength and mocked 'the fellow who "was born a man but died a clerk".'[17] The development of the modern office was not only constructed by class and gender, it was also a racialized process. In North America until after World War II, office workers of both genders were White and native-born, a factor that contributed to the image of clerical work as higher status in comparison to blue-collar labour, at least among those in the middle class.[18]

In North America today clerical work is almost synonymous with 'women's work'. In 1990 the largest single female occupation, employing nearly one in ten American women, was secretarial work.[19] In Europe and Australia, too, secretarial work is overwhelmingly the purview of women, though precisely what secretaries do varies in different cultural contexts.[20] Moreover, which women are considered appropriate for clerical work also varies across time and space. Until recently American women of both African-American and Chicana background were largely excluded from clerical work; today it is the largest occupational sector for both groups.[21]

In Canada, clerical work is the single largest occupation for women. In 1994 more than one in every four women in the Canadian labour force was employed in some type of clerical work. As Table 3 shows, there are differences in the employment patterns of women of colour and other women, but clerical work is the largest employment category for both groups.[22] Women of colour are less likely to be in managerial, professional, clerical, and sales positions and more likely to be in service and manual labour. When compared to the differences between women and men, however, these differences among women are fairly small.

In comparison to women of colour, men of colour are more likely to be in management, the professions, skilled trades, and semi-skilled and manual labour (Table 3). These patterns are more similar to other men than to women of colour. Still, in comparison to other men, men of colour are more often in clerical and service industries and less often in skilled trades or semi-skilled labour. While gender is a central organizing principle in the labour market, gendered patterns remain racialized. Moreover, as Table 4 shows, this racialized-gendered division of labour is manifest in a consistent wage gap in which White men prevail in better-paying and higher-status positions. Across every age group, men of colour earn less than other men on average, but both earn considerably more than women. Women of colour earned 63 per cent, other women 67 per cent, and men of colour 88 per cent of the average annual earnings for other (White) men in 1990.[23]

Broad aggregate trends in employment and wages tell us little about what is actually occurring in the workplace and there has been considerable debate about what causes this racialized-gendered division of labour. The more common explanations for labour market segregation include differences in human capital (levels of education and other human capital individuals bring to the job), statistical discrimination (a product of variation in market demand due to differential 'costs'), historical discrimination (the lingering legacy of past practices), status closure (practices to restrict access and maintain privileged positions), gender roles and socialization (especially differential family obligations), workplace competition and strategies to divide worker solidarity (split labour markets), or, most commonly, some combination of these.[24] These debates are shaped by different theoretical perspectives—economic liberalism, neo-Weberianism,

Table 3
Occupational Distribution of Visible Minority and
Other Persons in Canada, by Sex, 1991

Occupation	Visible Minority Women	Other Women	Visible Minority Men	Other Men
Upper-level managers	0.5	0.7	1.4	1.9
Middle/other managers	5.2	7.3	8.2	9.8
Professional	12.9	15.6	13.6	10.5
Semi-prof./ technician	4.8	5.4	4.4	4.3
Supervisor	2.4	2.4	2.8	2.1
Foremen/ women	0.4	0.4	1.9	3.8
Clerical	26.0	29.2	9.4	6.1
Sales	6.9	8.2	7.0	7.3
Service	15.5	13.7	11.1	6.6
Skilled crafts/trades	1.2	1.4	6.5	12.1
Semi-skilled manual	2.0	2.1	9.6	13.4
Other manual	14.3	8.2	17.3	17.7
Not stated	7.6	5.1	6.8	4.4
Total	100%	100%	100%	100%

SOURCE: Statistics Canada, *Women in Canada: A Statistical Report*, 3rd edn (Ottawa, 1995), 144.

neo-Marxism, and feminist theory—while sharing a common focus on macro-structural patterns in the labour market. Indeed, all of these factors can be seen to have some effect on how labour markets are structured but pay insufficient attention to the dialectical construction of social life or to the processes by which structures are created, re-created, and redefined.

A different level of analysis—often shaped by different strands of the same theoretical perspectives, including neo-Marxism and feminism[25]—focuses on the everyday negotiation of social life. The

Table 4
Average Annual Earnings, Full-time Full-year, of Visible
Minority and Other Persons in Canada, by Age and Sex, 1990

Age	Visible Minority Women	Other Women	Visible Minority Men	Other Men
15–24	$17,039	$17,268	$18,437	$20,674
25–44	$25,036	$27,147	$33,786	$38,572
45–54	$26,787	$27,819	$40,840	$45,867
55–64	$23,570	$24,580	$37,040	$41,519
Total 15–64	$24,712	$26,160	$34,597	$39,245
% of 'Other Men's' earnings	63%	67%	88%	100%

SOURCE: Statistics Canada, *Women in Canada: A Statistical Report*,
3rd edn (Ottawa, 1995), 145.

concern here is less with a description of the end product—social structures—and more with understanding the duality of structuration—the processes by which we produce, reproduce, and transform social structures and the concrete practices of meaning-construction that constitute these social relations.[26] How workers construct and reconstruct relations in the office—through day-to-day interactions mediated through meaning-systems and material relations inscribed in organizational forms—becomes part of the institutional formations that define the utility company and the office union.

Part of the negotiation of social life is expressed in the multiple ways we 'do gender' as an ongoing accomplishment.[27] Gender and race are understood as processes, not ascribed personal characteristics that can be counted as variables. In this sense a job, and not only its occupants, becomes gendered. As Cynthia Cockburn argues, for example, 'people have a gender and their gender rubs off on the jobs they mainly do.'[28] In the context of racialized-gendered identities and segregated labour markets this takes a racialized form. So, for example, a Chicana clerical worker accomplishes her Chicana identity, not just her feminine identity, on the job.[29] Similarly, Rosemary Pringle argues that what Australian secretaries are expected to do, or indeed who they are expected to be, includes performance of specific racialized, sexualized, and class-based gendered norms:

Those who make it into secretarial jobs are not only female and literate, they generally conform to the cultural criteria of white heterosexual attractiveness. Women who do not match up— Aboriginal and ethnic minorities, lesbians, feminists, older women or working-class women who have not been sufficiently incorporated into middle-class culture, are marginalised unless they can find some way of conforming.[30]

'Doing gender', then, is embedded in broader social relations that shape opportunities in the labour market and interactions on the job.

Not only are jobs gendered, so, too, are organizations. Organizations are cultural forms embodying values located in time and space; gendered assumptions are embedded in organizational culture.[31] Joan Acker has argued that the gendering of organizations can be seen in four interrelated processes: the production of gender divisions in jobs, wages, and hierarchies of power; the creation of symbols, images, and forms of consciousness about gender divisions; the enacting of dominance and subordination between and among women and men; and the internal mental work of individuals as we construct gender-appropriate personae.[32] Yet for all the evidence that gender is a central organizing principle in economic institutions, most organizational theory remains gender neutral:

What is problematic is the discontinuity, even contradictions, between organizational realities obviously structured around gender and ways of thinking and talking about these same realities as though they were gender neutral. What activities produce the façade of gender neutrality and maintain this disjuncture between organizational life and theory?[33]

Organizations are not gender neutral so we need to go beyond assessing how men and women are differentially affected by organizational structure and examine how gender is embedded in the logic of an institution.[34] One of the central ways in which gender is embedded in most workplaces is through job evaluation schemes that hierarchically rank jobs described through abstract gender-neutral language. According to Joan Acker, what the language of neutrality masks is that the idealized disembodied worker, from whom standards of job value are established, is in fact embodied in a married man whose wife takes care of the necessities of daily life.[35] As Acker suggests, job evaluation is one of the central ways the utility company *as a social institution* is gendered. BC Electric instituted a 'scientific' job evaluation scheme in 1946; it would be an object of union negotiations for the next 35 years.

All workplaces are gendered, but not all are gendered in precisely the same ways. Research on gender and technology suggests that technical environments, like that of the utility company, create specific types of masculine work cultures. Particular technologies do not just appear; technology is a social artefact that reflects the distribution of power and resources in a society.[36] Some technologies are rapidly developed, others are left to wither. The 'masculinity of technology' is evident in the types of technologies developed, in the production process (men design, women assemble), in the way technology is used in the workplace (men control and fix machines, women operate machines), and in ideologies about technical competence (men are 'naturally' mechanical, women are not).[37] 'By whatever contortion it takes, in masculine ideology women are represented as non-technical, as incompatible with machinery, except in [the] controlled, supervised, guided role of operator.'[38]

Perhaps not surprisingly, the valorization of technical competence and its association with masculinity is particularly strong in engineering, until recently an all-male profession.[39] As Sally Hacker has argued, the masculinity of engineering is clear from the classroom to the boardroom. Moreover, throughout North America those trained as professional engineers form a key source of managerial recruits. Engineers are deemed particularly appropriate candidates for management because, as one engineering professor said, 'they can treat people like elements in a system.'[40] Hacker notes that '[a]s engineers move into management, and as they create the technological background of industrial work, they also shape the social relations of work.'[41] Those technocratic social relations include a commitment to the 'neutral' values of science, technology, rationalism, and hierarchical organization steeped within a masculine culture that associates such qualities with men and other less desirable qualities (emotionality, intuition, and nurturing) with women.

An engineering culture shapes the entire utility company. Not only are its managers largely drawn from engineering, but a large cadre of professional engineers sits at the top of the non-managerial work hierarchy as technical experts. The organization of BC Hydro can best be described as technocratic,[42] with the polarization of jobs between experts and non-experts, between technical and non-technical positions, reflected in the value of jobs within the corporate culture. This organizational structure is gendered, segregating male experts from white-collar workers, who are then further divided into male technical and female clerical streams. Yet this distinction is misleading. The very definition of what work is more skilled or more technical than other work is socially constructed and politically contested between workers and managers and among workers themselves.[43]

It would be misleading to assume that the divisions of work in the office are the 'natural' result of an organizational hierarchy dominated by engineers. Managerial practices of gendering are only part of the picture, though certainly an important part.[44] Workers themselves, in the course of 'performing' gender at work, actively structure the workplace through practices as diverse as office gossip, sexual harassment, and decisions about whether to compete for particular job postings or with whom to have lunch. When women intrude in traditional men's jobs, men sometimes consciously heighten the sexualized work environment to exclude women.[45] In other contexts, gender issues are so taken for granted as to appear invisible to most participants.

Workers also identify jobs by gender through the collective bargaining process. Unions embody institutionalized forms of workers' resistance and legislated rights to negotiate conditions of work. Unions also embody a history of male dominance. As Cynthia Cockburn, among others, has shown, male unionists play a central role in defining and redefining skill by establishing control over technology and esteemed jobs on the shop floor.[46] Other research on trade unions documents a range of practices—from exclusion and differential rights to uneven representation and masculinist bargaining priorities—by which unions advance men's interests over their union sisters, and in so doing they help to construct the gendered division of labour.[47] Still other research points to unions actively constructing divisions around race and ethnicity in the workplace.[48] At the same time, the research on gender, ethnicity, and race in trade unions illustrates the contradictory nature of these processes, for many unions simultaneously challenge gender and racial inequality in the workplace and in society at large.

Negotiating White-Collar Masculinity

Clearly, the division of labour at BC Hydro cannot be explained without our taking seriously the role played by workers and their unions. Identifying how gender is embedded in the organizational logic of the union and its collective bargaining practices is essential for understanding how workers negotiate racialized-gender relations. As we can see, the end result of this process is the concentration of women and people of colour at the bottom of the office job hierarchies, with women segregated in clerical positions. However, negotiating 'men's work' and 'women's work' took place in a broader cultural context that in many respects was aimed less at the proper place of women than it was at relations among men. At the centre of the union's negotiating strategies was mediating the masculinity of white-collar men *vis-à-vis* blue-collar craftsmen, on the one hand, and professional engineers, on the other hand. As scholars of masculinity have pointed out, masculinity is first and foremost about negotiating relations between men.[49] The office union's competition with the IBEW over pay and status and its attempt to emulate the engineers through the creation of technical hierarchies were central to collective bargaining in the office.

There has been considerable debate about the class location of white-collar clerical workers: are they members of the working class or the middle class? Those arguing that clerical work is now, but did not used to be, part of the working class often point to processes of proletarianization, arguing that declining material rewards, control over work, and mobility prospects in the twentieth century have transformed clerical work.[50] These debates about the transformation of work assume previous sharp divisions between blue-collar and white-collar employees as if, until recently, the 'collar divide' between manual and mental labour was synonymous with class differences. Not only has the mental/manual division as a social cleavage among waged employees in North America been exaggerated,[51] but these lines were blurred even within individual families.[52] For other scholars, the question of class has hinged on class consciousness and why white-collar workers have often not acted like blue-collar workers in organizations like trade unions.[53] More recently, the growth of white-collar unionism across North America and Europe, particularly in the public sector, suggests that such distinctions have lessened. Meanings attached to distinctions between white- and blue-collar work change historically, as do the jobs so classified, and these meanings are mediated within the workplace and civil society. The clerical workers in this study were all wage-earners engaged in non-managerial white-collar (or non-manual) jobs. Although throughout this study they are referred to as white-collar workers, they were in fact engaged in ongoing negotiation between middle-class and blue-collar working-class definitions of their place in the workplace and civil society. For these white-collar workers at least, class was not lived as a homogenizing process, and they remained as distinct from their blue-collar counterparts as they did from their professional superiors. In important ways, the meanings of white-collar work were bound up with negotiating meanings of working-class masculinity.

As Bob Connell points out, at any given point in time a limited range of idealized forms of masculinity are hegemonic or socially dominant while other forms are subordinated.[54] Hegemonic forms of masculinity change over time and space, are contested in various ways by subordinate or marginalized ways of 'being male', and do not actually conform to most men's lived experiences. Nevertheless, dominant images of masculinity and femininity have a profound effect in shaping how gender is performed. In North America in the postwar period hegemonic masculinity and femininity were constructed around those who were White, heterosexual, able-bodied, and middle class. For White working-class men, part of masculinity was the attempt to attain a level of middle-class affluence so a working man could financially support a wife and children. The long struggle for a family wage, or what some have called a 'manly wage'—which simultaneously excluded women and children from various forms of 'men's work', raised men's wages relative to women's, and reinscribed familial ideologies of female domesticity—was central to working-class politics in the first half of this century.[55] Like other trade unionists in the postwar years, men in the Office Employees' Association negotiated their masculinity partly through demands for a breadwinner wage and limitations on women's work.

For these clerical workers the negotiation of masculinity was not so straightforward as for other trade unionists, however. Working-class men might seek middle-class affluence, but other norms prevailed to valorize physicality, toughness, strength, and craft skills associated with manual blue-collar labour while devaluing as sexually suspect ('effeminate' or gay) and physically weak ('sissies') those whose work did not involve such displays.[56] For men working in non-professional white-collar jobs at the utility company these hegemonic forms of working-class masculinity posed a problem. They were not able to demonstrate their masculinity in such blue-collar, working-class terms. By these standards clerical work was simply not masculine enough, especially as the office became more feminized over the course of the postwar decades. Working with all those 'girls' in an increasingly feminized environment, the masculinity of clerical men was questioned by their blue-collar counterparts in the union movement. Indeed, office workers were mocked by their blue-collar colleagues as a union of 'panty-waists' and a 'girls' union.[57]

At the same time, male clerical workers were unable to measure up to middle-class images of masculinity. By World War II middle-class norms of masculinity demanded a level of wages, social status, educational qualifications, and authority that, although perhaps once the purview of male clerical workers, was now clearly lacking. White-collar men in the utility office did not have access to higher-status positions, wages, or authority embodied in professional and managerial jobs. Moreover, although clerical men might opt for middle-class valorization of intellectual work over manual labour, they were consistently lower paid than blue-collar men at the utility company. No matter how much office workers might want to be middle class, then, their position in the work hierarchy suggested otherwise. Their decision to unionize at the end of the war, as part of a wave of mostly blue-collar union activity across the country, suggests that most cast their lot with other workers while seeking to set themselves apart as higher-status white-collar workers. Mediating between blue-collar working-class and professional middle-class masculinities was, in fact, central to strategies that focused on the creation of an intermediate group of technical office workers at the utility company.

Union strategies to achieve breadwinner wages and access to technical hierarchies also reinscribed gendered and racialized social dominance. Breadwinner wages were for men only, but this was clearly not meant for all men. The pursuit of 'suburban dreams'[58] of home-ownership and consumption of a wide range of consumer goods (from automobiles to processed foods) that marked North American prosperity in the postwar decades underlay demands for a single family income for the working-class man. But for non-unionized workers—largely recent immigrants, racialized minorities, and women who were already at the bottom of the labour market—breadwinner wages were not to be had. Unionization and breadwinner wage strategies helped to reinforce the economic advantages of White men relative to Aboriginals and people of colour whose economic and social marginalization was part of the legacy of British colonization and nation-building.

In this sense, then, the struggle for breadwinner wages can be defined as the negotiation of White masculine privilege. As White workers, office workers built on the privileges associated with being White in a North American context. The historical demarcation of race is different in Canada than in the United States, but the process is similar. In the context of British colonization, the First Nations were systematically stripped of access to land and resources and subjected to a host of state-initiated policies that created a racialized Indian 'other' in law and coercive forms of assimilation in practice that amounted to attempted cultural genocide. The legacy of this history continues in the form of economic, social, and political marginalization, on the one hand, and a strong Aboriginal rights movement of resistance, on the other.[59] Immigration policies formed a second prong of nation-building in Canada, with clear preference for British and Northern European migrants and various forms of exclusion towards non-Europeans that persisted until well into the postwar period.[60] Ideologies and material relations of British superiority and, later, broader conceptions of pan-European 'Whiteness' remained inscribed in the fabric of postwar social institutions.

To be racialized White in this context invokes a position of social dominance. As Peggy McIntosh argues, White privilege can be thought of as unearned assets that are rendered invisible through relations of dominance:

> I have come to see white privilege as an invisible package of unearned assets that I can count on cashing in each day, but about which I was 'meant' to remain oblivious. White privilege is like an invisible weightless knapsack of special provisions, assurances, tools, maps, guides, codebooks, passports, visas, clothes, compass, emergency gear, and blank checks.[61]

Union strategies should be understood as mediated through these material and discursive entitlements attached to the long history of White privilege in North America. To a large extent, in the postwar years this privilege was not addressed directly in collective bargaining because Whites' exclusive access to office jobs was never questioned. In later years, as more overt forms of state-sanctioned racism were replaced with multicultural and human rights discourses and office workers came from more diverse backgrounds, traditional approaches to collective bargaining reinforced the dominant position of more senior White members. Thus, White privilege was less a conscious element of collective bargaining than a foundation upon which bargaining proceeded and helped to replicate.

Breadwinner discourses embodied particular notions of femininity and familialism, as well. The heterosexual nuclear family was at the centre of these demands, permeated with notions of the separation of the public paid work of men from the private domestic sphere of women, with the latter characterized as a nurturing oasis away from the stress of the workplace.[62] Not only was this image far from the reality experienced by most women, it also devalued domestic work, which was excluded from the market economy and not seen to be real work at all.[63] The identification of domestic work with women predated these breadwinner struggles but the postwar realization of the one-income household among much of the working-class brought increased demands on wives and mothers that did not dissipate for those women who remained in the paid labour force.

Men's release from heavy domestic responsibilities, beyond furnishing a pay-cheque, indeed, the luxury of having someone else take care of hearth and home, was structured into job requirements, career ladders, and expectations of performance. Domesticated versions of femininity might involve the separation of home and work in popular ideology, but in reality the organization of paid work remained grounded in assumptions about the organization of the household.[64] Indeed, the gendered division of domestic labour forms an important if unacknowledged part of the organizational logic of economic institutions.

Clerical work was redefined in terms of ideals of femininity at the turn of the century, when women began to enter the field in large numbers. Work that was once thought unfit for women became appropriate for some women: those who were young, single, White, native-born, apparently heterosexual, from middle-class and blue-collar backgrounds. Indeed, the new feminized positions of typists and stenographers soon became quintessentially feminine, restructured along the lines of the deferential 'office wife' and no longer attached to upward career ladders.[65] Perhaps not surprisingly, the office union operated from similar assumptions about the proper place of women in the office as it negotiated femininity within the office and within the broader civil society.

Union Traditions: Equality and Solidarity

Negotiating gender and race in the office occurred in the broader context of union traditions in which particular notions of working-class equality and solidarity developed. Unions emerged through a long history of workers' struggles for decent wages and working conditions. Striving to modify an economic system that concentrates private ownership of productive resources in the hands of a few and a political system that privileges these rights over others, unions have played an important role in demands for greater class equality. Central to union traditions is the belief that greater equality can be achieved through the collective solidarity of workers. As a recent report by the Canadian Labour Congress reminds us: 'throughout their history, trade unions have fought for equality through both the collective bargaining and the legislative process.'[66] In spite of internal divisions within the labour movement and the shift away from militancy in the 1950s, the labour movement has helped establish higher wages, state regulation of working conditions through labour legislation, the de-commodification of some essential services (with a more developed welfare state in Canada than in the United States), and some movement towards the redistribution of income in the postwar decades.[67]

These struggles have involved men and women of all backgrounds, but White men have long dominated the union movement in North America. It should not be surprising, then, that racialized masculine culture is inscribed in union traditions and priorities.[68] In particular, traditions of equality and solidarity have been understood in ways that marginalize women and racialized minorities. For the most part, equality in the labour movement has been understood to mean sameness and identical treatment of union members.[69] This formal definition of equality runs counter to the way inequality is substantively lived. Workers do not all face the same situation in the labour market or in civil society. Nevertheless, equitable standards of treatment have been envisioned from the experiences of White men. As activists in many unions have recognized, equality for women and racialized minorities often means 'different' treatment or special provisions—ranging from day care to affirmative action—in order to level the playing field at work. More often than not, however, demands based on 'difference' have gained little support from White male co-workers holding fast to union traditions of equality through sameness. In the automobile industry, for example, Pamela Sugiman argues that 'most UAW leaders upheld the notion that "differential" treatment was "preferential" treatment or "privilege".' The result was that the union's vision of 'workplace equality', though central to collective bargaining, was really based on 'working men's vision of a just workplace'.[70]

Unions have not always held that women and racialized minorities are equal even in the formal sense. The belief that women should be organized, for example, often coincided with the conviction that 'the sexes were not only different but unequal', so men and women did not merit identical representation.[71] As explicit notions of gender and racial subordination dissipated in the postwar period, however, White masculine privilege was maintained through traditional definitions of equality as sameness. Democratic principles grounded in majority rule, an important element of the collective bargaining process itself, have also served to marginalize those whose interests might not be consistent with the majority of their co-workers.[72] Seniority rights, a central element of bargaining protection in North American unions, has similar implications, with those already most entrenched in the workplace receiving the greatest protection in the collective agreement.[73]

Representation is not only a question of numbers, however. Union leaders play a crucial role in defining strategies and priorities. The membership of unions has changed considerably over the last two decades but union representation has changed more slowly. In Canada women now make up 40 per cent of all union members.[74] Women of colour are as likely as White women to be members of unions (34 per cent of all workers); men of colour are less likely to be unionized (30 per cent), and White men are still the most likely to be members of unions (42 per cent).[75] In the United States 'today women of colour are more likely than their white sisters to be unionized.'[76] In spite of these changes, in Australia, Britain, and North America women are less likely than men to be job stewards, and proportionally fewer women and racialized minorities hold union leadership positions.[77] The culture of union activism remains steeped in a particular form of masculinity that makes it disquieting or uncomfortable for those who do not share similar traits:

> In the hierarchy of the union bureaucracy the image of the paid officer is a hardworking, hardnosed, thrusting, aggressive and competitive man, willing to work very long and irregular hours, to frequent pubs and clubs as the need arises. . . . It is a culture that does not exclude women but which makes very few concessions to the existence of any different set of values and patterns of behaviour. It is a culture where few women feel at ease and where most find difficulty expressing their views.[78]

Since the 1970s some unions have redefined equality in terms more amenable to women and racialized minority members. One response has been to reassert equality as 'difference' and form separate women's committees, human rights committees, and anti-racist caucuses to lobby for change. Women's committees, in particular, are now found in most Canadian unions, though the degree of autonomy and influence within a union varies, as does the degree of resistance to feminist activities.[79] As Cynthia Cockburn argues, autonomous organizing also has drawbacks:

> Feminists involved with unions . . . have arrived at an understanding that the weaknesses of demands for equality quickly led us to assertions of women's difference, women's specificity. That acknowledgement of difference leads us to demands for autonomy. Getting our autonomy, getting women-only committees, courses, and conferences, still leaves us marginal to the ostensible business of trade unionism: negotiation and bargaining with the employer.[80]

Progress in bargaining equity issues has been made over the last two decades—from pay equity to equality clauses and sexual harassment language—but tensions remain and, for the most part, special 'women's issues' and other equity issues remain secondary to more traditional union priorities.[81] The result is continued marginalization and internal struggles over power.[82]

Union traditions of solidarity make these struggles for change even more difficult. Membership solidarity is necessary for successful bargaining so internal divisions have the capacity to weaken a union. Making 'special' demands for some groups can be seen to compromise traditions of both equality and solidarity. As Ruth Milkman points out in the context of CIO unions during World War II, the focus on solidarity put women organizing for gender equality in a contradictory position:

> Unions are, after all, workers' organizations first and foremost. Their primary purpose was to unite their members in order to extract concessions from employers—always a difficult task. . . . Any effort to demarcate the special interests of subgroups within the larger membership was likely to be interpreted by union leaders as divisive and threatening. This severely restricted the political space in which female union activists interested in mobilizing women could operate. They had to provide continual reassurance to male union leaders of their loyalty to the larger organization, even as they sought to win broad support for women as a group with distinct interests.[83]

Feminist, anti-racist, gay and lesbian, and other activists in the 1990s face a similar contradictory situation. These activists are attempting to redefine union conceptions of equality, democracy, and solidarity that encompass rather than subordinate diversity among union members. Such struggles are complex, often contradictory, and always multivocal as unions both embody and challenge racialized-gendered relations of power and privilege in the workplace.

Weaving the Themes Together

The answer to the question of who gets ahead at the office is clearly complex. The racialized-gendered hierarchy of work at BC Hydro, as elsewhere in North America, has become more fluid and permeable over time. How these patterns change and persist and what role workers and their union play in this process are the focus of this study. Women and men actively negotiate the world around them, not just as they please, but in the context of power relations inscribed in meaning systems and material practices. Hierarchical relations of class, gender, and race form the context within which workers negotiate the workplace as well as part of what is negotiable. Following Patricia Hill Collins, we can think of these interconnections among race, class, gender, and sexuality as a 'matrix of domination' that is a historically contingent, often contradictory, system of power, privilege, and oppression.[84]

Both gender and race are socially constructed and constantly in a state of flux, rather than innate or primordial human essences. This is not to suggest that gender and race are discretionary and we can choose not to 'do' them; social relations that construct gendered and racialized differences in power and privilege are real enough in their consequences in our lives. We need to recognize that the practices of 'doing gender' become inscribed in racialized individuals, in cultural forms, in organizations, and in social institutions. Like people, jobs become gendered and racialized. So, too, do organizations such as trade unions. Exploring how the operation of the office union was inscribed through racialized and gendered assumptions helps us understand how workers both challenge and reproduce inequality in the office, sometimes in spite of their best intentions, as part of the collective bargaining process with their employer.

Recurrent themes weave together through the history of Local 378 as office workers negotiate their circumstances. These themes revolve around negotiating particular constructions of masculinity, femininity, technical skill, and equality and solidarity within the union, the company, and civil society. Pursuing these interrelated themes is critical for understanding the processes by which relations of privilege have become structural forms of inequality—embedded deep within the organizational logic of institutional arrangements, daily practices, and ways of thinking about the social world—that continue to shape contemporary attempts to achieve equity at the office.

2

Becoming a Union:
A Brief History of Local 378

The Office Employees' Association, 1921–1939

In 1921 the office employees at the British Columbia Electric Railway Company (BC Electric), a Canadian power company servicing the growing populations of Vancouver and Victoria, formed an association to 'enhance the mutual welfare' of the company and the company's employees.[1] There were nearly 3,000 employees at BC Electric in 1921,[2] including blue-collar craftsmen installing and maintaining the electrical systems, men working on the street railway, and men and women performing a wide range of office work. The first two groups were unionized under the International Brotherhood of Electrical Workers (IBEW) and the Street Railway Union (SRU), respectively, and both engaged in considerable labour militancy during World War I.[3]

Office workers benefited from the unionized environment at BC Electric, with wages and benefits that were generally considered above industry standards, but the initial organization of an office association was in no way an attempt to extend the benefits of collective action to white-collar staff. Instead, the early Office Employees' Association (OEA) was more social in nature, intended 'to encourage amusements, recreation and education' among its members while maintaining close ties with BC Electric managers.[4] The president of BC Electric, right up until union certification more than two decades later, was an honorary president of the OEA 'entitled to preside at all public meetings'.[5] In contrast, union members were not welcome in the OEA, clearly separating the association of office workers from their more labour-minded co-workers.[6]

Like many companies of its day, BC Electric was a paternalistic employer, extending various benefits to long-term employees in an effort to maintain a stable and loyal workforce. The company deducted $1.00 a year from office employees' salaries to fund the OEA and provided a club room for social activities complete with billiard table, records, and magazines. The club room was initially restricted to male employees, and it took nearly two decades for women members to gain equal access. Other employee benefits, such as life and medical insurance, home-building loans, coal, reduced rates for electricity, cloth for uniforms, and summer cottages in White Rock were also extended to OEA members in the 1920s.[7]

The Great Depression of the 1930s had a devastating impact in British Columbia, and BC Electric did not escape the economic upheaval. The Depression threatened the company's ability to maintain its social welfare policies and thus the OEA became involved in advocating on behalf of members' financial welfare. Fearful that reduced profits would result in lay-offs, the OEA encouraged its members to work harder to keep the company viable. The OEA expressed its 'confidence in our management, who have in the past and we feel sure, will in the future protect the interests of its employees who are at all times prepared to cooperate with them for our mutual benefit and that of the shareholders of the company.'[8]

Wages were cut during the 1930s and the OEA tried to negotiate restoration to pre-Depression levels. Economic conditions also put all company benefits in jeopardy. Loans and subsidies became scarce and soon disappeared. Medical and life insurance policies were no longer honoured by the issuing company, and BC Electric decided on a case-by-case basis whether to offer financial support. The OEA tried to fill these gaps. It contributed funds to particularly needy members who were laid off or ill and pursued individual claims with BC Electric. It was soon clear that the OEA was unable to marshal more than moral pressure, and as the Depression continued all company medical payments ceased. Similarly, death benefits ($500 for women and $1,000 for men) were continued only on a discretionary basis. Not surprisingly, then, health and life insurance was a major concern and the OEA established a special committee to design an employee-operated medical insurance plan. An OEA health insurance plan was implemented in February 1938, and when World War II began medical coverage was extended to the families of association members who joined the military.[9] This health insurance plan marked the beginning of the OEA providing employment services for its members.

It was clear that the Depression had a lasting effect on the OEA and its relationship with BC Electric management. As its members faced lay-offs and wage and benefit reductions, and as it tested its new-found

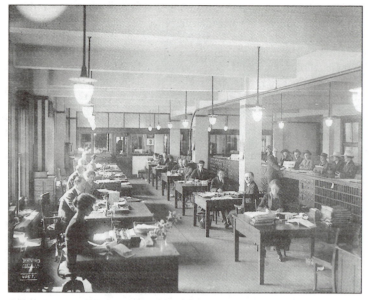

Office Interior, BC Electric, 1921. (Vancouver Public Library photo no. 21082.)

role as a collective representative, the OEA shifted its focus from social activities and amusements, though the latter by no means disappeared, to emphasize collective representation. The OEA not only tried to negotiate salaries and benefits, it soon expanded to pursue other employee grievances such as vacation leave and dress codes. Without the leverage of a union structure the OEA was often unsuccessful, however, as with its attempts to negotiate a contributory pension plan or to achieve extra bonuses for employees buying goods from the company store.[10] Employees began to recognize that stronger collective organization might be to their advantage.

While the OEA engaged in negotiation on behalf of its members in the 1930s, it remained essentially non-adversarial. The OEA and its members continued to have a close relationship with management, working side by side in the office with ready access to managers, and the company maintained a paternalistic management style that often treated employees better than did other companies of the day. In contrast, OEA members often saw little in common between themselves and the all-male blue-collar unions at BC Electric, whose relationship with management was more frequently adversarial. It was not easy to redefine such allegiances at a time when unionization of office work was almost unheard of. Nevertheless, by the time the Depression ended the OEA was regularly involved in negotiating on behalf of its members and began to recognize the advantages of having more than moral persuasion on its side of the negotiating table.

Becoming a Union, 1940–1949

World War II brought new changes to BC Electric. The company expanded greatly, employing more than 6,000 workers by the war's end.[11] Many OEA members joined the military, and women began to experience expanded employment opportunities as male employees became unavailable. The pre-war gender division of labour in the office was sharply drawn, with women confined to the bottom of the clerical hierarchy. Divisions between 'men's work' and 'women's work' softened somewhat during the war as women moved into previously all-male jobs both in and out of the office. At the same time the expansion of the company resulted in increasing bureaucratization of management practices and a new layer of management. The personal management style preferred by BC Electric was increasingly ineffective as the size of the organization prevented more personal knowledge of employees or an open-door policy for communication. At the same time the OEA grew more dissatisfied with the company's ad hoc provision of benefits. By the end of World War II, OEA members had decided to unionize.

In the early years of the war the OEA continued to negotiate discretionary benefits such as loans for home-building, wood purchase, cloth, and discounted rates on electricity and streetcar fares. Two issues would push the OEA towards the demand for standardized policies to provide workers with clearer employee rights: (1) company pensions, and (2) the reintegration of members who left to join the military. On both issues informal negotiations proved fruitless. With the successful implementation of a medical insurance plan the OEA lobbied for a contributory pension plan to replace a voluntary and ad hoc company system, but BC Electric management refused to consider a formal pension plan. Regarding returning veterans, the company provided assurance that servicemen would be rehired when the war ended.[12] The length of the war and the scale of mobilization made this prospect difficult to ensure and, combined with the general expansion of the labour force and the associated bureaucratization of employment and management practices, the OEA pressed for the creation of a personnel department to ensure that all hiring practices were transparent and fair to current members and those serving over-seas. BC Electric resisted, at least partly due to the additional costs involved and the desire to maintain the high degree of discretionary control in the absence of standardized personnel procedures.[13]

With the expansion of BC Electric during the war and private con-trol of the increasingly critical services of electric power and urban transportation, the City of Vancouver considered nationalizing the company in 1943. The OEA was disturbed by the threat of municipal control, with the city not renowned as a generous employer and BC Electric's voluntary pension plan in clear jeopardy. The threat of nationalization prompted the OEA in both Vancouver and Victoria to investigate the possibility of unionization.[14] OEA President Fred Arnott, a driving force behind unionization, contacted the Labour Board in Victoria in the fall of 1943. At the same time, the OEA began to consult more with the existing BC Electric unions (the IBEW and SRU) on issues of mutual concern, including demands for a contributory pen-sion plan, and the OEA began to use union wage increases as a basis for its own wage claims.[15]

In 1944 an advisory committee was formed to apply for bargain-ing agency under the terms of the new federal legislation, PC 1003. The last years of World War II were a period of labour turmoil across Canada. Strikes were frequent and often large, with union recognition a perennial demand. The federal government responded to the level of labour militancy by instituting a new era of collective bargaining rights with the passage of PC 1003. As a result unionization increased dramatically. Between 1940 and 1948 the number of union members in Canada increased from 362,000 to 987,000, constituting 30.3 per cent of the non-agricultural labour force.[16] The institutionalization of collective bargaining did come with a price, tying labour into a highly legalistic and restrictive framework of union certification and negoti-ation that, in the long run, fostered a less political form of business unionism rather than more politicized forms of social unionism.[17]

Alongside hundreds of thousands of other workers, mostly blue-collar men working in the resource and manufacturing industries, the Office Employees' Association at BC Electric entered the union movement. As an early activist explained, maintaining the relative status of white-collar work in relation to blue-collar work was a key factor in the decision to unionize:

> It [the OEA] had been primarily a social club, but it did sit down with management and talk about some of the working conditions and wages, but that was all it did. There were some people who

recognized that in the community collective bargaining was becoming widespread in other trades and the blue-collar field, and the feeling that probably the office and clerical people were getting left behind in the race to divide up the pie, it was a motivating factor. So . . . one or two people at that time suggested that perhaps the thing to do would be to get a bargaining certificate that would give us a legitimate ability to bargain with the employer rather than sit down and chat with them.[18]

Arnott and Vice-President Bruce Gleig applied for certification to negotiate on behalf of OEA members. On 19 May 1944, 90 per cent of eligible members in Vancouver and Victoria voted in favour of certification and in June the OEA became a legally recognized union. Negotiations for a first contract began immediately, focusing on salaries, merit pay, job evaluations, and a grievance procedure.[19] The path from office association to trade union was not accomplished in the single step of Labour Board certification—new procedures and relations with BC Electric still had to be worked out. Moreover, when the war ended federal jurisdiction over labour law also ended and new provincial legislation required recertification. Through the immediate postwar years, therefore, the OEA was involved in the complex process of becoming a union.

The unionization of the OEA, coupled with the increasing size and complexity of BC Electric, led to the establishment of a formal Personnel Department in 1945. Relations between the OEA and BC Electric management became more strained as formal bargaining occurred and contact with the director of industrial relations and the personnel manager displaced informal relations with the company president. In a move away from paternalistic management relations, BC Electric reneged on its commitment to re-employ returning servicemen and instead offered retraining: 'Returning servicemen [must] take a course, and upon completion, give up any connection with the company and its obligation to them.'[20]

The OEA underwent internal restructuring as its range of responsibilities multiplied and communication with its members became both more important and more difficult for the overworked volunteers staffing executive offices. Many OEA members remained uncomfortable with the notion that union and company interests were often contradictory and expected the union to be conciliatory. Relations with BC Electric's existing unions (the IBEW and SRU) also remained strained, with the latter hesitant to acknowledge that office workers, especially all those 'girls', could really become trade unionists. In reality, then, becoming a union was more difficult than OEA members might have imagined.

To deal with the new pressures of union organization the OEA amended its constitution. The ruling Executive Board took on more decision-making responsibilities and the larger Executive Council was less active in day-to-day decisions. The Executive Board—including an elected president, Victoria president, a vice-president, and secretary—maintained direct decision-making responsibility with an advisory Industrial Relations Committee overseeing negotiations. Advisory committees were drawn from the Executive Council, with councillors elected by job-specific (and sometimes even gender-specific) constituencies designed to represent the full range of OEA members. New members were also recruited, including steam plant workers previously organized in a separate company union.[21]

The new Personnel Department at BC Electric quickly formalized new salary scales and job classifications based on 'a scientific basis' of job evaluation.[22] Job evaluation and the 20 per cent 'female differential' that paid women less for equally evaluated work would form a central object of union negotiations for the next four decades (see Chapter 3). In the context of a job evaluation system that formally compared different male and female work, BC Electric's discriminatory pay practices were more explicit than was the case in many other companies, and the OEA became an early champion of equal pay for women. The first collective agreement negotiated in 1946 included separate male and female salary scales with the 20 per cent female differential and a truncated female classification system.[23] The first contract also provided language on grievance procedures (with the general secretary of BC Electric as final arbiter), vacancies and promotions (merit based, optional posting, and preference to internal candidates), vacations (two weeks paid after one year), overtime (time and a half), and hours of work (40 hours a week).[24] The OEA established a Grievance Committee to begin to enforce the terms of the collective agreement, quickly realizing that provisions are only as good as the union's ability to ensure compliance. For its part, BC Electric tended to do little to ensure its managers acted in accordance with the collective agreement, forcing the OEA to put considerable energy and resources into pursuing grievances.

In 1949 the OEA underwent recertification under the new provincial labour legislation that came into existence the previous year. This legislation had several implications. The OEA revised its constitution to remove the president of BC Electric as an honorary member. Members of the Executive Board ceased to be licensed as individual bargaining agents and the OEA hired its first professional business representative. And BC Electric took the opportunity to weaken the union by reclassifying 400 employees as supervisory staff, making them ineligible for union membership. For the first time the OEA hired a lawyer and fought the company at the Labour Relations Board. The union won a partial victory, gaining bargaining authority over 1,080 members, with the fate of 268 'supervisory' employees negotiated on an individual basis.[25]

Perhaps because relations between the OEA and BC Electric became more adversarial, or perhaps because the new Executive Board under President T. Collins was somewhat more radical, the union made it clear that it was no longer a company association by hiring a 'radical union man', Mr Gargraves, as its first business representative. BC Electric objected to the presence of Gargraves, and many OEA members also opposed the union's apparent radical turn. In the end Gargraves lasted only a few months, falling out with the Executive Board over affiliation with the rest of organized labour. Gargraves favoured affiliation with the more radical Canadian Congress of Labour (representing the industrial CIO unions), while the Executive Board, no doubt more in tune with the membership, favoured affiliation with the more conservative Trades and Labour Congress (representing the craft unions). Gargraves's contract was terminated and the OEA affiliated with the Trades and Labour Congress in early 1950. With recertification under the BC Labour Relations Board, affiliation with the Trades and Labour Congress, and the employment of a professional business representative, with Ev King, a labour moderate, replacing Gargraves, the OEA entered the 1950s having completed the transition from a company association to a bona fide trade union.[26]

Joining the OPEIU, 1950–1960

In the early 1950s the OEA sought to become more assertive in its dealings with BC Electric. The company continued to invoke a form of paternalism in its day-to-day managerial style, no doubt hoping that by maintaining closer ties with individual members the OEA would remain a more 'moderate' union than the IBEW or SRU. However, paternalism was now mixed with adversarial labour relations in direct dealings with the union. Grievances multiplied as the OEA encouraged its members to ensure that BC Electric live up to the terms of the collective agreement, with 10 to 15 new grievances filed each month.[27]

To handle the increased workload the OEA underwent internal reorganization, employing a full-time secretary in addition to a business representative, and the Social and Athletic Club was spun off as a separate enterprise. The OEA became active on the provincial and national labour scenes. King was particularly active in this regard, elected to the provincial Trades and Labour Congress executive in 1952 and called on as a mediator and arbitrator in other labour conflicts. Thus, the OEA simultaneously exerted more influence within BC Electric and within the 'House of Labour', though the stigma of being a white-collar and 'girls' union had not completely disappeared.[28] At the same time, as the union grew and its activities expanded, the gap between the Executive Board and the membership widened. Perhaps inevitably, the OEA itself became a more bureaucratic organization and the Executive Board and business representative possessed increasingly specialized knowledge not widely available to the membership. These two trends, union specialization and bureaucratization, translated into stronger representation within BC Electric, as well as occasional charges of authoritarianism as some members felt inadequately consulted.[29]

By 1953 members of the Executive Board were convinced that the OEA should join a larger union, the Office Employees' International Union (OEIU/OPEIU),[30] to increase its power by merging with other office workers. Few other Canadian office workers were unionized at the time and the generally low level of clerical wages limited the OEA's ability to keep pace with other BC Electric unions, such as the IBEW, that had a strong unionized environment with which to draw wage comparisons. Moreover, the advances in unionization among blue-collar workers in the postwar period were widening the wage gap between blue- and white-collar wages. It was argued that seeking affiliation with an international office union would provide the OEA a basis to organize other office workers. Bill Kyles, vice-president of the OEA, explained the reasons for affiliation with the OEIU as follows:

> He gave three reasons why, in his opinion, office workers have been slow to organize: the white collar feeling of privilege, personal individuality, and their distaste for certain union practices. . . . However, in connection with the first two reasons, other workers have become so well organized and strong that the differential between them and office workers has become substantially narrowed. With regard to the third reason, distaste for trade union practices, Mr. Kyles felt that the logical solution was to affiliate

BC Electric salesmen, 1941. (Vancouver Public Library photo no. 25528.)

with a group having the same general interests and problems. In the past we have bargained on the basis of increases, fringe benefits, etc., that the other unions have obtained. However the time has come when the company will no longer allow such comparisons, but point out that we compare very favorably with other office workers in the community. Mr. Kyles suggested that we seek affiliation with the OEIU with a view to raising the status of other office workers in the area so that no unfavorable comparison will be possible. Also, we would be able to obtain specialized help under OEIU affiliation which we cannot get under outside affiliation.[31]

Led by OEA President W. Mann, Kyles, and Ev King, the union put the question to referendum. In spite of strong pressure from the union Executive, many members remained suspicious of joining a larger American-based union and fearful of possible pressures towards greater militancy. In the end members in Vancouver voted against affiliation while those in Victoria voted in favour. Consequently, both Mann and Kyles resigned. In light of the split vote Victoria chose not to affiliate, but the process produced new tensions between members in the two cities.[32]

The issue of affiliation with the OEIU was put to a second vote two years later, in 1955, under the direction of President Bill Lowe, in the midst of difficult negotiations with BC Electric. Frustrated by smaller wage increases than their blue-collar counterparts had received, this time OEA members in the Lower Mainland and Vancouver Island both voted in favour of affiliation. The Lower Mainland OEA officially became the BC Electric Office Employees' Association, Local 378 of the Office Employees' International Union, while Vancouver Island became Local 300. For the first time the OEA joined forces with other office workers in North America and began to operate from a broader frame of reference external to BC Electric.[33]

On the negotiating front the OEA continued to make headway. A medical plan was first negotiated in 1953, with full premiums covered by BC Electric in 1954. Grievance procedures were improved after 1949 with provisions for an arbitration board. Hours were reduced to 37.5 (1953) and overtime provisions improved, with double time after four hours (1956). The pension plan became negotiable in 1956. Paid sick leave (1958) and leave of absence without pay (1958) were covered in union contracts. In the 1958 contract the company agreed to negotiate financial assistance for employee training, moving allowances for promoted and transferred employees, job security for those displaced through office automation (through retraining or severance pay), lay-off notice (lay-off based on merit and seniority), a recall list, and three weeks' paid vacation after eight years.[34]

The latter half of the 1950s was a period of expansion for the OEA as it moved to embrace new workers in the expanding company and began to consider organizing office workers in other companies. Depending on seasonal employment, the OEA's total membership in both Locals 378 and 300 fluctuated between 1,350 and 1,700 members. As BC Electric acquired a new engineering branch, BC Engineering, the OEA applied for bargaining authority over its office employees. New provincial labour law excluded professionals from unions, so professional engineers were excluded from OEA jurisdiction, but the growth of technical jobs brought new technical workers into the union. Diversification was further reflected in constitutional changes, with three vice-presidents and a treasurer on the Executive Board in 1958.[35]

By 1960 BC Electric was undergoing a process of restructuring. Office work expanded as the company grew. Technological change resulted in the introduction of automated office equipment and new forms of job rotation and temporary supervisory training were introduced. BC Electric sold its transit division and then turned BC

Engineering into a separate subsidiary, International Power and Engineering Consultants Ltd (IPEC), in 1959. This process separated administration and customer service from the development of new power projects, while also separating core BC Electric employees from more 'flexible', often temporary, workers.[36]

The creation of IPEC brought increased difficulties for the union as IPEC tried to evade OEA jurisdiction by recruiting temporary workers and claiming non-union status. The OEA managed to retain bargaining authority for office employees at IPEC but was forced to bargain a separate contract. Unable to bargain a first contract with IPEC that matched BC Electric's contract, and with greater difficulty policing the IPEC agreement, the union filed numerous grievances. Though a subsidiary of BC Electric, IPEC was more intransigent in negotiations and less likely to comply with the letter of the collective agreement.[37]

The OEA entered the 1960s as a more professional union, having acquired considerable labour expertise and confidence and a more efficient, though perhaps necessarily more specialized and bureaucratic, operational structure. A part of the House of Labour in much more than name only, the OEA was now part of an international union of office workers trying to organize other office workers in the local community. In recognition of these changes, and to better appeal to office workers in other companies, the OEA officially changed its name to the Office Employees' International Union (OEIU Local 378) in 1960. A visible sign of its size and resources was the first building the union purchased, on Hornby Street in the heart of downtown Vancouver. In May of 1960 the president of the international OEIU, Howard Coughlin, journeyed to Vancouver to celebrate the opening of the union's new offices.[38] From its new headquarters on Hornby Street, OEIU Local 378 would negotiate very different terrain in the coming years as members were suddenly transformed from private- to public-sector employees and as growing labour militancy emerged among the membership.

Becoming a Public-Sector Union, 1961–1963

In 1961 the province of British Columbia nationalized BC Electric, thereby transforming union members into public-sector workers. BC Electric Island and the BC Power Commission (another Crown corporation servicing the rest of the province) were merged later that year, and the following year all three were united under British Columbia Hydro and Power Authority. At this time, unionization in the public sector was weak and the OEIU and other unions at

BC Hydro were placed in a very precarious position. Existing labour law did not apply to Crown corporations, so unless the government chose to recognize existing collective agreements the latter would have no force. The OEIU made an application to the Labour Relations Board to bring Crown corporations under the Labour Relations Act and secure their bargaining rights. Locals 378 (Vancouver) and 300 (Victoria) merged and the OEIU applied for certification for office workers at the BC Power Commission as well. For their part, BC Hydro and IPEC sought to use this occasion to demand concessions in the collective agreement.[39]

The transition to a Crown corporation provided a new avenue for inter-union co-operation, with the Allied Hydro Council of BC bringing together the building trades unions (including the IBEW) and the OEIU working on the Peace River dam project. Though initially a challenge to the union's existence, the nationalization and expansion under BC Hydro led to the expansion of the OEIU. The Labour Relations Board ordered a vote on certification in 1962 and the OEIU won representation of office workers throughout BC Hydro. As of January 1963 all BC Hydro OEIU members were covered under a single contract, albeit one that included concessions from the previous BC Electric agreement. In many respects management of the new Crown corporation was more aggressive than had been the case with its predecessor, and the remnants of BC Electric's historically paternalistic management were jettisoned. In the early years some believed that decision-making was shared by BC Hydro management and the government in Victoria, and there were frequent threats to outlaw collective bargaining altogether.[40]

At the same time union operations became more streamlined and power more consolidated. The union redefined its executive, providing new job descriptions and transforming the union presidency into a full-time position, with Ron Bone as the first long-term president (1962–74). Elections for president and the Executive Council became biannual, with the rest of the Executive Board elected annually. Authority to appoint shop stewards and delegates was transferred from the Executive Council to the Executive Board, while authority to appoint the business representatives was transferred from the general membership to the Executive Council. General membership meetings were reduced to two per year, with Executive Council meeting bimonthly and the Executive Board meeting biweekly.[41] A more professional union structure resulted, though with less frequent participation by the general membership. Like all large unions, maintaining sufficient activism among the membership became a constant challenge. Moreover, increasingly powerful union leadership positions continued to be dominated by men in a union whose membership was about half female, and it would be nearly two decades before women began to play a major role within union leadership (see Chapter 5).

Increasing Labour Militancy, 1964–1979

The 1960s and 1970s saw increasing labour militancy among Canadian workers, and members of the OEIU were no exception. Relations with BC Hydro and its subsidiaries were often adversarial, and strike votes and work stoppages were increasingly common elements of collective bargaining where the government was now also the employer. Expansion, restructuring, and new technology altered the nature of much office work at BC Hydro, adding new groups of workers with high levels of technical skill. In an attempt to remake its image and broaden its claim to represent such workers, the union changed its name to the Office and Technical Employees' Union (OTEU Local 378) in 1964.[42] By the mid-1960s the OTEU had also successfully organized office workers in companies outside of BC Hydro, and its membership, resources, and bargaining power grew considerably.

By 1966 the OTEU encompassed over 3,000 members covered under six collective agreements. Within BC Hydro the OTEU had become the company's largest union. Steady gains were made at the bargaining table but negotiations were often protracted and bitter. As new bargaining units were organized (at Caseco, CBA Engineering, Inland Natural Gas, Dominion Glass, Federal Pacific Electric, and Hertz and Avis Rent-a-Car), the OTEU sought to use the BC Hydro contract as a benchmark with which to bargain other contracts. Monitoring several collective agreements was labour-intensive, and additional staff were hired in the union office. By 1969 the OTEU employed three full-time business representatives to service its membership and organize new units. With more staff, and probably a more knowledgeable membership, the union became increasingly successful in grievances and bargaining. In 1965 the OTEU conducted its first government-supervised strike vote in negotiations with Inland Natural Gas.[43] A strike was narrowly averted with the intervention of mediators from the international union, and the Inland contract was brought into line with the BC Hydro contract.

The union also won arbitration cases against IPEC, which continued to flaunt the collective agreement.[44] Following a strike vote in 1966 IPEC concluded an agreement that, for the first time, outpaced the existing contract at BC Hydro. The contract negotiated at IPEC the following year was even stronger (with wage increases between 20 and 34 per cent over two years), and the OTEU executive considered it 'one of the best agreements in Canada for the period concerned'.[45] The increasing militancy of IPEC members, demonstrated through two illegal work stoppages the following year, was a key factor in achieving better contracts. Even so, by 1968 IPEC management became more aggressive in attempts to undercut contract progress and adopted an intransigent bargaining position, first rejecting a Conciliation Board award, and only narrowly averting a strike by finally accepting the Board's recommendations.[46]

At BC Hydro the union continued to try to expand its jurisdiction into the higher-level technical and professional job categories and created a new staff position to oversee job evaluation grievances. BC Hydro began to hire technical institute graduates for higher-level technical positions rather than train members for new jobs. As a result the union refused to participate in the company's Manpower Development Committee pending a commitment to train existing employees.[47]

Distrust at the bargaining table between the union and the company appeared to intensify in the mid-1960s. The OTEU was the largest union at BC Hydro by this time but it was also the weakest, without a militant history. Just as good agreements were being negotiated at IPEC, and without the right to strike at a Crown corporation for most of the 1960s, BC Hydro contracts often ended up before a Conciliation Board under the jurisdiction of the Labour Relations Board.[48] In negotiations in 1969, with government employees now legally allowed to strike, OTEU members took their first strike vote at BC Hydro and a new collective agreement was reached without conciliation or mediation.[49] Like their counterparts in other units, BC Hydro members, too, were demonstrating their readiness to strike for decent contracts.

Though the 1960s experienced increasing tension at the BC Hydro bargaining table, the union accomplished many new initiatives. New language on bumping (1961), demotions (1965), income continuance (1965), banking vacations (1963), isolation allowances (1969), life insurance (1960), maternity leave (1965), and a new pension plan (1963) added to the ongoing effort to strengthen existing provisions.[50] Much less successful were union attempts to end wage discrimination against women still embodied in the company's pay scales through the female differential (see Chapter 3).

For a white-collar union still operating in a largely blue-collar union environment, it was clear that expanding union organization to other office workers was crucial for future security. In the newly organized bargaining units it was sometimes necessary to strike for a first contract, for example, at Federal Pacific Electric, Dominion Glass, and Hertz and Avis. Organizing and strike support took considerable energy and resources, and consequently some BC Hydro members were less than enthusiastic about the union's expansion.[51] In the long run, however, expansion increased the union's resources to better represent its members.

In the late 1960s the labour movement across Canada was becoming more involved in social activism, a move away from the conservatism of the 1950s. The reunification of the Canadian labour movement under one umbrella in 1956, with the Trades and Labour Congress (TLC) and the Canadian Congress of Labour (CCL) joining to form the Canadian Labour Congress (CLC), marked the end of a radical Communist influence in the labour movement.[52] With fewer ideological divisions the CLC became the single voice of Canadian labour outside Quebec. In 1961 the CLC joined with the Co-operative Commonwealth Federation to form the New Democratic Party (NDP), a political party with one of its main aims being to represent labour. By the end of the decade CLC and BC Federation of Labour conventions included resolutions on many political issues of the day, and some unions played an active role in election campaigns for NDP candidates. At the same time a wave of public-sector union organizing swept across the country, heightening the political dimensions of collective bargaining. For the OTEU the organization of public-sector workers also added dramatically to the white-collar, and female, composition of the Canadian labour movement and provided new points of comparison in contract negotiations and potential allies in the struggles ahead.

Labour unrest became common in Canada and British Columbia during the early 1970s. With inflation and unemployment rising, BC Hydro began to contract out more work, particularly within IBEW jurisdiction, and the latter struck twice in 1971. On both occasions OTEU members supported the IBEW and respected picket lines.[53] In general, labour relations were in crisis at BC Hydro, with '30 grievances in process' in early 1972 and 'resolution only occurring when a case is on its way to arbitration'. Moreover, compared to 25 years with only two strikes at BC Hydro (one each by the IBEW and the Amalgamated Transit Union—formerly the SRU), there were two strikes (by the IBEW) and one walk-out (by the OTEU) in a 12-month period.[54]

The OTEU walk-out in 1972 was precipitated by a time-management study by the consulting firm WOFAC Management Systems Limited that recommended a 25 per cent reduction in staffing levels in some departments. The union advised its members to work to rule and not to co-operate by refusing to fill out further WOFAC questionnaires. Seventeen OTEU members were threatened with disciplinary action for refusal to co-operate with the WOFAC research, and nearly 1,200 members walked off the job over a two-day period to express their solidarity. As the union executive explained: 'The union being bound by the collective Agreement, had no choice but to advise the members to return to work. Individual members however placed justice ahead of legal processes and refused to accept this advice.'[55] The resistance of union members was successful and the WOFAC plan was never implemented. At the same time, however, contracting out, the downgrading of some jobs, and the hiring of new categories of 'technologists-in-training' who were exempt from the bargaining unit signalled new job insecurities for OTEU members. The change in provincial government with the election of the left-leaning NDP in 1972, ending the 20-year rule of the more conservative Social Credit government, contributed to instability within BC Hydro management, but it brought a somewhat more favourable labour climate for unions.

In line with the move towards more social activism among unions the OTEU also began to adopt broader measures recommended by the CLC, the BC Federation of Labour, and the international OPEIU. For example, OTEU delegates attended a BC Federation of Labour conference on women's rights and pressed the labour movement to lobby for amendments to the Equal Pay Act so that BC Hydro could not circumvent equal pay provisions through job classifications that only applied to female employees. The union convened a Political Education Committee to consider possible affiliation with the NDP, though the latter recommended against affiliation.[56] Some councillors became more active as union delegates to conventions, previously the purview of executive officers and business representatives, another indication of increasing activism among the membership. In the mid-1970s broader representation of the membership on the Executive Board resulted in constitutional changes to replace three vice-presidents with a diverse range of directors representing workers from BC Hydro, the Insurance Corporation of British Columbia, and the smaller units in the local, as well as a new committee structure that involved councillors in bargaining and other matters.

In the fall of 1973 IPEC was officially merged into the engineering division of BC Hydro and all IPEC workers became subject to the BC Hydro agreement. This government decision deprived BC Hydro of a subsidiary that absorbed 'flexible' work needs related to development projects. From the union's perspective the move consolidated collective bargaining and eliminated the need to specially police the IPEC agreement. The OTEU also continued to expand to other companies, organizing Rayonier, Kaiser Resources, and the Insurance Corporation of British Columbia (ICBC).[57]

ICBC was the largest of the newly organized groups. Organizing ICBC began in the fall of 1973, as the OTEU competed with the Canadian Union of Public Employees (CUPE) and the BC Government Employees' Union (BCGEU) for certification of the newly created provincial automobile insurance agency. CUPE and BCGEU united to form a single association to organize ICBC, and the Ministry of Labour unsuccessfully pressured the OTEU to join this group rather than compete for certification. In the fall of 1974 the Labour Relations Board ordered a certification vote among ICBC's 1,800 employees and the latter voted 63 per cent in favour of affiliation with the OTEU. In one act the membership of the OTEU increased dramatically, and BC Hydro was no longer the only large unit in Local 378. Two ICBC delegates were added to the Executive Board and two assistant business representatives and two clerical staff were hired to service ICBC members.[58]

Negotiation for the first ICBC contract was difficult and the union believed the government wished to set an example to restrain the bargaining aspirations of other public-sector workers. The OTEU struck ICBC for 14 weeks in 1975, at which point they were legislated back to work by the NDP government. Parity with the BC Hydro contract was not won, but the union pronounced the ICBC agreement a 'good one to build on'.[59]

At BC Hydro, too, the 1974 negotiations brought the union to the brink of a strike. With a 93 per cent strike vote, including a commitment to make a new job evaluation system a strike issue, and coming out of a three-year contract during a period of high inflation, OTEU members demonstrated a new level of militancy. A strike was narrowly averted through the mediation of the Industrial Inquiry Commissioner, resulting in arguably the best contract BC Hydro workers ever achieved. Significant wage increases coexisted with a new dental plan, flexible starting hours, a 35-hour week (with the implementation of the reduced workweek leave or one day off every two weeks), and commitment to design a new OTEU-BC Hydro job evaluation system.[60] The job evaluation system, considered inconsistent and subject to manipulation, was a continuing bone of contention among OTEU members. With the departure of Ron Bone as president in 1974, Fred Trotter became the new president of the OTEU (1974–84). Having previously served as the business representative in charge of job evaluation grievances, Trotter was well aware of the problems of job evaluation and committed to developing a system with full union input. The 1974 agreement provided for a joint union-management committee to construct a new job evaluation plan, the terms of which would be a continuing negotiating issue until its implementation in 1981 (see Chapter 4).

The first OTEU strike at BC Hydro occurred in the next round of bargaining, in 1976. This time members had to walk the picket line in order to keep up with the wage increases awarded other BC Hydro unions. Having learned of the hardships in large units caused during the ICBC strike, the executive adopted an innovative strategy to avoid all-out strike action while effectively disrupting BC Hydro services:

> No overtime unless authorized by the union; work to job descriptions and [work to] rule; rotating strikes, i.e. members would be requested in various departments to withdraw their services at critical times for periods determined by the Negotiating Committee.[61]

Those not on strike at any given time donated 10 per cent of their wages to support those on the picket line. The rotating strike was highly effective, without undue hardship to OTEU members, other BC Hydro unions, or the general public, and in a matter of days BC Hydro nearly doubled its wage offer.[62] Thereafter, escalating job action ending in tactical rotating strikes became a staple of OTEU negotiating strategies.

By the late 1970s the OTEU had been transformed into a major union in the province, with five business representatives servicing an increasingly activist membership. The postwar economic boom had ended, marked by the dual events of the early 1970s oil crisis and the end of the gold standard, heralding an era of simultaneously rising rates of unemployment and inflation. These trends signalled tougher adversarial labour negotiations at BC Hydro and elsewhere as workers sought to maintain, or increase, real wages while managers and employers sought to contain costs eating into profit margins or, in the public sector, to hold the line on public debt. In provincial politics, the defeat of the NDP government in 1975 and the return of a Social Credit government produced a spate of legislation that the BC Federation of Labour characterized as among the worst 'anti-labour legislation' in the history of the province.[63] In hindsight, the legislation of 1977 was but a prelude for measures instigated by the same government after its re-election in 1983.

Neo-Liberal Restructuring, 1980–1994

The numerical and political growth of the OTEU coincided with a demographic shift in the working population. Women had always formed about half of the union's membership at BC Hydro and its predecessor, BC Electric, but by the 1970s women's work patterns were becoming increasingly similar to men's. Thus women, too, expected career mobility at BC Hydro, access to better jobs, higher pay, and promotions into management or technical fields. Some women began to resent their marginalization in the power structure of the union and a new gender politics began to reshape the OTEU. The 1980s were marked by the formation of an activist Women's Committee, the election of the first woman president of Local 378 (Anne Harvey, 1984–90), and the achievement of gender parity on the Executive Board (see Chapter 5). The 1980s also witnessed internal divisions within the union and the appearance of competitive Executive Board elections. In 1990 Anne Harvey was defeated in her re-election bid by Ron Tuckwood (1990–).[64]

The 1980s were also marked by the processes of economic restructuring and the politics of neo-liberal market reform. The provincial government embarked on a program of fiscal restraint, public-sector downsizing, and regressive labour and social legislation that exacerbated the early 1980s recession and precipitated massive public resistance through the Solidarity Coalition and a near-general strike in the province. For the first time in its existence BC Hydro embarked on massive lay-offs, and the membership of Local 378 moved firmly onto the defensive (see Chapter 6).

The 1981 negotiations at BC Hydro[65] brought the last gains union members would see for some time: adoption leave, bereavement leave, improved maternity leave, better pension, medical, and health benefits, and the resolution of women's pay inequity stemming from the old dual wage scale (see Chapter 4).[66] The recession of the early 1980s began to affect BC Hydro employees in 1982 and for the first time in decades lay-offs occurred.[67] Following a three-month strike in 1983–4 the union accepted its first concession contract in 20 years. Weeks later the corporation began massive lay-offs that cut union members by one-quarter, halted career mobility for a decade, and undermined further labour militancy (see Chapter 6). For the rest of the 1980s contract bargaining involved attempts to shore up seniority rights and stave off increasing concession demands, with the membership determined to avoid another strike at all costs.

By the late 1980s corporate restructuring had turned to privatization, contracting out, and other forms of workplace flexibility. In 1989 OTEU members took job action for the first time since the lay-offs, adopting a work-to-rule strategy with selective picketing at BC Hydro offices and construction sites.[68] With the help of mediation, the union won a number of improvements, including a broad job security clause. The trade-off was corporate flexibility, and as regular employees won employment security the use of temporary workers escalated, creating a new problem for the union. Still, the gains in the 1989 contract suggested that the OTEU had weathered economic restructuring and the membership had regained its determination to resist concessions.

By the early 1990s it was clear to everyone that global trends had restructured work across Canada. The election of a new NDP government in British Columbia in 1991 only marginally improved the labour climate for unions. Computer technology and automation were rapidly reducing the number of workers needed for all types of jobs, in the office and elsewhere, and 'lean production' and 'flexible specialization' became corporate buzz-words in the private and public sectors. It was now more difficult to make gains at the bargaining table, especially any that challenged the trends towards flexible use of labour and the downward pressure on costs. This had particular implications for attempts to bargain pay equity and employment equity measures in the office, and in the end results were disappointing (see Chapter 6). Some new gains were bargained in the early 1990s, however, including protection against contracting out, a sexual harassment policy, paternity leave, and protection for sexual orientation. These gains were traded off against other flexibility concessions around temporary employees, shift work, non-standard hours, and experiments with homework.[69]

Peeling Back the Layers of History

There was much for the members of Local 378 to celebrate as they marked their fiftieth anniversary in 1994. Collective bargaining seldom leads to complete victories for workers, especially during periods of economic restructuring, and every improvement in the terms and conditions of work is a victory born of struggle. At the same time, it is easy to see obstacles to winning progressive measures as emanating solely from management policies. This is especially true when union histories are read as linear movements forward, with occasional unavoidable steps backward, when the story is presented as one of bargaining in the interests of a homogeneous group of workers. The above history of Local 378's first half-century can certainly be read this way. What such a reading ignores, however, is the multivocal character of workers. In particular, it ignores the broader power relations of gender and racialization within which collective bargaining occurs; these social relations shape union practices, traditions, bargaining agendas, and priorities. In very concrete ways Local 378 negotiated racialized-gender relations among its members at the same time that it negotiated general conditions of work with its employer. The chapters that follow attempt to peel back some of these more opaque layers of the union's history to explore ways in which racialized-gender relations were, and continue to be, produced, reproduced, and challenged through the processes of collective bargaining.

3

Normalizing Breadwinner Rights

*It is possible to segregate those jobs which can definitely
be done by females from those revised ones which
can be done by males on the basis of group #4 and up.*

(Union bargaining proposal, 7 January 1948)[1]

The Postwar Labour Market

The period of postwar economic expansion in Canada greatly
increased the demand for office workers and opened up new employment opportunities for women. As Table 5 shows, not only did the
number of clerical jobs expand in the 1940s, but these jobs were also
in the process of feminization.[2] In 1941 male clerical workers out-
numbered female clerical workers by a considerable margin: nearly
60 per cent of clerical workers were male. Within 10 years these
numbers were reversed, with females comprising almost 60 per cent
of clerical workers. The number of women employed in clerical work
more than doubled in the 1940s, while the number of men so
employed increased by less than 20 per cent.[3] In particular, jobs classified as office clerks, the largest occupation for men clerical workers,
dropped from over 70 per cent male to 57 per cent male. Employment
expansion was concentrated among stenographers and typists, whose
numbers increased by nearly 70 per cent in the 1940s; 95 per cent of
stenographers and typists were female.

Clerical work was becoming dominated by women, but considerable gender segregation remained within office work, not unlike that
found in other sectors of the labour market.[4] The broad classifications
of census data tend to mask the full extent of clerical job segregation.

Table 5
Clerical Occupations in Canada, by Sex, 1941–1961

1941	Male	Female
Accountants/auditors	34,096	2,992
Bookkeepers/cashiers	16,550	20,931
Office appliance operators	411	2,634
Office clerks	124,083	49,860
Shipping Clerks	25,385	937
Stenographers/typists	4,141	77,914
Total	204,666	155,268

1951	Male	Female
Bookkeepers/cashiers	33,686	54,713
Doctor/dental assistants	0	2,626
Office appliance operators	1,237	9,764
Office clerks	158,229	118,025
Shipping/receiving clerks	45,710	3,196
Stenographers/typists	5,038	133,485
Total	243,900	321,809

1961	Male	Female
Bookkeepers/cashiers	59,050	98,781
Office appliance operators	6,007	22,372
Stock clerks/storekeepers	33,064	3,835
Shipping/receiving clerks	52,476	3,782
Baggage handlers	1,819	0
Ticket/station clerks	7,258	1,324
Stenographers	4,704	160,843
Typists/clerk-typists	2,319	48,799
Doctor/dental attendants	137	3,761
Other clerical	157,977	165,848
Total	324,811	509,345

SOURCE: *Census of Canada*, 1941, vol. 3, 34; 1951, vol. 4, 4–1, 4–2; 1961, vol. 3, 6–4, 6–5.

Nevertheless, census data show that some clerical work, such as shipping and receiving clerks, ticket station clerks, and baggage handlers, remained men's employment. Jobs that involved typing, as more and more office work did, were strictly women's domain.

As World War II ended, having brought more married women and mothers into the labour force to fill jobs created by the war economy or vacated by men serving in the armed forces, a movement ensued to push women out of the labour force in preference for returning ser-vice*men* and other men in need of work.[5] Federal, provincial, and municipal levels of government, employers, and working men all participated in this movement to restrict women's paid labour and assert men's right to work and wages. Yet in some respects this move-ment was less than successful; the number of women working for pay did not drop to pre-war levels, and then it subsequently rose in the decades to follow.[6] Moreover, not only did the number of women in paid employment climb, but so, too, did the number of married women who were employed. Nationally, the percentage of women clerical workers who were *single* declined from 90 per cent in 1941 to 70 per cent in 1951 and 47 per cent in 1961.[7] The age of employed women also increased progressively, so that by 1961 one in five female clerical workers was over the age of 45. In the province of British Columbia this figure was closer to one in four women (23 per cent) over the age of 45, and 54 per cent were married.[8]

The immediate postwar period was, therefore, a period of continu-ity and transition, with many more women in the paid labour force, including more married and older women, yet considerable pressure continued to restrict women's employment opportunities. The gen-dered division of paid labour, disrupted somewhat by the war, was renegotiated in its aftermath.[9] It is clear, moreover, that in unionized environments this renegotiation was one in which trade unions played an active role.[10]

The postwar labour market was not only segregated by gender, it was also shaped by processes of racialization.[11] Just as men and women were deemed suitable for different types of work, whether paid work or unpaid domestic work, so, too, were descendants of var-ious cultural communities differentially incorporated into the social, political, and economic domains of Canadian society. The legacy of British colonialism was vested in what John Porter first called the 'vertical mosaic',[12] a hierarchy of power and privilege that placed those of British origin at the top of the political and economic sys-tems, controlling economic development and immigration, followed by those from Northern Europe, Southern and Central Europe, and non-Europeans in descending order. At the bottom were the First Nations of Canada, disenfranchised through colonization, and descendants of immigrants from Asia and Africa, many of whom had arrived as indentured labour. In British Columbia segregation between those of European and those of Asian origin, the latter con-sisting of immigrants from China, Japan, and India, was a marked feature of the labour market by the late nineteenth century. Immigration from China, Japan, and India was either prohibited or seriously curtailed in the early part of this century.[13] In 1941 the Asian-Canadian population of British Columbia was over 5 per cent, in decline from 11 per cent in 1901.[14] Most people of Chinese, Japanese, and Indian descent were relegated to manual labouring jobs in the resource sector or worked in small family-owned businesses. Women, in particular, seldom worked outside of the confines of the ethnic labour market.[15]

Though not usually higher paid than unionized blue-collar work, office work retained some of its higher status in the postwar period, providing a patina of middle-class respectability. Office work was typically clean, salaried rather than hourly waged, with regular hours, better job security, often better benefits (such as pensions), and less subject to seasonal downturns than many other sectors of employment.[16] It was also clearly the purview of those of British origin. In BC in 1941, 91 per cent of men and 90 per cent of women in clerical work were of British ethnic origin, and most were Canadian-born.[17] Less than 2 per cent of men and 1 per cent of women in clerical jobs in the province were of Asian origin; nationally, these figures were less than one-fifth of 1 per cent.[18] Moreover, the number of Aboriginal men and women employed in clerical jobs was but a fraction of Asian office employment.[19] Two decades later, in 1961, the proportion of Asian Canadians and First Nations people in clerical work remained unchanged.[20] The gendered division of clerical labour was in a period of renegotiation, but the racialized division of office work was unaffected by recruitment during the war or the expansion of clerical jobs in the postwar boom economy. In the decades after World War II in Canada, office work clearly belonged to White men and women.

The racialized-gendered construction of office work in the postwar years formed the context in which 1,200 newly unionized office workers at BC Electric set about negotiating conditions of work with their employer. With the division between men's and women's office jobs in transition and the racialized division of labour uncontested, these workers, through their trade union, set about normalizing the superior rights of White men in an attempt to fulfil the postwar aspirations of working-class men and women for a middle-class income and better job security and working conditions. The pursuit of suburban dreams[21] was explicitly gendered and racialized, evoking different idealized roles for women and men, as homemaker and breadwinner respectively, embodied in images of White nuclear families. Drawing on trade union traditions steeped in a masculine culture,[22] and perhaps especially in an office union operating in an increasingly feminized environment, the White male breadwinner was the centrepiece of postwar negotiations, setting in place a hierarchy of entitlements to office work and wages that was normalized and then rendered invisible. Less transparently, but equally central to labour negotiations, was the mediation of white-collar masculinity in a blue-collar union environment. In the process of negotiating conditions of work the union negotiated the meanings of masculinity and femininity in the office and the gender composition of its own membership at the same time.

Men and Women in Their Proper Places

Like its earlier incarnation as an office association, the new OEA union was headed by men in the upper ranks of the clerical jobs. Under wartime federal labour legislation individual members were certified as bargaining representatives, so the president and vice-president of the OEA were usually also the bargaining representatives. In addition, the executive of the union included a secretary (in the early years the only woman on the executive), a treasurer, and, sometimes, an additional member also certified as a bargaining agent.[23] Councillors were elected from specific areas of the company by floor or department and with consideration for gender representation. Until the late 1950s women constituted about 40 per cent of councillors. In 1949, for example, there were 12 women among 28 elected councillors.[24] One reason women fared so well in union representation was due to the specifications for councillor positions. Not only were councillors identified by departments or floors to reflect gender divisions in the office, some positions on the Executive Council were specifically designated as male or female.[25] By the early 1960s this practice was in decline and fewer positions were set aside for women.[26] As a result women's representation dropped, with women comprising about 20 per cent of all councillors.

In the early years bargaining strategies were discussed by the Executive Council. Later, as the union expanded and professionalized, business representatives were hired to service union members, beginning with the first hiring in late 1949,[27] and separate bargaining committees were formed. The open nature of bargaining discussions at Council and the significant presence of women on Council suggest that men and women both played an active role in early postwar negotiations. At the very least, men union activists did not devise strategies in secret. Nevertheless, the OEA's first order of union business was to stabilize the gender order in the office.[28] The division between men's and women's office work had become more permeable with the expansion of women's employment during the war, and the OEA adopted a negotiating stance intent on sharpening the postwar gendered division of labour. In contrast, the racialized division of labour was not permeable, and the assumption that the subjects of contract negotiation remained White men and women was held by both parties. As one former union activist noted: 'you would never have seen a Chinese or Japanese [person] working in the building or on the streetcars or anywhere' in the 1940s and 1950s.[29]

In the first round of collective bargaining union proposals opened with a demand that the company should not employ married women: 'The only conditions under which married women should be retained in the employ of the company is where [a] woman receives no support from her husband, such as the husband may be an invalid or may have deserted his wife.'[30] BC Electric agreed: 'In principle the Company agrees with your request under this heading, although there may be the odd case where special circumstances would warrant an exception being made.'[31] BC Electric further proposed that married women who were retained be confined to temporary status. The OEA agreed, even though temporary employees were not eligible for union membership.[32] In light of the significant number of married women who remained in the BC labour force in the 1940s—one-third of all female clerical workers by the end of the decade[33]—this union-initiated policy to deny married women access to jobs closed to a large number of women one of the only avenues of unionized clerical work in the province.

Barring married women from clerical jobs ensured a high turnover of women at the office while simultaneously assuring men access to promotions tied to seniority and experience. The hierarchical organization of work in the office did not provide enough senior clerical positions for all male employees, however. Entry-level jobs with prospects for future mobility remained an important source of men's employment. Negotiating a sharper and less permeable division of labour between men's and women's work, with promotion opportunities reserved for men, was the OEA's chief concern at the bargaining table.

The first round of negotiations occurred in the context of the reorganization of the office. In 1945 the growth of the company precipitated the creation of a new Personnel Department with a director of industrial relations in charge of union negotiations. At the same time scientific management was welcomed into the office as the company jettisoned ad hoc pay rates and hired consultants to implement a new job evaluation and classification system. In a letter to the union, BC Electric promised that the new job classification system would rely on the 'clear-cut and scientific basis' of job evaluation.[34] A new system of job evaluation was implemented for office workers but not for blue-collar workers at the utility company. These workers, organized in two separate unions (the IBEW and SRU), continued to negotiate flat rates for specific jobs. In contrast, the job evaluation scheme implemented in the office resulted in a much more differentiated and hierarchical pay structure than anything experienced by blue-collar workers and fostered negotiation over increases to the overall wage system rather than negotiation of pay rates for specific jobs.

BC Electric's job classification system was based on a factor point plan with all office jobs measured along ten factors grouped into three categories of knowledge and ability, responsibility, and physical conditions.[35] Detailed job descriptions were compiled and each job was evaluated according to the number of points awarded for each factor. On the basis of the total score, jobs were then classified into one of sixteen different job groups with salary scales tied to the job group.

This job evaluation scheme, not unlike others, was weighted towards valuing managerial tasks such as supervision most highly, followed by cognitive and finally manual skills in descending order. In this way job evaluation reinforced and rationalized pre-existing hierarchies of authority, status, and pay differences within the office environment. The rationalization of pre-existing office hierarchies also involved overvaluing men's jobs while undervaluing women's jobs. So, for example, heavy or dirty work was valued more highly than clean or light work; outdoor hazards (like rain or cold) more highly than indoor hazards (like machine noise or repetitive movements); contacts across departments more highly than those within departments; and communication with suppliers and senior managers more highly than communication with sometimes difficult customers.[36] At the same time these gendered evaluative criteria were redefined in neutral management language, thereby providing the appearance of an objective assessment of job-related skills. Even with these gender biases built into the job evaluation system, however, the company designed two separate salary scales for men and women that pushed women's wages lower still. Women's jobs spanned Groups 1 to 11 and were soon reduced to only nine job groups, while men's jobs ranged from Groups 1 to 16. More important, there was a 20 per cent wage gap between male and female salary scales in the same job grouping, so that a Group 4 women's job was paid 20 per cent less than a Group 4 men's job. Demands to end this wage gap, which quickly became known as the female differential, were central to bargaining for decades to come.

Two different sets of concerns underlay the OEA's resistance to the female differential. On the one hand, for women the issue was one of simple discrimination. The female differential established lower pay for women in jobs that were evaluated as equal in the company's 'clear-cut and scientific' job evaluation process. In 1946 more than 300 women, half of the union's female membership, signed a petition protesting lower pay and demanding a single wage scale. The union president forwarded the petition to management but the issue did not become a contract demand in negotiations later that year.[37] For men, the question of discrimination against women was, at least temporarily, superseded by concerns that cheaper women might displace men from their jobs. Initially, the latter concern made it onto the negotiating table. The union's chief negotiating demand leading to its first contract was to ensure a clear separation between women's and men's jobs and, in the meantime, to insist that if women performed men's work they must be paid according to the male wage.

These demands were embodied in the first collective agreement, which included separate male and female salary scales, truncated for women by the female differential, and a commitment to differentiate clearly between men's jobs and women's jobs. The latter commitment (in clause 6–C) read as follows:

> The Company agrees to undertake a study of the jobs performed by employees eligible for membership in the Association in order to determine which may be classified as jobs ordinarily done by men and jobs ordinarily done by women; a further study will be made to determine which jobs may be classed as 'professional' in the sense that a particularly high degree of training will be required for the carrying out of such jobs. In any case where a woman is employed in a job which is classified as one ordinarily done by men or as 'professional', she shall be paid for her work on the basis of the male salary schedule.[38]

Although strong language, it soon proved to be unenforceable, with the company choosing to interpret 'jobs ordinarily done by men' to mean those always and only ever done by men. By definition, then, any job in which a woman was employed was not a man's job and she received lower pay. Strategies to ensure the intent of clause 6–C soon dominated the union's bargaining agenda.

Tabular room, BC Electric, 1943. (Vancouver Public Library photo no. 70433.)

The permeability of the gender division of labour was in lower-level jobs, particularly in Groups 3, 4, and 5, which constituted the higher end of women's work and the bottom end of men's work. The OEA expressed concern that if men's entry-level jobs were reduced by the upward creep of women's jobs, women would soon staff the office and there would be fewer office jobs of any kind for men at BC Electric. According to the OEA leadership this situation 'would constitute a real blow at the existing social order of employment'.[39] In a letter to management in late 1947 the union accused management of adopting a hiring policy that gave preference to women and was therefore unfair to men:

> Recently it has been the undeclared policy of the company to employ women in every job from group #1 to #7 inclusive as and when replacements are required. This policy has greatly undermined the confidence of the majority of the male employees of the company. Groups #1 to 7 contain the greatest density groups of the whole employee structure.[40]

It is not clear whether women were really making inroads into Groups 6 and 7, but the perception of a threat to men's employment prospects led the OEA to propose radical intervention: the union proposed tinkering with the job evaluation system, first to upgrade the content of men's jobs, and then to reserve promotion opportunities for men. In this way a clear gender division could be enforced in the office. In January of 1948, the union advanced these demands in the following proposal:

> Wherever male jobs occur in group #3 every effort should be made to increase those job contents to a group #4 value if possible. It being realized that the earning power of a group #3 job for male employees is barely enough to meet the needs of a man supporting a family. With reorganization of job content throughout group #1 to #7, it is possible to segregate those jobs which can definitely be done by females from those revised ones which can be done by males on the basis of group #4 and up. Thus, in the process, establishing increased job value for men and marking an avenue of promotion for male employees within those groups.[41]

Women would be left with clerical work considered to be less skilled and, no matter how experienced or competent, they would be ineligible for most promotions.

At the heart of the union's proposal, like its resistance to employing married women, was securing men's rights as breadwinners to enjoy a 'family wage'—wages and career opportunities commensurate with a man performing his role as a good provider for his wife and children (whether he had any or not). Why the company chose to accept the union's proposal rather than continue to expand women's employment in the office is less clear, especially in light of the 20 per cent female differential, though it is likely that an important factor was management's acceptance of the breadwinner norm. In a memo to the union a month later, BC Electric outlined its acceptance of the union proposal in an official employment policy that would upgrade men's jobs and restrict women's access to promotions:

> The following rules should apply to the matter of filling vacancies in job groups 1 to 7 inclusive: 1. When such a vacancy occurs, it is to be filled, if possible, by a male employee who holds a lower grouped job, if that is possible, and so on down the line. 2. If it is not possible to promote males in lower group jobs to vacancies occurring at job levels 1 to 7 inclusive, then female employees should be promoted to such vacancies or females should be

recruited from outside the company. 3. When a male employee is promoted, as outlined under the several possibilities suggested in #1 above, the final vacancy resulting should be filled by a female employee if it constitutes a promotion for her, or alternatively a female recruited from outside the office. 4. Division heads will make the final determination of the point whether or not a vacancy at job levels 1 to 7 inclusive can be filled by a female. . . . This will serve to merely formalize the routine now in operation.[42]

The development of these hiring and promotion practices solidified gender divisions between men and women in the office and more clearly defined all male work as skilled office work that warranted a higher job classification. Thus, what was promised to be a 'scientific process' of job evaluation was soon shaped not only by the pre-existing hierarchy of jobs in the office, but also by union demands for a male breadwinner wage.

The definition of which work was more or less highly valued, and who might perform such tasks, was mediated by union arguments that 'the earning power of a group #3 job for male employees is barely enough to meet the needs of a man supporting a family.'[43] Breadwinners required higher incomes and, by definition, men were breadwinners and women were not. Several union strategies were advanced for achieving breadwinner rights through the job evaluation system: (1) job evaluation could be reworked to reassign men's tasks a higher value; (2) men themselves could be promoted to higher-ranked jobs; and (3) men's jobs could be removed from the job evaluation system altogether. All three strategies were negotiated to separate higher-level male from lower-level female work, including redefining some union jobs as non-office jobs excluded from the job evaluation process. At the same time the segregation of 'those jobs which can definitely be done by females'[44] was redefined as a measure of skill validated through the job evaluation system. In this way the OEA not only initiated sharper gender divisions between male and female office workers, it also played an important role in constructing the value of different tasks that men and women performed in the office,[45] encoded in a job evaluation system that remained in place unchanged until the early 1980s.

It should be remembered that in the late 1940s the OEA's bargaining strategies were clearly set out in Executive Council meetings. If women activists in the union objected to the privileging of men as breadwinners, such dissent was not recorded in Council or bargaining minutes. Women did express opposition to the female differential through a mass petition and, as we shall see below, by the end of the 1940s the union took this up at the negotiating table. It is possible, however, that most female members also supported the family wage strategy, which conformed to conventional ideals in the postwar years. But it is also the case that the OEA's explicit privileging of men's breadwinner rights was soon rendered invisible within collective bargaining. Such assumptions were quickly normalized and the union's role in establishing the gendered division of labour ceased to be visible in bargaining or in the terms of the collective agreement.

Even as masculinist hiring and promotion policies were being negotiated between the union and the company, and expressed clearly in bargaining talks, these policies were not hinted at in the final language of collective agreements. The 1949 collective agreement, for example, included provisions on hiring and promotions framed entirely in gender-neutral (not to mention racially neutral) language, with no mention of the formal company policy established the year before. Clause 6–B of the 1949 collective agreement read as follows:

> The company will whenever possible give preference to Company employees when filling vacant positions, and before filling a vacant position with a person who is not a Company employee, post the said position with its classified group rating so as to give employees of the Company an opportunity to apply for it. Subject to the foregoing, all promotions may be made by the Company solely on the basis of merit without posting the position to be filled.[46]

According to the collective agreement, employment status with the company and performance-based merit were the bases upon which jobs were filled. In reality, this was clearly understood to occur within gendered and racialized parameters. Over time the union also negotiated greater promotion rights based on seniority. But the gendered hierarchy of jobs, upon which the OEA and BC Electric had reached full agreement, was to remain invisible; in fact, it was to be strengthened by establishing seniority rights because the policy on married women precluded most women from attaining much seniority. Similarly, when White-only hiring practices began to break down in the 1960s, seniority rights helped to maintain the privileged position of White workers long after this ceased to be a precondition for employment at the utility company. In this way, racial and gender privilege became part of the organizational logic of the office and of union bargaining traditions, about which office workers might remain completely unaware but be affected by just the same.

On occasion the gendered parameters of job hierarchies did become more visible in the collective agreement. So, for example, it surfaced tangentially after the provincial government legislated the Equal Pay Act for men and women in 1953. The Equal Pay Act stipulated that men and women doing the same work in the same establishment must be paid the same wages.[47] Since women and men who were evaluated as doing work of comparable value (that is, in the same job group) received different wages due to the female differential, the company changed the female job classification scale from numerical to alphabetical values to emphasize that this was *different work* for different wages. This change in describing the male and female job groups resulted in reference to the gender specificity of promotions for men and women in contract language. The 1953 collective agreement included the following language on the monetary implications of promotions in clause 6–A:

> Provided that, *in the case of males*, no employee shall step down to a salary which gives him an increase less than (1) In the case of promotion to a job in Groups 1 to 3—$5.00 per month. (2) In the case of a promotion to a job in Groups 4 to 7—$10.00 per month. . . . *In the case of females*, no employee shall step down to a salary which will give her an increase less than (1) In the case of a promotion to a job in Groups A to C—$5.00 per month. (2) In the case of promotion to a job in Groups D to G—$10.00 per month.[48]

The gendered job structure was inadvertently and briefly rendered visible in the collective agreement, making it clear that promotions could only occur within gender-specific job hierarchies. In spite of this, clause 6–C, dealing with the conditions of hiring and promotions *in the same contract*, retained neutral language to suggest that seniority, merit, and employment status were the only factors considered in hiring decisions:

> A permanent employee already on staff of a department in which a vacancy occurs may be promoted to such vacancy without that vacancy being posted on Company bulletin boards. Such promotions shall be made on the basis of merit and seniority in that order. If promotion is not possible within the department, then the position shall be posted showing job group rating on Company bulletin boards, in order to give employees an opportunity to apply for it. Candidates for all vacated or newly established positions will be considered in the following order: (1) Employees on permanent staff. (2) Employees on temporary staff. (3) Non-employee applicants.[49]

In this way neutral language rendered racialized-gendered processes at work invisible. Hiring and promotions appeared instead to be the product of different skills, aptitudes, job performance, and seniority, rather than a badge of unearned entitlement that restricted top competitions to White men.

By the end of the 1940s gender divisions in office work had been firmly established. The number of office workers had expanded from 1,200 at the end of the war to over 1,500 by 1949.[50] With the company's preferential hiring and promotion policies, men moved into the majority in the office; by the end of the decade men constituted nearly 60 per cent of BC Electric's office staff. Moreover, the union's goal of segregating 'those jobs which can definitely be done by females from those revised ones which can be done by males on the basis of group #4 and up'[51] had become reality. As Table 6 shows, 81 per cent of women were employed in jobs in Groups 1 through 4. Two-thirds of all female clerical workers were employed in jobs in

Table 6
Distribution of Office Workers by Job Group,
Maximum Monthly Salary, and Sex, 1949

	Men				Women		
Job Group	No.	%	Max. Salary	Job Group	No.	%	Max. Salary
1	20	37	122.00	1	34	63	118.00
2	8	10	158.50	2	70	90	138.00
3	50	22	184.50	3	176	78	157.50
4	85	26	208.50	4	243	74	176.50
5	90	55	230.50	5	75	45	196.00
6	63	70	257.00	6	27	30	218.50
7	184	94	286.00	7	12	6	241.50
8	107	96	316.00	8	4	4	265.50
9	76	99	345.50	9	1	1	289.00
10	53	100	376.50				
11	46	100	407.00				
12	27	100	443.00				
13	27	100	483.00				
14	28	100	523.00				
15	17	100	564.00				
16	12	100	605.00				
Total	893	58%		Total	642	42%	

SOURCE: Bargaining Files, Box 21, File 7: Salary Scales, 1 Nov. 1949.

Groups 3 and 4. Less than 7 per cent of women were employed in jobs higher than Group 5. In contrast, 82 per cent of men worked in jobs in Groups 5 through 16. Moreover, unlike women, those men who were in lower-level jobs could reasonably expect promotions. The largest concentration of men (one-third) was found in Groups 7 and 8, where they enjoyed salaries nearly twice as large as those of most of their female co-workers. Once set, the gendered division of the office remained remarkably stable, with the ceiling for women's work inching upward over the next four decades.

Although the gender order in the office had been destabilized during the war it was firmly re-established in the late 1940s. As we have seen, the organization of clerical work was not defined solely by management practices. Through the collective bargaining process workers themselves advanced demands privileging the rights of male breadwinners to better jobs, promotion prospects, and higher wages. This process was led by union men, but it was initiated with the participation and knowledge of women who held positions on the Executive Council, and there is no indication that these women, or other female members, resisted breadwinner strategies. By integrating these masculinist demands into the job evaluation system, however, the OEA did much more than embrace heterosexual familial ideologies of the postwar period; it helped structure the gendered division of clerical work, skill, and value at BC Electric for decades to come.

Equal Pay for Women

By the late 1940s the OEA had negotiated men and women securely into their 'proper places' in the office. The union then began to pursue issues of gender in a different direction. In 1949 the OEA took up the position, first expressed in the 1946 petition of 300 women members, that the female differential was unfair and unacceptable to women.[52] It was not a coincidence that BC Electric formalized its preferential male hiring and promotion policy in early 1948 and union resistance to the female differential on the grounds of wage discrimination against women (rather than hiring discrimination against men) appeared on the bargaining table the following year. The previous year, in 1947, the union endorsed a policy of equal pay for women doing men's work; but its concern was the potential to create a 'cheap labour market' that would disrupt the 'existing field of employment for males' by replacing them with women.[53] With this threat removed the union might have followed most of the labour movement after the war and abandoned all concern with equal pay for women.[54] Instead, in its 1949 bargaining proposals the OEA sought to end the female differential and demanded equality for women: 'Equal Pay for Male and Female Employees: No Female Differential'.[55] The job evaluation system, it was argued, demonstrated the equality of male and female work ranked in the same job group. Equal pay for equally evaluated work would remain on the bargaining agenda for the next two decades.

The struggle over equal pay for women illustrates the complex nature of gendering processes embedded in union concerns with equality. The rights of male breadwinners clearly received primacy in postwar union politics, but issues of equality for women were also addressed very early on. Thus, while the timing of the campaign to end the female differential turned on protection gained for men's jobs and breadwinner wages, the struggle for equal pay was an important recognition of women's right to equality in the workplace. In this regard the OEA was a pioneer in the equal pay movement, moving beyond equal pay for identical work to equal pay for equally evaluated work well before most of the labour movement.

That the OEA negotiated a sharper gendered division of clerical work, skill, and value to the disadvantage of women while pioneering demands for equal pay for women speaks to the multifaceted and often contradictory ways that working-class gender relations were lived. The female differential ceased to divide the perceived interests of men and women when the threat to male wages was eliminated through sharper segregation. Building solidarity around women's equality was easier when lines of job segregation were less permeable and men and women were not competing with each other for the same jobs.

Equal pay became a central union issue largely because the job evaluation system, championed by the company as rational, scientific, and fair, made gender discrimination so visible. Unlike in most workplaces, men's and women's work at BC Electric was subject to a single job evaluation system that made it possible to compare gendered jobs, and once compared, the female differential demonstrated systematic discrimination based solely on a worker's gender. As male union activists in the postwar years summed it up, they knew 'it just wasn't right.'[56]

Women also played an important part in making the female differential a central union issue. Women formed a critical mass in the OEA, constituting 42 per cent of the local's membership in 1949 (see Table 6). A union that ignored blatant discrimination against almost half of its members might have difficulty maintaining its legitimacy. The OEA sought to represent all of its members and, as already discussed, defined councillor positions to achieve this. The union's electoral structure ensured that women were present on Council. Although women did not play a major leadership role in the 1940s and 1950s,[57] the presence of a significant number of women on Council helped keep the female differential on the negotiating table. On the other hand, it should also be noted that beyond the petition women circulated in 1946, there was little indication in the immediate postwar decades that women were vocal about the female differential. Once in place, and perhaps especially for those who were hired later on, the female differential tended to be accepted as a normal part of the labour market.[58] Women office workers at BC Electric were not earning less than their female co-workers in other offices; indeed, because they were unionized, OEA women were most often earning more money.

Equal pay for women was a staple at the bargaining table for decades but movement was painfully slow. For years BC Electric refused to negotiate this issue. The company used a host of justifications for the female differential: community standards for similar male and female work; the lower level of skill and complexity of women's clerical work; two 15-minute coffee breaks that women received but men did not that reduced women's workday by 6.6 per cent (a vestige of an early Factories Act); the high turnover of female employees (no doubt related to the company's policy on married women); and charges that women had more absenteeism than men.[59] Because coffee breaks proved a useful argument against the union the company refused to extend coffee breaks to men, although twice daily tea and coffee wagons did deliver to men at their desks. The central issue for the company was conformity to community standards of pay. The lower value of women's work, even when men and women performed the same work, was a normal employment practice in the postwar period. BC Electric was not inclined to pay women more than was required to attract good employees or to give up profits due to misplaced benevolence towards its workers, and the OEA was not strong enough to make it do so. Moreover, the cost of eliminating the female differential was not insubstantial: in 1958 it was estimated that such a move would cost $344,000 per year.[60] Finally, as the company pointed out, the female differential was not in fact an issue of equal pay for women and men as it commonly understood at the time. According to provincial legislation of 1953, equal pay applied only to identical work; and, thanks in part to the union's initiatives in gendering office jobs after the war, men and women did not perform identical work at BC Electric.

The OEA was not in a strong position to force the company to abolish the female differential. Unlike the situation faced by the company's blue-collar unions, the broader community of office workers was almost entirely unorganized; thus, community comparisons could always be used against their demands for higher pay. Indeed, the OEA prided itself on securing wages above community standards;[61] at the bargaining table the union did not want to be compared with other office workers at all. At the same time, although it was on every bargaining agenda beginning in 1949, the OEA never put the female differential at the top of its bargaining priorities. Thus, the union did not bargain equal pay as strongly as it might have. General wage increases always topped the list of bargaining demands and these were invariably tabled as percentage increases that over time widened the gap between higher and lower (and thus male and female) wages. Across-the-board wage increases that might have lessened the effect of the female differential were rejected as contrary to community practices and the principles of the job evaluation system.[62] Instead, the union's top priority in negotiations was parity between higher-paid male office workers and those in the blue-collar unions, rather than parity between equivalent groups of clerical men and women.

Nevertheless, the abolition of the female differential remained an important union goal and it reappeared on every bargaining agenda during the 1950s and 1960s. Following the Equal Pay Act of 1953 the OEA redefined its demand from 'equal pay for equal work', defined in law to mean identical work, to 'equal pay for equal job evaluation'. In this way the union argued that BC Electric was circumventing the intent, if not the letter, of the law:

> The union contends that with the present job evaluation system all jobs are measured with the same yardstick and therefore only one salary scale should apply. . . . The company maintains that they are governed by community practice.[63]

> To deny equal remuneration to a male and female rated the same number of [job evaluation] points is to base a difference in pay on sex alone; and [that] infringes the law. [64]

In the 1950s the OEA proposed a number of ways for the company to bring women's salaries gradually up to the male scale. These included transferring women with several years' experience to the male scale; transferring women in higher job groups to the male scale; transferring those women who supported their families ('female breadwinners') to the male scale; and gradually eliminating the gap between the two scales over a number of years.[65] These gradualist arguments implicitly accepted many of management's claims for lower pay for women, including their lesser experience, lower skill levels, and the importance of the breadwinner norm. This strategy had the effect of validating the company's arguments by suggesting that women who did fit these masculine stereotypes had a greater claim to equal treatment with men. On the other hand, the OEA's intent was to use the cases of anomalous women strategically to make the first cracks in the two-tier system of remuneration.

It is worth recounting in some detail the slow movement to abolish the female differential. After a decade of negotiations, the OEA won its first concessions in 1958 when female employees gained an additional 1 per cent pay raise and a joint union-management committee was struck to study the issue of equal pay.[66] It took more than two years for this committee to report, but when it did the committee sided entirely with the union's position. The report recommended that 'management give early consideration to the elimination of its dual pay scales . . . [and accept] the moral responsibility placed upon it by the enactment of the Equal Pay Act in British Columbia.'[67] BC Electric simply ignored the report. Within months the company was nationalized by the provincial government and the following year it was incorporated into a much larger province-wide utility company, BC Hydro and Power Authority, with the female differential still intact. As the union grew to include all office workers in the new, larger BC Hydro and also began to organize office workers in other companies, Local 378 formally changed its name to reflect its affiliation with the international union. The OEA became the Office Employees' International Union (OEIU) in 1960, and then the Office and Technical Employees' Union (OTEU) in 1964.

Once it became a Crown corporation, BC Hydro showed more concern with the appearance of wage discrimination than had its predecessor. The OEIU pointed out that other public-sector workers did not have separate male and female wage scales. On the other hand, the company remained just as eager to keep wage costs in line with community standards, still arguing that the skill and complexity involved in female clerical work did not warrant higher wages.[68] Picking up some of the union's proposals for the gradual elimination of the dual wage scale, over the next four collective agreements (1963 through 1969) BC Hydro agreed to eliminate the female differential. In essence, however, the female differential was restructured rather than eliminated.

Steno pool, BC Electric, 1957. (Vancouver Public Library photo no. 29616.)

As a prelude to negotiations for the 1963 agreement BC Hydro informed the OEIU that it was willing to replace the dual wage scales with 'a common salary scale [that] would result in a composite scale reflecting the average level' of male and female wages.[69] What the company had in mind was lowering the male scale and raising the female scale in the lower job classifications (where most women and few men were employed) to a single mid-range scale. Not surprisingly, this was unacceptable to the union. Lowering the male scale would have undermined men's support for equal pay for women. Moreover, by the early 1960s women were becoming increasingly vocal and demanded their lateral merger directly onto the male wage scale. It is perhaps not coincidental that this demand intensified as the ban against married women began to break down and when, for the first time, two women were members of the negotiating committee.[70] As a letter from one member indicates, by the early 1960s masculinist assumptions were being openly challenged by some women:

Men are supposedly paid a better wage or salary because they have to maintain a household. What about women, like myself, that have to maintain a household, raise a family, educate our children and try to hold up our heads in the community? Are we any less worthy of maintaining a high standard of living than our male counterparts?. . . Most men would sneer at my pay check were they asked to work and keep their family on it, yet I have to— because I am a woman. This is discrimination.[71]

The OEIU was still in a weak position in regard to community comparisons for clerical work, in a largely unorganized sector of the workforce, and without a history of membership militancy on this or other issues, and so it sought a compromise through gradualism. The gradual elimination of the dual wage scales maintained male wages but it also allowed the company to manipulate the job classification system at each stage and thereby restructure the female differential.

In the 1963 contract, women won an additional 3 per cent increase each year for two years, narrowing the female differential to just over 10 per cent. In exchange, women lost their two coffee breaks each day.[72] Both men and women received coffee and tea service at their desks, and in the following contract all members received the same 15-minute coffee breaks. The first significant step in abolishing the female differential occurred in the 1965 contract. Accepting the union's long-standing suggestion that the small number of women in higher-level jobs should be paid at men's wages, the corporation moved all women in Group F (6) and above to the male salary scale. Nearly two decades after the union had helped to segregate women in lower-level jobs and circumscribed their promotion opportunities, very few women were affected by this partial merger of the job classification system. Only 69 women, 9 per cent of the union's female members, were in Group F or above. Ninety-one per cent of all female clerical workers were in jobs classified as Group E (5) and below, and for these women the female differential remained in place.[73]

The dual wage scale was formally eliminated in the following contract, in 1967. This should have been a victory for the OTEU, 18 years in the making, but the terms were unacceptable to the union. Women did not receive 'equal pay for equally evaluated jobs', so the OTEU had little to celebrate. Women fully expected the completion of their merger to the male scale for those in Groups 1 (A) through 5 (E) and the union proposal was worded as such. BC Hydro proposed the creation of a single classification system but designed it so that female clerical workers would not receive the expected increase to male wages. They hoped to achieve this by placing women one group lower on the new single scale than where they previously had been on the female scale. Women below Group 6 would need more points than men in job evaluation (still ostensibly an objective and scientific way of evaluating the skill level and value of a job) to be assigned to the same job group. In this way the female differential was restructured within a single classification system. In bargaining, the union insisted on a lateral transfer of women to the male scale but eventually agreed to the company proposal, provided that wage rates were substantially raised. The company refused the union compromise. With the workers having no legal right to strike at the time, the contract impasse went to conciliation. The Conciliation Board ruled in favour of the company and its new single job classification system was created.[74] As one irate woman councillor commented, the 'award added job evaluation discrimination to salary discrimination.'[75] As she went on to point out, this was doubly ironic because a non-discrimination clause was also negotiated in the collective agreement that year to protect members from discrimination based on 'race, colour, creed, national origin, age, sex, or marital status'.[76]

From the OTEU's perspective the new job classification system was old wine in new bottles, and so the struggle to end pay discrimination against women continued. In contrast, BC Hydro sought to prevent unwarranted wage increases for women and argued with some justification that its staff were already among the best-paid clerical workers in the province. The visibility of the female differential was the problem the company sought to address. From the company's perspective, then, the solution adopted in the 1967 collective agreement had not sufficiently eliminated the appearance of discrimination. It, too, sought to revisit the issue.

Thus, equal pay was on the bargaining table yet again in the following negotiations in 1969. The OTEU called for the lateral merger of women onto the male wage scale by upgrading those women who had been downgraded in 1967. BC Hydro proposed another revamping of the job classification system that would, at least on the surface, acquiesce to union demands. Women in Groups 1 through 4 were upgraded to their previous job group, so that a former Group B moved from Group 1 to Group 2, and so on. In addition, however, all men's office jobs below Group 5 were transferred out of the job evaluation system altogether. From here on in, there would be no men at all employed in office jobs in Groups 1 to 4. Such men's jobs, most of which were in Group 4, were redefined as non-office jobs and as such were not subject to job evaluation or to comparison with similarly ranked women's jobs. Instead, wage negotiations for these jobs took place as a separate part of union negotiations and resulted in higher wages than for equivalent office jobs.[77] In addition, and most important for women's pay, the entire pay scale for office workers was restructured with a skewed pay grid so that those in the lower groups earned proportionately less than those in the middle and upper groups. For example, those in Group 1 (all women) had only a 7 per cent spread between their minimum and maximum salary levels, while Group 6 (almost all men) had a 17 per cent pay spread; previously, every job group had a 21 per cent pay spread between minimum and maximum salaries. As a result of such tinkering with the pay scales, a general 15 per cent wage increase over two years produced salary increases ranging from 0.5 per cent in Group 1 to 19 per cent in Group 12.[78]

Although the OTEU had recently gained the right to strike and did take a strike vote to strengthen its bargaining demands, no job action was forthcoming to gain a more equitable settlement for women.[79] This did not mean that the union simply acquiesced to restructuring job evaluation or that it then abandoned the struggle to end pay discrimination against women. In fact, the demand for a rationalized pay grid that would end the hidden female differential remained on the union's bargaining agenda for the next decade, and was finally achieved in 1981 (see Chapter 4). It did mean, however, that equal pay for women was not sought with as much determination as it could have been, and in the end this goal was sacrificed for good general wage increases. Moreover, in 1969 BC Hydro was successful in finally ending the *appearance* of wage discrimination. The female differential was completely hidden, with lower-level men's jobs forever removed from easy comparison through designation as 'non-office' (something the union never sought to change), and community standards, whereby women were paid less than men for similar work, were maintained. With the female differential restructured and buried in a complicated pay system that few people understood, the grassroots demand among women for equal pay for equally evaluated work soon subsided. Outside the doors of OTEU bargaining committees, most members were no longer aware that pay discrimination continued in a new form.

Wage Parity for Men

The struggle against the female differential embodied resistance to prevailing gender norms but coexisted with strategies to preserve men's right to better jobs and higher wages. In fact, demands for women's equality were embedded in demands for equality among men. OEA bargaining strategies were shaped not only by simultaneously embracing and challenging conventional relations between the sexes, but also by conceptions of masculinity and demands for wage parity between men in the company's blue-collar and white-collar unions.

As we have seen, time and again the OEA raised the issue of equal pay for women at the bargaining table. But such demands were always secondary to other wage concerns: wage demands that revolved around men's wages. How did male office workers compare with men in other industries? More importantly, how did their wages compare with other men in the utility company? These concerns were prioritized and set the context for general wage demands that used an exclusively masculine measure of comparison. This strategy helped make more persuasive claims at the bargaining table, because in the broader community men enjoyed higher wages than women, but it also embodied concerns over white-collar masculinity.

In its survey of salaries for collective bargaining in 1955, for example, the OEA outlined the following reasoning for its bargaining strategy:

> Throughout we have utilized the wage rates of male employees only. We have done so for obvious reasons. *It is to these employees that justice must be done. Their responsibilities do not differ from those of other workers in the industrial field.* Therefore *equity demands* that their remuneration should at least keep pace with the advance of wages in the industrial field.[80]

Prioritizing demands for wage parity between men signalled the extent to which concerns with wage justice and equity were encompassed within a breadwinner discourse. Men's right to keep pace with other men superseded women's right to equal pay because men's responsibility as (real or potential) family breadwinners took precedence over other considerations. Moreover, it was clear that different conceptions of masculinity were bound up with status differences among men. Comparisons with other men invoked the notion of comparable worth: 'Our members are comparing themselves with such other higher paid employees whom they consider are either doing work which is *comparable in terms of value or is even of less value than their own.*[81]

The office job evaluation system was the union's measure of skill, placing supervisory, mental, and manual labour in descending order of value. Thus the OEA viewed its men as highly skilled and worth higher wages than their blue-collar counterparts. The starting point for wage comparisons was 1945—the year job evaluation was implemented and collective bargaining began between the OEA and BC Electric—and a Group 7 men's salary was used as the benchmark to compare wage increases among different groups of men in the intervening period. In 1953, for example, the union concluded that its members were at least '20 per cent behind wages paid for directly comparable [men's] work in the community'.[82] The most important wage comparisons were between men in the office and those in blue-collar unions at the utility company. Demands for wage parity were grounded in a growing gap between these white-collar and blue-collar men working at BC Electric. For example, in 1953 the OEA argued:

> We found that the S.R.U. Operator at 85 cents per hour was almost exactly comparable to the average hourly rate of the standard step of group 4 at 86 cents per hour [in 1945]. In terms of our progress at this level, the S.R.U. Operator at his present level is now 19.7 per cent above our present group 4 standard salary. Similarly, [in the IBEW] we found that the Lineman was comparable to our group 7 and the Groundsman was comparable to our group 4. In these cases, they are now 23.6 per cent and 33.2 per cent respectively above the standards in these groups.[83]

On one level it was assumed that wages reflected the value or skill of the worker and the relative scarcity of these skills, in short, his or her economic worth to an employer. At the same time, it was clear that definitions of skill and levels of remuneration reflected struggles between workers and employers and among groups of workers. As the OEA acknowledged, political realities—including higher union density in the community, all-male bargaining units, and blue-collar traditions of aggressive bargaining backed by periodic bouts of labour militancy—placed blue-collar unions in a much stronger position to make claims for higher wages. But in a brief to the Conciliation Board in 1960 the union argued that these political differences ought not to deny equality to white-collar men. The Conciliation Board could choose to rectify the growing power imbalance among men at BC Electric:

> Our brother union (under whose jurisdiction other occupations lie) having superior bargaining power by virtue of their ability and willingness to strike and a more inelastic demand for the labour within its jurisdiction. . . . Members of [our] union, for reasons which need not be discussed in this submission, but which include a high degree of community responsibility and loyalty as well as desire to maintain an atmosphere of harmony with management with whom they work so closely, are not as willing to withhold their labour. This consequent weaker bargaining position has been taken advantage of by the Company, or conversely the Company

has been forced to accede to the stronger Unions and so the wage gap has steadily increased. The Union asks the Board to lend its power to rectify this growing inequality.[84]

Identifying the stronger position of blue-collar unions with their greater militancy, the OEA pointed to the more ambiguous working-class position of white-collar unionists, with an emphasis on 'harmony', 'loyalty', and 'responsibility'. The greater bargaining strength of the blue-collar unions was not just a function of militancy, however; it was also related to a broader unionized environment for similar work and, above all, the existence of all-male bargaining units.

The relative decline in the salaries of male office workers in relation to their blue-collar counterparts was clearly at odds with the union's own notion of the superior value of men's white-collar work: 'To make it even more difficult for our members to accept this drastic worsening of their comparative position is the fact that the skills required by a Group 7 [man] in our jurisdiction are superior to those required by a lineman.'[85] This conception of relative levels of skill was embodied in the company's job evaluation system. In office job evaluation manual work was not highly rewarded. Yet in the company as a whole, as in the broader community, manual work associated with unionized men was often highly rewarded.

For its part the company tried to rationalize the growing gap between its blue-collar and white-collar men by reference to principles of job evaluation, even though blue-collar jobs were not subject to any form of job evaluation and end rates were negotiated for specific jobs. BC Electric argued that any historic link between office and blue-collar jobs in 1945 was superseded by changes in the content of blue-collar jobs. The IBEW linemen, for example, were paid proportionately more because the job required greater skill than it had in the past.[86] Community standards of pay, which were higher for such jobs, were argued to reflect differences in skill levels.

This line of reasoning was made more questionable in light of tinkering with the job evaluation system to exclude some members of the office union from job evaluation. These were the so-called non-office jobs, originally a handful of men's jobs that ranked too low in job evaluation for wages comparable to similar men's jobs in other companies or other sections of the utility company organized in blue-collar unions. After restructuring the female differential, as we have seen, all men's jobs below Group 5 were redefined as non-office jobs.[87]

The OEA was keen to redefine lower-level men's jobs as non-office since this allowed them to negotiate end rates, and higher wages, for many men's entry-level positions. On the other hand, non-office jobs were also used to demonstrate that men's office jobs were undervalued. If community pay standards measured skill, and so, too, did the company's job evaluation system, why was there such disparity between men's office and non-office pay rates?

> Our studying of the Company's so-called 'non-office' job descriptions which have been developed as a means of adjusting certain of our members salaries in order to bring them into line with the salaries of other union employees whom they are either working with or their work is directly comparable. In every case, these examples prove the fact that their salaries as determined by job evaluation are all well below the salary necessary to provide the comparability required. One outstanding example is that of the Utility Man, evaluated at our group 1 salary level, whose non-office rate was 70 per cent above our present standard rate for a group 1 [male] by virtue of the fact that his job compared directly with the Janitors rate under the s.r.u. agreement, and who was just recently transferred to i.b.e.w., and thereby advanced a further 19 per cent by virtue of his now being covered under the latter agreement. Another is the Platen-Pressman who is evaluated at a level of group 4 under our salary standard, but whose salary is adjusted to provide comparability with the local Printers' Union scale and which in turn puts him 42.7 per cent above our scale.[88]

These comparisons between office and non-office union jobs were raised only within the context of men's work and were used as grounds to argue for parity between men's white-collar and blue-collar wages. When all men in the lower groups were transferred to non-office classifications in 1969 the union did not extend this argument to the general undervaluing of women's work. Had the union considered these two issues together—undervaluing women's work and undervaluing men's office work—it might have considered how these two trends were interrelated in the context of feminization. Moreover, the union itself was complicit in this process of gendering notions of skill that defined women's clerical work as low-skilled, and in the long run tended to undermine claims that men's office work was highly skilled.

Collective bargaining at the utility company operated within a larger masculine union environment that, in general, valorized manual labour. Office workers, operating in a largely non-union environment in their own trade, were at a serious disadvantage in pressing their claims since community comparisons were central to the company's remuneration policies. The arbitrary removal of some jobs from office job evaluation made it clear that job evaluation was little more than a process of rationalizing community practices, to be discarded when it proved inconvenient.

Indeed, when utility men defined as unskilled in the job evaluation system earned more than almost all female clerical workers and more than men below Group 4,[89] job evaluation was being used to suppress wages and maintain levels closer to those in non-unionized offices. This was not only a blow to office workers' incomes, it was a blow to the masculinity of male clerical workers as expressed through the value of their work and their own sense of skill *vis-à-vis* blue-collar workers. According to company pay practices, male office workers were less skilled than blue-collar workers, an injustice the union sought to rectify by restoring male office workers to their rightful place in the male status hierarchy. For all the union's recognition that the female differential 'just wasn't right', therefore, wage discrimination against women took second place to the demands for equity and justice for white-collar men. Masculinist assumptions did not prevent union men and women from recognizing and resisting the injustice of the female differential, but prioritizing breadwinner rights put the struggle for equal pay for women, like the women themselves, in their proper place, second in line to the interests of their union brothers for wages in accordance with their proper worth in the company's male status hierarchy.

Challenges and Contradictions

Office workers played an active role in gendering work at BC Electric through their strategies in collective bargaining. Collective bargaining simultaneously reproduced and challenged gendered hierarchies in the office: privileging the rights of White men to better jobs, higher salaries, and promotion opportunities; demanding equal pay for women as part of women's equal rights as workers; and demanding wage parity between white-collar and blue-collar men. These struggles were bound up with contradictory constructions of white-collar working-class masculinity and femininity in the postwar years.

As we have seen, women and men were literally and figuratively negotiated into their proper places in the social order at BC Electric. Collective bargaining embodied contradictions between familial ideologies of breadwinner rights and working-class aspirations for equality among all workers. These contradictions can be read in terms of relations between men and women in the office, where breadwinner rights and equal rights for women were often at odds. In such cases breadwinner rights usually trumped women's rights at the bargaining table. On the other hand, such contradictions can be viewed in terms of broader gender relations outside the office. Women's apparent support for breadwinner strategies in the 1940s may reflect broad acceptance of conventional familial roles that located women first and foremost as wives and mothers, and a standard of breadwinner wages for men could forestall women's need to do a double shift of paid and unpaid labour.

Contradictions between breadwinner rights and equality for women deepened as women's labour force participation changed in the decades after the war. By 1961 a majority of female clerical workers in British Columbia were married and nearly one-quarter were over the age of 45.[90] Wage labour and homemaking were no longer discrete phases in most women's lives. By this time, however, masculine privilege no longer formed an explicit part of union strategies discussed at Council meetings or in bargaining committees. Men's access to better jobs, higher pay, and promotion opportunities was structured into job evaluation and job classification, pay rates, and hiring, promotion, and job security provisions that formed the foundation for further bargaining. Rather than being an issue up for renegotiation, masculine privilege had been normalized as a central element of the organizational structure at the office and in collective agreements between the OEA and BC Electric, and this privilege was rooted in union traditions and practices. As part of normalization, masculine privilege had also been rendered invisible through abstract gender-neutral language.

Another reading of these struggles over masculine privilege is interpreted through the negotiation of masculinity. Breadwinner rights were defined at least as much in relation to other men as in relation to women. In fact, the determination of what wage was adequate to support a wife and family was always drawn in comparison to other men. Breadwinner wages were in essence a measure of heterosexual working-class masculinity; and masculinity, as we saw in Chapter 1, is about how men relate to other men in a social world where, to a considerable degree, relations with women are of much less consequence. Male office workers, becoming part of a larger union culture in which masculinity was valorized through physical manual labour, experienced status inconsistencies over the value and masculinity of white-collar work. Rejecting and rejected by blue-collar working-class norms of masculinity and aggressive styles of trade unionism, white-collar workers sought a middle road. In its first three decades the OEA was not a militant union by any definition, and certainly not in comparison to the IBEW. The OEA never struck BC Electric, and after nationalization and the formation of BC Hydro the right to strike was legally prohibited for several years. This lack of labour militancy, in itself, doubtless raised questions about the credibility of the OEA in the eyes of many blue-collar co-workers. The escalating gap between IBEW and OEA wages was tied to these different styles of trade unionism; it was also tied to feminization of the office and constituted a challenge to the masculinity of male office workers. Failure to win wage parity with the IBEW threatened to undermine the status of white-collar men in the company and in broader relations among working-class men.

Struggles over the value and masculinity of male white-collar work were negotiated, first, in relation to other White men, and only secondarily in relation to women or to men of colour. In general, men's work was deemed to be worth more than women's. The union's struggle against the female differential challenged such a view, but restricting women to the lowest jobs reasserted it. There were no such challenges to or contradictions in the racialized order of office work in the postwar years. Well into the 1960s office employees of the utility company remained Euro-Canadian. This was a hiring practice that the union had no direct role in shaping. However, absence of discussion at the bargaining table should not lead us to underestimate the importance of White privilege in shaping the union's practices. Comparison with particular workers and not others, the sense of entitlement to breadwinner wages, and their place in the social order of workers were very much shaped by racialization. In the period before World War II the labour movement in the province had a long history of anti-Asian organizing and exclusionary practices.[91] Although explicit forms of exclusion subsided after the war, the 'Whiteness' of white-collar workers was an unearned asset upon which the union's bargaining demands were built.

Together with BC Electric—which maintained racialized hiring policies after the war and fought to maintain community standards of lower wages for office work, especially for women's work—the OEA negotiated the normalization of superior claims for White male breadwinners at the office. As the union grew, practices initiated in the 1940s and 1950s became part of the invisible weight of custom and tradition embedded in the terms of the collective agreement, the traditions of bargaining strategies, and, equally important, the very structure of jobs and pay in the office. In the following chapter we will examine more closely the embodiment of these practices on the job through the construction of separate streams of clerical and technical work at the office.

4

Transforming Clerical Work
into Technical Work

*When it comes to comparing, for instance, the clerical
job I hold on a full time regular basis to my temporary
drafting job, the justification for the difference in the two
is, well, 'drafting is technical'. . . . Having done the two
jobs, the clerical job is more technical.*[1]

Negotiating Corporate Culture

With the exception of women's recent entry into management the gender division of labour at the utility company has changed little over the
last 50 years. As we saw in Chapter 1 gender divisions in the 1990s are
such that most work remains male-dominated. Men perform a broad
range of jobs, including blue-collar or manual labour, white-collar
office work, and management and professional engineering. In contrast, women are seldom employed in the blue-collar trades or as engineers. Moreover, even the entry of women into management has been
slow. For the most part women's work remains within the office.

The general parameters of the gendered division of labour have
remained much the same, but the jobs of office workers have changed
considerably. Office work is more or less evenly assigned to women
and men and, as we have seen, it, too, is clearly segregated along gender lines, though the division between women's and men's work in
the office has inched upward over time from Group 4 to Group 6. At
the same time, office work has been transformed through automation,
the computer revolution, and increasing educational credentials.

These changes have not been unilaterally defined by management; office workers have negotiated the gendered nature of contemporary office work through the construction of two gendered streams of clerical and technical office work. In the 1960s and 1970s negotiating technical work became a central union preoccupation.

Labour negotiations have been shaped by the broader corporate culture of engineering. Professional engineers not only dominate management, they form a large block of technical experts near the top of the corporate hierarchy. Thus, engineering culture shapes how work is organized and defined within the company. Engineering is an important part of the habitus,[2] or networks of shared cultural/social capital and esteem, that valorizes skills attached to applied science and technology.[3] Few women share this culture; in the 1990s engineering remains a male-dominated profession. Thus, engineering culture is a defining quality of the utility company environment from which women have been excluded. Exclusion from engineering culture has been based as much on gender as on formal education in engineering. Men without training in engineering have been groomed into engineering-related work. In contrast, women have been unable to gain admission to entry-level positions in which they might begin to forge the experience necessary to move to the bottom rungs of the technical office hierarchy.

Unlike other gender divisions at the utility company, which resonated with unchallenged cultural assumptions about the masculinity of physical blue-collar labour and the scientific expertise of professional engineers and managers, the rationale for gender divisions among office workers after the war was more contradictory. Office work was increasingly feminized and considerable effort was required to imbue some office jobs with masculine gender identities. Much of this effort involved attempts by white-collar men to recast themselves in the image of their engineer-managers. The creation of the technical office worker who performed clerical support work for engineers, differentiated from the feminine typist and general support clerk, in fact formed part of the negotiation of masculinity at the office.

White-collar men simultaneously negotiated between working-class blue-collar and professional middle-class images of masculinity, creating skilled technicians somewhere between the electricians and linemen in the IBEW and the professional engineers in the company. Building on the links between clerical support work tied to the engineering functions of the company, union and management created a complex system of career ladders that all but prevented those who did not begin in traditional male entry-level jobs from moving up the office hierarchy. For those men who did move up this hierarchy the esteemed label of technical office worker was bestowed. With few exceptions, men who played leadership roles in the union worked their way up the job hierarchy to these technical positions. These men carried with them a knowledge of and respect for the value of engineering that was inscribed into the culture of the union and reflected in the collective bargaining process.

For the most part, men's entry-level jobs were designated as non-office jobs that provided higher salaries than job evaluation suggested they merit. Many non-office jobs were closest in kind to manual blue-collar work, but they were historically linked to white-collar career ladders and were thus included within the jurisdiction of the office union. The single largest entry-level job for men was meter reading, which involved reading utility meters at homes and businesses; this position served as a recruitment funnel into higher-level office work. Although meter reading cannot be considered a technical job, experience in meter reading and other non-office jobs was redefined as technical or field knowledge necessary for advancement up the job hierarchy. Long after women were officially denied promotion to higher-level office jobs, this so-called technical or field experience remained a barrier that most women were unable to breach.

In the early 1970s the growth of post-secondary training in related technical fields added a new dimension to the process of separating technical from clerical work. Courses and certificates from technical institutes provided recognized expertise that vaulted some new employees past other men with more seniority. Formal technical training outside the office thus began to circumvent the normal male career ladder in the office. Soon, post-secondary courses and certificates were combined with experience acquired in men's entry-level jobs for career mobility within the office. This added a new set of externally acquired criteria for promotion up the office ladder, just as racialized hiring patterns broke down and provided a basis for job mobility for some young men of colour. Post-secondary technical training did not have the same impact for women, who remained greatly underrepresented in technical training. If anything, reliance on externally acquired technical qualifications added a new gender barrier for women at a time when employment equity policies might otherwise have enhanced women's access to technical jobs. This chapter explores how these clerical and technical divisions were negotiated in the 1960s and 1970s and were inscribed in processes of collective bargaining and the organization of the office.

Creating the Office Ladder

By the end of the 1940s, as we saw in Chapter 3, the OEA and BC Electric had negotiated a sharp gender division of labour that defined the experiences of men and women in the company. In 1949, 81 per cent of women were in Groups 1 through 4; 93 per cent were in Groups 1 through 5. In contrast, 82 per cent of men were in Group 5 and above (see Table 6). This pattern changed little over the next two decades. In 1960, 92 per cent of women were in Group 5 (E) and below; men continued their movement upward, with 82 per cent of men in Group 6 and above (Table 7).[4] The 1960s were a period of rapid growth for the utility company as it became a Crown corporation and expanded province-wide. The number of office workers grew by more than 50 per cent in the first half of the decade, to more than 1,800 men and women. Although this expansion coincided with more

Table 7
Distribution of Office Workers by Job Group,
Maximum Monthly Salary, and Sex, 1960

Men			Women		
Job Group	*Number of Employees*	*Maximum Salary*	*Job Group*	*Number of Employees*	*Maximum Salary*
1	0	239.00	A	6	210.00
2	1	278.00	B	32	239.00
3	8	312.50	C	124	267.00
4	18	345.50	D	224	296.50
5	61	385.00	E	80	329.50
6	86	427.00	F	15	363.00
7	106	470.50	G	24	397.50
8	135	513.50	H	1	433.00
9	57	558.00	I	0	468.50
10	9	602.00			
11	13	653.00			
12	0	711.50			
Total	494*		Total	506**	

*Plus 148 men in non-office jobs; total men: 642.
**Plus 46 women in non-office jobs; total women: 552.

SOURCE: Bargaining Files, Box 20, File 14: distribution of office employees, Dec. 1960; Collective Agreement 1960, Salary Scales in effect 1 Oct. 1960.

Table 8
Distribution of Office Workers by Job Group and Sex, 1966

Job Group	Female Employees	Job Group	Male Employees
A–E	739 (89%)	1–5	160* (15%)
6–12	63** (8%)	6–12	694 (66%)
Non-office	25 (3%)	Non-office	198 (19%)
Total	827 (100%)	Total	1,052 (100%)

*56% of these men were in Group 5; 94% were in Groups 4 and 5.
**Women above Group F were transferred to the male job groups as part
of this contract. There were no women above Group 8. A more detailed
breakdown of women was not provided, though a complete breakdown
was provided for men. The highest concentrations of men were in Group 8
(18%), Group 6 (16%), Group 9 (14%), and Group 7 (13%).

SOURCE: Bargaining Files, Box 20, File 1: Employee Distribution and
Salary Scales, 12 Dec. 1966.

married and older women remaining in the labour force, women who
might be expected to enjoy more career mobility in the office, the pattern of gender segregation remained just as sharp. In 1966, 89 per
cent of women, and only 15 per cent of men, were working in the bottom half of the office hierarchy, Group 5 (E) and below (Table 8).

This ghettoization of women was reflected in lower salaries and
limited career prospects. In 1960, for example, the average monthly
salary of women in the union was 63 per cent of the average salary for
men ($270.83 compared to $429.31); nearly two decades after unionization the wage gap for office workers was still tied to the traditional
gap between men and women in the Canadian labour market.[5]
Equally telling, employment tenure with the company, and thus
seniority rights negotiated by the union, continued to favour men. In
light of postwar restrictions on married women's employment it is not
too surprising that in 1960 over 70 per cent of men, but less than 40
per cent of women, had been employed with the company for more
than five years.[6]

In the postwar years restrictions against married women effectively prevented much upward job mobility among women. As labour
market needs increased in the 1960s and more married women sought
to retain employment, these restrictions began to break down. By
1968 fully 40 per cent of female office workers at BC Hydro were
married.[7] In recognition of its changing membership needs the union
negotiated unpaid maternity leave of four months in 1965.[8] As social

conventions around women and work liberalized and more women embarked on longer careers with the company, the exclusion of women from promotions and higher-level jobs did not change; instead, gender segregation remained an unexamined part of the organizational culture of the office and the union.

The construction of gender differences began with recruitment into the company. Women were recruited right out of high school or secretarial school with limited previous work experience, while men were expected to have some previous work experience and tended to be a few years older. As a report presented to the Royal Commission on the Status of Women in 1968 explained: 'Approximately 70% of the females hired by the Company are in the age bracket of 18–20 years. A slightly lower percentage of male hiring is in the 21–23 age bracket. The qualification of "maturity" is stressed when males are hired.'[9] Moreover, women's entry-level jobs were at the bottom of the office hierarchy, whereas men entered about midway in what was, by the 1960s, a 12-group job classification system: 'At least 70% of the females are hired into Salary Grade Levels 1 or 2, while approximately 70% of the males are hired into Salary Grade levels 4 or 5.'[10]

Men and women were hired for different types of jobs and their gendered career prospects were made clear in job interviews. One woman remembered these messages in her initial interview in the mid-1960s:

> My very first impression was when I was sitting in this little glass office having my interview and the selecting supervisor was asking me why I wanted a job and all these questions, and then he asked me if I had any questions. And I said, 'Well what do all those people do?' And he described them and their names and what they did. And I said, 'Would I be able to move up to those positions?' And at that point he said, 'Well, I'm very sorry, B., but these particular jobs are women's jobs, and those other jobs are men's jobs.'[11]

Women were hired for shorthand, typing, and other clerical abilities acquired largely in high school. These skills were possessed by increasing numbers of women after the war. Combined with the appropriate demeanour of support-worker and helpmate, the clerical skills women brought to the job were often considered innate or unlearned feminine attributes.[12] In this way the mastery of technology in the form of typewriters and other office equipment, and later computers and complex software, was redefined as non-technical clerical tasks.[13] It was a management truism that 'women are usually more adaptable to strict clerical routine and highly repetitive jobs'.[14] Once employed at BC Electric women enjoyed limited promotion opportunities and found themselves confined within a female job ghetto: 'The normal progression of the majority of females is from Salary Grades 1 and 2 to Salary Grades 3 and 4. . . . The normal progression of the majority of males is from Salary Grades 4 and 5 to Salary Grades 6 to 9.'[15]

In the decades after World War II the ceiling between women's and men's jobs inched upward, from Group 4 in the 1950s to Group 5 in the 1970s and finally to Group 6 in the 1990s. There were always a few 'exceptional' women who crossed the barrier, and their exceptionalism reaffirmed the gendered order at the office:

> Anything above a five was a man's job, and there was one little, tiny, old lady that must have been very close to retirement age and she had bridged the gap, and she was a Group Five position. And she was held to be quite remarkable by everyone in the section and probably in the company.[16]

> If a comparable man that came in at a meter reader, worked his way up, it was an expectation that he'd be an office supervisor. Or he'd be a Group Ten, that was quite clear. It was an expectation. . . . On the other hand, if a woman works her way up and becomes a supervisor it's written up in [the company newsletter] and 'wow'. You know, it's not an expectation.[17]

In contrast, men's career expectations were considerable and promotion into the higher ranks was expected. Like women, most men were hired for office work with a high school education. Men's high school studies seldom included typing or shorthand and more likely included drafting, mechanics, or electronics, which might serve as an initial introduction to technical work. The typical entry-level job for men, meter reading, required few skills of any kind beyond general fitness for walking and the ability to read consumption figures on utility meters.

> Every man I have ever talked to, it seems, that is a Group Ten or Eleven job or higher, and unit management jobs, they all started out as meter readers. So that's always been the entry position for men; whereas accounts payable, cash accounting, the pay department [that's where women enter].[18]

> When I started I went in at a Group Three, cashier clerk, where I was responsible for thousands of dollars of money every day,

balancing it and everything else, at a Group Three. And my brother when he went to work went in as a meter reader which was equivalent to a Group Six. And I went in as a Three. And all they did was go out and read the meters. And my brother would be finished at one o'clock in the day, you know, they would learn how to short circuit the routes, do the documents, read the meters, and they learned all kinds of techniques to speed it up, and they had half the afternoon off.[19]

Once in the company, a man could expect a lifelong career with considerable mobility up the office ladder. Mobility out of the union and into management ranks, on the other hand, was limited by the corporate dominance of engineers. Working his way up from meter reader, or another similar entry point, a typical man was recruited into one of a broad range of jobs in Groups 7 and 8; these jobs accounted for nearly half of all men in the office in 1960 (see Table 7).[20] Many men moved even higher up the office ladder. For men, meter reading was the first step in a varied career at the office:

I remember meter readers were an entry-level position. That's where everybody drew when they wanted, say, a Group Six rep, or going into the men's jobs, like the engineering technicians or engineering clerks, the sales reps, those were all men's jobs. . . . A man that came in at a meter reader worked his way up, it was an expectation that he'd be an office supervisor. Or he'd be a Group Ten. That was quite clear.[21]

I can think of three [senior men] right off the bat that started out as meter readers. I think one was the vice-president of human resources, another one was the personnel officer, and one was a manager in stores department. As they were retiring, reviewing their career, you would hit that they'd started out as a meter reader.[22]

Women, on the other hand, were denied access to this and other men's jobs, so important for later recruitment up the ranks, due to the 'dangers' of the work.

Their reason for not hiring women into meter reading was because of the rubby dubby places that women couldn't go into.[23]

We had probably 500 meter readers in this company. And this person [in charge of hiring], he said, 'We don't want female meter readers because if they get down on Water Street, they are going to get raped or something.' . . . So therefore, we can't have female meter readers anywhere. There were 500 of them, and there was probably one route in town [that was dangerous], you know. So this turkey was just not letting any women meter readers in.[24]

Danger perceived to be lurking outside of the office was a familiar theme barring women's entry into other jobs outside the protective environment of the office: danger should a car break down on an isolated highway or even danger on construction sites.

Other rationales were used to maintain a pool of the 'right kind' of men in meter reading, men worthy of promotion to higher-level office jobs:

[The company] maintained male entry-level jobs [like meter reading] at the higher pay scale so they could attract good men and then subsequently get them into jobs up the line.[25]

Meter reading was always for men. I was told by B., who was my manager, that they were told to hire White Anglo-Saxon males. That was their mandate.[26]

Meter readers served as the primary pool for male office workers well into the 1970s. Thus, those charged with hiring meter readers and for other non-office jobs were really the first level of screening for virtually all upper-level office positions. Hiring the right kind of men mattered, even for such low-level positions. Meter reading also served as an important shared experience for most men in the office; this initial familiarity with utilities in the field (or outdoors) began the journey to technical competence. As one observer commented, even in the 1990s 'it is still better to start as a meter reader than as a clerk . . . because the guys who are making the decisions on promotions, some of them started as meter readers. It's a shared experience.'[27]

Differences between men's and women's work went much deeper than job groups and career ladders. Women's jobs were thought about differently, in subtle and not so subtle ways, which evoked gendered notions of skill and of the lower value of women's work. For example, women's jobs were lumped into a handful of generic positions; in contrast, most men enjoyed specialized job designations. These differences embodied beliefs that women were interchangeable; men, however, possessed recognizable individualized skills.

These patterns are illustrated in a detailed examination of OTEU job titles in effect in 1967, just before the formal elimination of the female differential also eliminated separate listings of jobs designated as men's and women's. Authorized jobs for 1967 appear in Tables 9, 10, and 11. As Table 9 shows, for every female job title in the office there were seven titles for men's jobs—58 compared to 409

Table 9
Authorized Job Groups and Job Titles, 1967

Female Job Titles		Male Job Titles	
Group	No. of Job Titles	Group	No. of Job Titles
A	4	1	5
B	12	2	6
C	13	3	9
D	16	4	20
E	13	5	30
		6	78
		7	84
		8	83
		9	62
		10	21
		11	10
		12	1
Total	58	Total	409

SOURCE: Bargaining Files, Box 19, File 12: List of Authorized Job Groups and Job Titles, 1967.

different job titles. The largest number of women were concentrated in Group 4 (D); 224 women in Group 4 were crowded into only 16 jobs (Tables 7 and 9). [28] In contrast, the largest number of men were in Group 8; 135 men in Group 8 were distributed among 83 separate jobs (Tables 7 and 9).

A closer look at the titles of these jobs shows the skills of women recast as non-technical general abilities. At the same time, men's clerical skills were elevated to specialized technical categories. Table 10 lists all authorized job titles for office workers in Groups 1 through 5 (A to E). Table 11 lists all authorized job titles in Group 8, where the largest number of men were employed (21 per cent in 1960 and 18 per cent in 1966) (see Tables 7 and 8). These tables raise six related points about gendering at the office.

First, the higher up the job ladder, the larger the number of discrete job titles. The number of job titles peaks in Groups 7 and 8, with a combined total of 167 job titles. At the top of the job ladder Groups 10 to 12 had fewer job titles but also a much smaller number of employees in the highest classifications (Tables 7 and 9).

Second, and in contrast to the first point, the limited number of job titles in the lower ranks did not result from small numbers of employees in these positions. Groups 3 (C) and 4 (D) comprised a total of 29 separate jobs for 348 women, and another 29 jobs for far less than half as many men (Tables 7 and 9).[29] The small range of job titles at the bottom of the office hierarchy was clearly gendered. Women were more readily classified in large generic groups of workers than were men.

Third, the designation of some jobs as non-office jobs was also gendered and worked in opposite ways for men and women (Table 10). Both men and women held some non-office jobs. Women's non-office jobs were all positions in the cafeteria, including dishwashers, waitresses, salad makers, cooks, and cafeteria assistants, with the one exception of senior matron. In contrast, only one men's non-office job was in the cafeteria—the kitchen helper. Clearly, cafeteria work was considered women's work that was different in kind from clerical work. However, the designation of non-office work separating white-collar from more blue-collar women's work was used to pay non-office women even lower wages than clerical women in the same job group. As the report to the Status of Women Commission explained:

> Non-office rates (sometimes called floor rates) are salaries set at a level other than their job evaluation warrants. Generally they reflect community levels. This Firm has about 14 such jobs for men and 6 or 7 for women. The women (i.e. waitresses, cooks) are paid salaries comparable to office rates or, in some cases, slightly less. The men (i.e. messenger clerks) are paid salaries one to two Salary Grade levels above the job evaluation.[30]

As we saw in Chapter 3, non-office jobs were created by and large as a way to remove some lower-level men's jobs from the job evaluation system so they might be remunerated at higher market levels. For men, unlike women, non-office designation was financially beneficial. By the mid-1960s, as Table 10 shows, a wide range of men's jobs were classified as non-office. Some of these jobs, like the female jobs in the cafeteria, were more similar to other blue-collar work than to white-collar work (for example, bill distributors, mail truck drivers, patrol guards, fire equipment servicemen, and meter readers); but other male non-office jobs seemed indistinguishable from the men's clerical jobs subject to job evaluation (such as messenger clerks, transit cashiers, meter reading schedule clerks, and storemen/counter-men). Within two years all men's jobs in Groups 1 through 4 were reclassified as non-office jobs as part of restructuring the female differential. Thus, for women non-office designations separated out a limited range of manual jobs included in the office union, while for

Table 10
Authorized Job Groups and Job Titles, by Sex,
Groups 1 to 5 and A to E, 1967

Female Job Titles	Male Job Titles
Group A	*Group 1*
Building services attendant	Bill distributor (n/o)
Bus girl/dishwasher (n/o)*	Farebox receipts attendant (n/o)
Junior clerk 2	Kitchen helper (n/o)
Waitress (n/o)	Messenger clerk (n/o)
	Records clerk
Group B	*Group 2*
Accounting clerk 4	Farebox attendant (n/o)
Addressograph operator 2	Mail truck driver (n/o)
Bindery clerk	Messenger
Coin machine operator	Messenger driver
Diazo print & misc. clerk	Patrol guard 2 (n/o)
Farebox receipts clerk	Transit cashier (n/o)
General clerk 4	
Mail clerk	
Pastry cook (n/o)	
Salad maker (n/o)	
Typist clerk 2	
Waitress-cook (n/o)	
Group C	*Group 3*
Accounting clerk 3	Chart changer
Addressograph operator 1	Delivery truck driver
Consumer services clerk 3	Farebox attendant leader (n/o)
Cook (n/o)	Patrol guard 1 (n/o)
Employee services attendant	Senior mail clerk
General clerk 3	Senior transit cashier
Keypunch operator	Tobacco & sundries clerk
Printing clerk	Travelling timekeeper
Relief varityper	Utilityman
Senior matron (n/o)	
Stenographer clerk 2	
Switchboard operator receptionist	
Typist clerk 1	

Table 10 *(continued)*

Female Job Titles	Male Job Titles
Group D	*Group 4*
Accounting clerk 2	Armoured car attendant (n/o)
Cafeteria assistant (n/o)	Assistant work scheduler clerk
Consumer service clerk 2	Attendant clerk
Control checker clerk	Depot clerk 3
Drafting clerk	Draftsman fieldman 3
General clerk	Fire equipment serviceman (n/o)
Information clerk	Materials & equipment clerk
Layout & lithograph assistant	Meter reading schedule clerk (n/o)
Senior keypunch operator	Meter reader (n/o)
Senior waitress (n/o)	Receiver shipper
Sightseeing clerk	Receiver shipper clerk
Stenographer clerk 1	Supervisor of day janitors
Switchboard operator receptionist 1	Supervisor of night janitors
Tour agent	Senior fire prevention equipment server (n/o)
Varityper & layout assistant	Senior transit cashier (n/o)
Verifier operator	Stock clerk
	Storeman/counterman (n/o)
	Stores clerk & charger
	Tracer draftsman
	Traffic checker
Group E	*Group 5*
Accounting clerk 1	Aut. stock service & shop clerk
Computer clerk	Chainman
Consumer service clerk 1	Clerical assistant 2
Control clerk B	Depot & information clerk
General clerk 1	Depot clerk
Home lighting consultant 2	Depot clerk North Van.
Keypunch operator leader	Diesel records clerk
Power districts clerk	Draftsman 3
Secretary	Draftsman fieldman 2
Senior telephone operator	Electrical service order clerk
Senior tour agent	Electrical system clerk
Switchboard information clerk	IBM operator

Table 10 *(continued)*

Female Job Titles	Male Job Titles
Switchboard inf. clerk-relief	Inventory checker
	Invoice & materials clerk
	Laboratory assistant
	Mail clerk leader
	Mapping assistant 2
	Materials clerk
	Maintenance records clerk
	Output clerk
	Pay distribution clerk 3
	Power records clerk
	Rate clerk
	Rodman
	Schedule maker B
	Senior district meter reader (n/o)
	Stock clerk 1
	Stock service & shop clerk
	Stockroom & shop clerk
	Traffic analysis clerk

*OTEU jobs classified as non-office jobs.

SOURCE: Bargaining Files, Box 19, File 12: List of Authorized Job Groups and Job Titles, and List of Non-Office Jobs, 1967.

men this designation rested less on the non-clerical character of the work and more on agreement to exclude them from job evaluation in order to provide higher wages.

Fourth, if we look closely at the distinction between men's and women's jobs in the lower groups it seems clear that several related factors served to gender particular tasks. These included considerations about inside versus outside work and spatial restrictions versus spatial mobility on the job. Jobs that involved some outside work or more spatial mobility were designated men's jobs. Apart from cafeteria work, jobs involving more manual or physical labour were also relegated to men.

Fifth, both men and women worked in jobs as clerks. In fact, almost all women were defined as clerks or operators. In Groups 4 and 5 large numbers of men were defined as clerks and cashiers. What was the difference between male and female clerks? The titles in Table 10 suggest that even in Groups 4 and 5 men's roles as clerks

Table 11
Authorized Job Groups and Job Titles, Group 8, 1967

Accounting assistant 1	Lighting sales rep.
Area development assistant	Manpower development asst.
Assistant deputy registrar	Material stds. analyst
Assistant publication editor	Meter & service planner
Branch sales rep.	Methods analyst
Builder sales rep. 2	Office rep. 1
Buyer	Operating budget clerk
Car accountant	Paint tester & inspector
Claims investigator	Paving inspector
Columbia project analyst	Plant statements accountant
Commercial sales rep. 1	Power & spec. building leader
Commercial service rep.	Protection tech. 2
Commitment analyst	Purchase traffic clerk
Comms. draftsman 1	Records & dispatch leader
Computer tech. 2	Reg. T & D assistant
Construction estimator	Residential sales rep. 2
Contracts clerk leader	Revenue accounting leader
Control clerk leader	Safety & fire inspector
Customer service inspection instr.	Safety & inspection instructor
Dealer sales rep. 2	Sales rep. 2
Display assistant	Sales tax analyst
Disposal salesman	Service centre clerk 2
District distribution estimator	Senior computer operator
District sales rep.	Senior corrosion tech.
Distribution planning assistant	Senior design draftsman
Draftsman surveyor	Senior distribution clerk
Electrical tester 2	Senior draftsman-planning
Electrical trade train co-ord.	Senior home service adviser
Equipment maintenance asst.	Senior instrument fieldman
Field planning assistant	Senior project cost clerk
Freight accounting leader	Senior records & control clerk
Freight traffic rep.	Senior service rep.
Government reports clerk	Staff auditor
Heating sales specialist 1	Systems analyst programmer 3
Heating sales rep. 2	Tab systems designer
Hydrology tech.	Transitman
Industrial safety officer	Transmission engineer assistant
Industrial radiologist	Transportation planning clerk
Instructor	Underground distribution tech.
Insurance assistant	Vehicle analyst
Invoice clerk leader	Work order distribution clerk
Land rep. 2	

SOURCE: Bargaining Files, Box 19, File 12: List of Authorized Job Titles, 1967.

were defined in a more specialized language to reflect their individualized skills. For example, female clerks' titles in Group 5 (E) were more generic, such as accounting clerk, computer clerk, and general clerk. In contrast, men's job titles were more specialized—e.g., automotive stock service and shop clerk, depot and information clerk, and electrical service order clerk. This may less reflect differences in clerical duties performed and more the career ladders these jobs were located within. Men performed clerical support in departments that were more technical or engineering-oriented, such as the automotive and electrical departments. Clerical support work in such departments appeared to imbue male clerks with additional technical skills. Women's clerical support roles in accounting or computing, however, did not seem to confer experience relevant for promotions in those departments. Men were thus able to move up the various department hierarchies on the basis of the experience gained in their jobs as clerks in technical departments; women enjoyed no such upward mobility and were not presumed to have learned anything towards becoming accountants or computer technicians on the basis of clerical support functions in these departments.

Sex-typing of clerical jobs occurred not only between more masculine and feminine departments, it also occurred within technical departments and prevented women in these departments from acquiring jobs on the bottom rung of the promotion ladder. As one union business representative commented:

> The engineering hierarchy basically was a training hierarchy, where you came in at the bottom and did some basic, very basic technical things. And then you moved up. It was a natural progression, and men who were engineering clerks could get into this bottom hierarchy engineering job very easily. Women who worked as clerks in the same area, who did very much the same work, couldn't get in.[31]

Many different rationalizations were used to exclude women from jobs that formed the bottom rungs of the technical career ladder. The most common of these, still expressed in the 1980s, relied on the rights of male breadwinners to higher incomes, women's lack of relevant (even if fictional) specialized knowledge or ability, and exposure to adverse conditions inappropriate for women. Women who tried to compete for men's jobs related similar experiences:

> There was discrimination and I've heard it rumoured that the man would get the job because he has the wife to support and the mortgage to pay.[32]

A woman job steward wanted to know how I was doing with the [job] grievance that failed, it didn't go to arbitration. She said, 'Oh well, D. really needs the job, he has a family to support.' And I said 'I have a family to support, I have the same needs. I lost my house.'[33]

When I finally did get that Group 6 job I actually had a number of people say to me that they weren't happy me getting the Group 6 because that was considered an entry-level job for the men that were planning on staying in that job for about a year, and then going through on promotions . . . a lot of the guys there felt I was going to block that position.[34]

The manager there actually phoned my supervisor and asked him, like in Revelstoke it snows a lot, and you're sometimes travelling up to the Mica Dam. How would I be if I had a flat tire?[35]

[A manager told me] there is absolutely no way a woman could have a job in the interior past a Group 6 because all jobs, even the inside office jobs, were so connected to construction that if you didn't know construction terminology and what it was all about, you couldn't communicate with the people working outside. So you couldn't even have an inside job past a Group 6.[36]

I applied for a drafting job and I didn't get an interview. But I got a telephone call from the guy [manager] saying that he wouldn't be interviewing me because part of the job was to go down into manholes and look at wiring in manholes, and there was rats down in the manholes and things like that. And he said, 'So, of course we wouldn't be hiring any women for that job.' About two years later I was going out with a guy that was an electrical engineer at [the company] and I told him this whole story. And he said, 'Boy, they pulled the wool over your eyes.' He said there is no such thing as going down into the manholes to look at electrical wiring.[37]

They didn't want to expose a woman to the spirit, the atmosphere of the drafting floor. Now, I never asked what is the great danger, but I assume that they couldn't use the familiar language which became pretty common later. . . . It's okay if you work for them, but not to compete with them. If you are one of them, then you interfere with the comfort level.[38]

Gender segregation was not just a matter of excluding women from particular jobs, it was a process of actively defining jobs themselves as gendered, and therefore as only appropriate for one gender.

The definition of a job as technical, as more skilled, and thus ranked higher in job evaluation, was never independent of the gender of its occupant; to define a job as technical was to define it as masculine. As one woman who had performed work defined as technical and as clerical at BC Hydro commented, these distinctions seemed arbitrary:

> When it comes to comparing, for instance, the clerical job I hold on a full time regular basis [Group 4] to my temporary drafting job [Group 6], the justification for the difference in the two is, well, 'drafting is technical'. . . . Having done the two jobs, the clerical job is more technical. Now look at the computerized equipment a person has to use. Look at how you have to be a mediator, a negotiator, you have to be able to juggle demands, you have to do so many things at once. I would take this drafting job over secretarial. Drafting is a piece of cake. Quite frankly, I think the secretarial job deserves more money.[39]

The gendered nature of these job definitions sometimes became clearer when jobs changed gender and were re-evaluated. This was almost always a one-way transition from men's to women's jobs, and in the process of changing occupants the designation of the job was often re-evaluated downward. As one woman remembered:

> I can remember when I got a Group D (4), I was doing mostly clerical work. There was a man in our office, and he was a Five. So not only did he get a level higher than me but the pay scales were adjusted higher, too. So when he left, got a promotion and went somewhere else, the job was rewritten. And mine was now a Five, it had gone from a D to an E, mine was a Five. The job that he did was rewritten and it came out a Three![40]

The sixth and final point drawn from this examination of official job titles relates to the increasing specialization of jobs as one moves up the office hierarchy. The range and terminology used in the higher job groups, to which men alone had access, showed how male clerical work was transformed from support functions to technical expertise in the office. As Table 11 shows, there were more job titles for Group 8 men (83) than for all female office workers combined (58). Moreover, the terms used to describe Group 8 work were qualitatively different from those in the lower job groups. This change in language began to occur in Group 7, coincident with the transition to all-male jobs. Some Group 8 jobs were still designated as clerks, but usually with extensive modifiers; at the same time, other more powerful terms emerged. Group 8 men were variously described as analysts, investigators, representatives, technicians, estimators, inspectors, surveyors, testers, co-ordinators, specialists, officers, instructors, planners, accountants, advisers, auditors, and designers (Table 11). These job titles clearly indicate decision-making rather than support functions in the office.

Specialized job titles at the higher levels were not merely symbolic. Transition to a 'men's job' represented a qualitative change in the way employees were treated at the utility company. As two woman remembered this transition:

> I found that the way I was treated by my department managers when I hit about a job Group Eight was different. They would ask my opinions. If they knew that there was someone I had worked for in the past that was retiring, or something, they'd actually ask me if I was interested in going to the dinner, and that sort of thing. They started treating me as an equal person, as opposed to a subservient person.[41]

> [When I worked in a male technical job] there was a secretary who looked after my phone. I could wear whatever I wanted to wear to work. I could wear jeans, running shoes and a sweatshirt. I could eat at my desk. We had the radio playing all the time. . . . Our day was our own, just get the work done, and we were on our own. Such a different way to be treated. You are treated with respect, you are treated like a person, like a somebody. So when I went to this clerical work [after being laid off], no one knew I was there. Say 'Good morning' and they would look right through you. They wouldn't even acknowledge that you existed.[42]

This improvement in the way workers are treated occurred not only within the company but also, as a product of more authoritative job titles, outside of the workplace:

> One of the big perks when I went from a Group Seven to a Group Eight is I suddenly became, instead of being referred to as a clerk, my title included the word accountant in it, or analyst, or something like that. If you're applying for a credit card, to have to say that you're such and such clerk, as opposed to 'I'm an accountant or an analyst' or something like that, it holds a lot more weight for your general life and all. And it makes you feel better about yourself, too.[43]

The organizational culture that identified higher-level office work with men was also manifest in more subtle ways of organizing the office.

Office Interior, BC Electric, 1956. (Vancouver Public Library photo no. 29368.)

For example, one woman recalled that as she rose up the ranks even the size of the office furniture established her place as an outsider:

> Most of the women had a small-size secretarial chair. But once you hit about a Group Seven or Eight level they had a much fuller-size armchair. It worked out that these chairs were really designed by, or for, male body size, because when I sat in the chair, the back of my knees right against the edge of the chair, my back was still about two inches from the back of the chair. So I had absolutely no

back support. And I spoke to a few of my supervisors about this and they pretty well refused to believe me.[44]

In all kinds of ways, then, the gender of jobs was made apparent at the utility company: by the sex of incumbents, a job's designation as office or non-office, clerical or technical, the nature of job titles, even the arrangement of furniture. Moreover, it should be remembered that, like the women, men holding higher-level technical office jobs in the 1960s and 1970s had moved up through the office ranks, having trained in non-office and lower-level clerical support positions on their way to becoming technical office workers. Most of these men did not possess post-secondary credentials of any kind:

> Men were hired just the same as the women, probably with less skills because they wouldn't know how to type. They just graduated from high school. But the men got trained on the job.[45]

> There is sort of a snobbery, I think, that goes on. Because the technicians work very closely with the engineers they are considered power professional. They would never call themselves clerical . . . [even though] they were trained on the job and promoted gradually within the company.[46]

This suggests that the language used in upper-level job titles tells us less about the complexity or skill levels involved in different jobs and more about who was expected to occupy the positions in question. In spite of rationalizations that suggested otherwise, access to technical office jobs was less the result of aptitude, pre-existing knowledge, or specialized training *per se* than it was the ability to translate experience in clerical support functions into recognized expertise required for promotion to the first rung on the technical career ladder. The possibility to do this was firmly circumscribed by gender.

Negotiating Technical Work

So far the reinscription of men's clerical work as technical office work has been discussed without reference to the union's role in this process. Yet the union did play an important role and, like its approach to the female differential, one that both challenged and reinforced the lower ranking of women's clerical jobs. As we have already seen, the union played a central role in redefining the skill levels of men's office jobs after the war and establishing career ladders that only men could access. In addition, the valorization of men's work as technical, highly skilled and inherently masculine occurred alongside the devaluation and homogenization of women's clerical jobs. This was embodied in a number of union practices, including OTEU participation in designing a new job evaluation system. At the same time, however, the union actively pursued women's grievances contesting job evaluations.

The segregation of male and female jobs was well established by the end of the 1940s, but the clustering of women in Groups 1 through 4 and men in Groups 4 through 9 did not tell the whole story of gendering. The shift towards the rigid job titles and gendered job content we see in the 1960s was in flux in the decade after the war. In the early 1950s, for example, some men were still employed in jobs such as shop clerk-stenographer and clerk-typist, the former a Group 5 position and the latter a Group 3.[47] By the 1960s these jobs had disappeared for men. Similarly, in the 1950s a few women were still employed as bus conductors (or conductorettes) and draftswomen, jobs that women held during the war, and with few exceptions this ceased. In one case a woman employed as a conductorette for seven years was unwillingly transferred to a lower group as a radio control clerk in 1951.[48] Similarly, 'draftswoman' disappeared from the job titles for women. While 'draftsman' appeared under male job titles in Groups 4 and 5 in the mid-1960s, the closest title for women was 'drafting clerk' in Group D (see Table 10).

The hardening of divisions between masculine technical domains and feminine clerical domains in the office was initiated by the OEA to normalize the rights of male breadwinners to higher pay and career mobility. In 1949, a year after the company had agreed to preferential hiring and the upward reclassification of men's jobs to at least Group 4, the union launched a grievance to implement this agreement for all men still in Group 3. The OEA insisted that Group 3 men be raised to 'the same salary step in group #4 as he may now have in [the] group #3 salary scale'.[49] Promotion prospects were monitored by the union throughout this period. By the mid-1950s the pattern was well established of hiring new male employees at Groups 4 and 5, especially in non-office jobs like meter reading, and women at Groups 1 and 2. Appointments to higher-level jobs were almost always based on internal promotions, and the OEA tried to ensure that all its members, including women, were considered for promotions. For example, in 1957 the union pressured BC Electric to 'compile data on present job titles, education, length of service, test results, performance records, etc. and conduct a study as to what action can be taken to expedite promotions for those who appear eligible for them.'[50]

This study focused on men in Groups 1 through 5 and women in Groups 1 through 3 (A to C). As a result of the study BC Electric instituted training lectures for supervisors to outline to their employees 'future possibilities within the company, what career fields they should aim for and what training should be provided to see that they could progress in those fields'.[51] In general, men were encouraged to learn specialized skills peculiar to the utility company, while women were encouraged to hone their more generic office skills. In regard to women, the company advised supervisors to:

> concentrate on unearthing those with the shorthand skill, for example, who are not using it. Competency in shorthand presents the best avenue of promotion for these girls. They should be encouraged to make use of their basic training, take refresher courses if necessary and then we will have a pool from which to promote. So many of them are now barred from advancement because they have not kept up their shorthand. [52]

The OEA was concerned about the promotion prospects of woman and men, but both union and management envisioned gendered career ladders that restricted women from learning more specialized skills. This distinction between men's specialized and women's generic skills provided greater job security for men as well. In response to union concerns about the use of temporary office services, BC Electric assured the OEA that office overload services were only used to hire temporary clerical staff in women's jobs; men would not lose overtime opportunities to temporary employment because their 'specialized' skills could not readily be replaced. [53]

Seniority became more important for the expression of numerous union rights during the 1950s and 1960s, from access to promotions to bumping rights and job security. As married women became more common in the office the method of calculating seniority ignored the realities of women's lives. Seniority was calculated on the basis of the length of 'continuous membership' and did not include short-term or temporary employment. A member who left and then re-entered employment at BC Electric was treated like a new member with no seniority. The only exceptions were for 'military leave-of-absence' or 'leave-of-absence on union business'.[54] Beginning in the late 1950s women were able to continue work while they were pregnant, and in 1958 a policy was adopted to terminate employment of pregnant women six weeks prior to their due date and consider them for reappointment six weeks after the birth of the child. The effect of this policy was to eliminate all union seniority for women who became pregnant; none the less, the OEA expressed its view that the policy was 'quite reasonable'.[55] Language on seniority negotiated two years later did not make any allowances for maintaining seniority after maternity leave. In 1965 unpaid maternity leave of four months was negotiated into the collective agreement for the first time; continuous seniority was not amended to include exceptions for those on maternity leave.[56] Moreover, the company's restrictions on re-employment within six weeks of delivery remained in the Collective Agreement until the late 1970s, when women complained that it contravened the Human Rights Act.[57]

The OEA's role in constructing gendered career ladders did not prevent it from pursuing grievances launched by female members while it simultaneously resisted any change to masculinist practices it had helped to entrench. In the case of the bus conductorette reassigned as a radio control clerk, for example, the union launched a grievance on her behalf, demanding that her experience gained in seven years as a conductorette be recognized and applied to the pay scale in her new job. BC Electric argued that there was no correlation between the two jobs and thus there were no prior skills to merit a higher salary. For its part the union tried to demonstrate how a range of skills used in her previous job were applicable in the new position.[58] Though this grievance was not won it was noteworthy because the union followed the same rationale used when transferring experience from men's non-office jobs to skills needed in men's clerical work.

Both men and women filed grievances over job evaluation as they compared themselves to similar jobs in higher job groups, and the union pursued these grievances with equal vigour. Men continued to enjoy preferential promotion and the overall upgrading of their jobs in terms of technical career paths, but management resisted efforts to re-evaluate individual jobs regardless of the gender of the incumbent. In some instances workers reportedly faced intimidation to dissuade them from filing grievances.[59] In other cases the company apparently accepted grievances brought by men more readily than those brought by women. In one instance, for example, the OEA pursued the grievances of three workers, two men and one woman, seeking temporary promotions for performing the duties of co-workers in higher positions. The men were eventually granted temporary promotions but the woman was denied because she failed to perform 'all of the duties' of her male supervisor and continued to do her own job at the same time (thereby doing two jobs at once).[60]

Perhaps the most important job evaluation grievance pursued by the union in the 1950s involved a small number of draftswomen denied equal pay with draftsmen. The Equal Pay Act legislated in 1953 required the same pay for identical work in the same company. As we saw in Chapter 3, BC Electric changed women's job groups from numerical to alphabetical values and continued to pay lower wages in an attempt to differentiate male and female work and continue to apply the female differential. The following year the OEA filed a grievance on behalf of three draftswomen, arguing that lower pay violated the Equal Pay Act. The case went to a hearing before the Equal Pay Board. The company argued two issues: women did not perform identical work because, unlike draftsmen, women never went out into the field; and women worked shorter hours because they enjoyed coffee breaks not available to men. Using direct comparisons with individual draftsmen the OEA was able to demonstrate identical work: many draftsmen did not, in fact, go out into the field, and some women had done so in the past. The practice of women going into the field had only been stopped after passage of the Equal Pay Act in an attempt to enforce some difference among men and women drafters. The union won this grievance, and the company was ordered to pay women the same rate as men. The Equal Pay Board accepted BC Electric's contention that women worked shorter hours, however, so equal pay was construed as men's salary minus 6.7 per cent for two 15-minute coffee breaks.[61]

Having lost once at the Equal Pay Board, BC Electric was more careful to differentiate male and female work. However, this could be difficult in jobs that underwent feminization. At some point in such transitions men and women were likely to be engaged in identical tasks. One example of this involved the feminization of machine billing operators in the tabulating division. In the late 1950s, for the first time, women moved into these jobs, which were ranked in Groups 4 and 5 (or D and E), with promotion to Group 5 after six months. Men who worked as machine billing operators were in Group 6. For a time men and women machine billing operators existed side by side while classified in different groups. When the union questioned this practice BC Electric made three arguments: (1) the change in staffing offered new promotion opportunities for women key punch operators; (2) if the union threatened an equal pay grievance women would be removed from these jobs immediately; and (3) women were not doing the 'full male job' since the remaining Group 6 men were work leaders.[62] In this case the union decided not to proceed with a grievance. The OEA unsuccessfully challenged the six-month training period before promotion to Group 5 (E), arguing that women transferring from the key punch section already knew all about the operating system and did not require any training on the billing machines.[63] This dispute over machine billing highlights three issues: first, feminization corresponded with the downward re-evaluation of jobs; second, job content was often manipulated to attain some degree of gender difference; and third, even when women's skills were directly transferable from one job to another it was difficult to have these skills recognized.

Weak language on grievance procedures and the generally non-militant tenor of the membership in the 1950s and 1960s prevented many union victories on job evaluation. As a result, by the 1960s job evaluation had become a central issue at the bargaining table and would be an object of increasing union demands for participation in designing a more transparent system. The union continued to pursue individual job evaluation grievances and it also began to pursue broader solutions at the bargaining table. In the 1967 collective agreement, for the first time, the union won the right to see job descriptions and evaluation information before new jobs were posted. It also succeeded in having a joint Labour-Management Committee formed to review the office job evaluation system. While the OTEU interpreted this language broadly to mean it would be consulted in the evaluation of new jobs, BC Hydro insisted it need only inform the union of decisions made; conflict over job evaluation intensified.[64] By the early 1970s dissatisfaction with job evaluation became a strike issue.

Another trend affecting gendered job hierarchies was emerging by the end of the 1960s. A growing number of men were hired with 'some University, College or Technical training' and other men were beginning to enrol in 'evening or correspondence courses to improve their qualifications' and prospects for promotion.[65] On the one hand, post-secondary educational credentials would not change the overall shape of the clerical/technical divisions created in the fifties and sixties, but it would become a flash point for union conflicts over the mobility rights of men. These external credentials provided an apparently objective rationale for promotion into technical support jobs just as the ideological justifications for excluding women began to break down. Post-secondary qualifications provided a new avenue of job mobility when racialized hiring practices began to change and men and women of colour became part of the general labour pool recruited into the office. Thus, although seniority remained the key to mobility for women within the limited clerical office hierarchy, maintaining a privileged position for more senior White women, men seeking to climb the office ladder began to require night courses at a technical institute. Men with the right educational qualifications could bypass the seniority system. At the same time, gender streaming in education and work, combined with uneven domestic responsibilities, prevented most women from acquiring the post-secondary credentials increasingly required to climb the technical office ladder. Within a few less technical sections of the company, such as finance and personnel, educational qualifications in accounting began to provide some women with possibilities for upward mobility.[66] The majority of upper-level jobs remained decidedly male, however, as technical courses and certificates formed new gender barriers for promotions.

The growth of post-secondary education of all kinds created new entry routes into white-collar jobs at BC Hydro and conflicts multiplied over who could perform jobs within the jurisdiction of the OTEU. Conflicts between the office union and blue-collar union had always existed, particularly over OTEU jobs in the field, but these conflicts grew as more and more white-collar work was redefined as technical work, a term the IBEW, as a craft union, believed ought to come under its jurisdiction. Another long-standing jurisdictional conflict occurred over clerical workers designated as confidential staff, a significant group of personal secretaries and others excluded from the union on the grounds that they had access to sensitive company information. The company periodically tried to expand the confidential designation while the union challenged such designations.

With the increasing educational qualifications of the labour force, new divisions emerged around a series of special training programs. These included 'commerce-graduates-in-training' (recent university graduates routed into the middle and upper end of finance and accounting); 'engineers-in-training' (men with university degrees in engineering who were routed into the upper end of the technical positions and excluded from the union on the grounds that they would become professional engineers); 'technologists-in-training' (graduates from the two-year certificate programs at a technical institute routed into the middle and upper levels of the technical stream and remaining within the union); and 'in-office-training' (unpaid high school 'girls' excluded from union work while becoming familiar with office routines). This patchwork of special training programs was a source of continual negotiation whereby the union aimed to keep technical jobs within its purview and ensure promotion prospects for men based on work experience and seniority rights. With the exception of the in-office-training program, which was intended to place women in entry-level jobs upon graduation from high school, none of these training programs competed for women's clerical jobs. Needless to say, the latter program caused the union the least worry.

The engineers-in-training had the longest history with the utility company, stretching back through the 1950s. Professional engineers were excluded by law from joining a union. The exclusion of those training to become professional engineers was accepted by the union after they proved to be a conservative political force. The engineers-in-training were blamed for the OEA's initial rejection of affiliation with the American-based Office and Professional Employees' International Union in the early 1950s.[67] However, these non-union workers performed the same work as union members and it was impossible for the union to monitor whether such people ever became professional engineers.[68] More important, the jobs they filled were skilled ones lost to union men. In the early 1970s the OTEU again moved to include engineers-in-training and professional engineers within the union.

The technologists-in-training program began in the late 1960s as BC Hydro sought to recruit men with post-secondary technical training into 'sub-professional' jobs in the middle of the technical office hierarchy. This program represented a shift away from reliance on in-house training, the traditional way to groom men for promotions. The company continued to offer a range of short, specialized, technical courses peculiar to company jobs, but internal promotion prospects declined. The union negotiated the number and location of these training positions, including the departments and job titles to be recruited, as exclusions to the general provisions of the collective agreement that covered job postings and internal competition. The OTEU sought to keep the number of technologists-in-training to a minimum.[69] At the same time, and unlike the engineers, the technologists were members of the OTEU that the union also had a duty to represent.

Five issues dominated negotiations over the technologists-in-training: (1) the extent to which the program denied promotions and training opportunities for existing union members; (2) abuse of the training designation by hiring fully qualified technologists rather than trainees into these positions; (3) more effective consultation over job descriptions for them to prevent conversion of existing regular jobs to trainee positions; (4) demands for higher wages for them, as the union sought parity with apprentices in the IBEW; (5) the role of post-secondary educational credentials in defining technical skills.[70] Thus, by the early 1970s there were two paths up the technical office ladder for men, and those who entered the company through traditional entry-level positions, such as meter readers, soon found it necessary to avail themselves of night courses at technical institutes, in addition to specialized in-house courses, if they hoped to continue their ascent up the office ladder.

In contrast to men, women remained firmly shut out of promotion possibilities outside of the feminized clerical hierarchy. Women did not have equal access to in-house training, constituting only 6 per cent of employees in courses in the late 1960s,[71] nor did they have similar access to courses at technical institutes. Few women possessed the prerequisite experience from high school or on the job for such courses, the current career trajectory, or the time afforded by a domestic partner caring for home and family. Moreover, although in 1958 the union negotiated company contributions for the financial cost of training, post-secondary studies had to be approved by management on the grounds of pertinence for promotion within the company.[72] Thus, women were less likely than men to have tuition reimbursed.

> The females seeking career counselling are interested in problems affecting their present job performance or a possible single salary grade promotion. Interest is shown in the traditional female professions (e.g. Teaching, Nursing, Social Worker) but this Company has very little help to offer along these lines as the interests are outside the limits of the Company. A female must take the decision to quit work and go to college, and few do so. Career counselling for females is most effective on short term advice on the traditional female roles in business (e.g. on how to increase typing speed).
>
> The males seek career counselling on matters affecting their whole future, anticipating promotions of at least three or four salary grades. They are interested in advice on Accounting, Sales and Engineering programs requiring study of up to five years in duration; courses which fulfil the needs of the Company [and thus the company will pay for these courses].[73]

The shift from promotions based on experience gained in male entry-level jobs to a combination of experience and specialized educational qualifications in no way provided a more gender-neutral career ladder. Emphasis on individual educational choices and accomplishments can lead to such erroneous conclusions, however.[74] None the less, short-circuiting the usual male mobility path based on seniority did provide men of colour with a possible route to higher-level office jobs.

With the election of a more labour-oriented provincial government in the early 1970s[75] the OTEU sought to influence new labour legislation and expand its jurisdiction within BC Hydro. The union wanted to increase the technical component of its membership and resolve some of its ongoing jurisdictional conflicts. Its submission to the Minister of Labour highlighted its increasing focus on male technical jobs, already symbolized in the name change to the Office and Technical Employees' Union. In light of its ongoing difficulties with the company's blue-collar union, the IBEW, it is not surprising that the OTEU argued that white-collar and blue-collar workers at the same company should not be organized in a single union; different work skills, physical location, and many more women in the OTEU indicated that the two unions did not share a single 'community of interest'.

What is surprising was the attempt to expand the OTEU to include groups until then legally excluded from unionisation, including much of the MPC category: managers, professionals, and confidential staff. The union argued that its members already included people doing the same work as those designated MPC; both were evaluated under the same job evaluation system and enjoyed the same wage structure and benefits. MPC and OTEU employees were thereby presumed to share a single 'community of interest'.

> This particular bargaining unit [the OTEU] represents employees in salary groups, ranging from $426 per month to $1474 per month. These employees work in offices, in the field (survey and construction), in generating stations (technologists or technicians; graduates of B.C.I.T.), and include the whole range of sales staff (including sales engineers and those with agriculture degrees), draftsmen and designers (B.C.I.T. graduates), senior audit clerks and cost accountants (requiring accounting diplomas, but not Chartered Accountants), programmers and system analysts (requiring university degrees), senior construction inspectors (required to pass or reject work of contractors), land representatives (buying land and property) *as well as typists, secretaries, and clerical help of all kinds up to senior levels.*[76]

As this description suggests, male technical positions were becoming more differentiated and specialized as post-secondary credentials, in combination with the traditional requirements of experience in various entry-level men's jobs, were factored into promotion opportunities. In contrast, in the union's own representation women's clerical jobs were increasingly homogenized and merited no differentiation whatsoever.

The union's attempt to place MPC staff within union jurisdiction focused on the engineers, not on managers or on confidential staff. Managers were perhaps less likely to become eligible for union membership even under a revised labour code, given the history of Canadian collective bargaining traditions. The union's lack of attention to confidential staff, most of whom were at the top end of women's clerical job hierarchy, was more surprising. The possibility that engineers-in-training and professional engineers might form their own separate union,[77] increasing jurisdictional conflicts at BC Hydro and potential loss of skilled union jobs, was a motivating factor behind the union's focus on engineers. So, too, was the OTEU's ongoing attempt to raise the skill level of jobs in the technical office hierarchy by attaching these jobs more closely to engineers. These concerns were central to the union's focus on the engineers and those in training. As the OTEU argued:

> We believe that the majority of professional engineers would fall in the homogeneity of our bargaining unit by their filling the next one or two levels in a hierarchy of jobs starting in our bargaining unit. For example:
> i) Draftsman
>   Senior Draftsman
>   Designer/ [or] Professional Engineer
>   Professional Engineer
> i) Computer Operator
>   Programmer/ [or] Professional Engineer
>   Systems Analyst/ [or] Professional Engineer
>   Professional Engineer
> i) Junior Inspector
>   Inspector
>   Senior Inspector/ [or] Professional Engineer
>   Professional Engineer
> i) Technician-in-Training
>   Technician
>   Senior Technician/ [or] Professional Engineer
>   Professional Engineer
> . . . We contend that many professional engineer employees of the company are not employed in their professional capacity . . . because in many cases they are performing work which is identical with that performed by union members.... [Thus] their being placed in separate bargaining units could lead to severe jurisdictional disputes.[78]

In the end the OTEU did not succeed in including engineers or engineers-in-training in its bargaining unit. It is unlikely that engineers perceived a similar 'community of interest' with office workers well below themselves in the office hierarchy, and one largely female at that. The attempt to include engineers, however, illustrates that the process begun in the 1940s continued for decades as the union sought to upgrade men's office work and redefine it as more esteemed, and rewarded technical designations, increasingly differentiated from the homogenizing trends affecting women's clerical work.

At the same time that technical jobs were being credentialized, women's clerical jobs were undergoing a process of devaluation. For example, job grievances were increasingly fought against downgrading positions that involved shorthand dictation (Groups D and E). With the introduction of new technology in the form of tape-recorder dictaphones, dictation relied less and less on shorthand, which had constituted the pinnacle of skill recognized in women's clerical work. In such cases stenographers were downgraded to clerk-typists, usually one group lower in the job hierarchy. Dictaphones were perceived to involve no particular skills beyond typing, itself considered a generic female ability.[79] As occurred time and again, the introduction of new technology in feminized clerical jobs seemed not to imbue its operators with additional technical expertise.[80] The OTEU pursued numerous grievances related to downgrading women's jobs, a practice that usually occurred when a position became vacant. In general, its success with such grievances was mixed, and the union was unable to make any headway in cases involving stenographers.

Ironically, alongside pressures to devalue clerical work went rising educational requirements for clerical employment. These educational qualifications were ignored in the job evaluation system. For example, in the early 1970s the union launched an unsuccessful grievance on behalf of all typist positions in Groups 1 to 3. The OTEU argued that the company ranked these positions as requiring less than grade 12 education; in fact, however, high school graduation was a requirement for all typists and so typists should be reclassified.[81] This argument challenged the entire structure of the job evaluation system, rather than an individual job description, so the union was unable to proceed to arbitration under the terms of the collective agreement. Frustration over such arbitrary elements of job evaluation led the union to demand equal partnership in designing a new job evaluation system. Line management, too, was frustrated with the company's job evaluation system and eager to see a new system developed. Run by a former military intelligence officer, job evaluation was administered in a secretive and arbitrary manner that alienated management.[82] Negotiations for greater union participation in job evaluation occurred in every collective agreement from 1967 until it was won in 1974.[83] A joint union-management task force on job evaluation was established to design a new system for office workers. During this period of expansion and technological transformation of office work in the 1970s, the union became a real partner in job evaluation, with effective consultation over new job descriptions and partnership in designing a complex job evaluation system that was finally implemented in 1981.

Union-Made Job Evaluation

During the mid-1970s labour militancy in the OTEU increased, with strong strike votes and occasional strikes by office workers at BC Hydro.[84] As the union shook off three decades of limited labour militancy, job evaluation was one among a number of strike issues for which the membership was ready to withdraw their labour to achieve. The joint Job Evaluation Task Force won in the 1974 collective agreement must, therefore, be seen as a hard-fought victory for the union.[85] In this new era of union partnership in job evaluation, the OTEU was able to win resolution on a number of outstanding grievances:

> The undernoted outstanding Job Evaluation problems are hereby resolved as follows:
> 1) Jobs requiring technological institute graduation, or the equivalent, will not be established at a level below Group 9.
> 2) Jobs which require a competent typing skill will not have an education factor grade below high school graduation [raising most to Group 4].
> 3) Stenographers to be at Group 4 level if either shorthand or dictaphone utilization required.
> 4) Land Representatives will be upgraded to the Group 10 level.
> 5) Switchboard Operators (Receptionist) to be upgraded to Group 4 if they are required to operate PBX [switchboard] or replacement as major part of duties.
> 6) a) In District Offices where there is only one Customer Clerk, such position will henceforth be established at Group 5.
>   b) In District Offices where there are two or more Customer Clerks, one Clerk will not be less than Group 6 level.[86]

As the above resolutions illustrate, the OTEU advocated upgrading jobs at the bottom and the top of the office hierarchy, among male and female jobs, finally resolving outstanding issues affecting female typists, stenographers, and switchboard receptionists and male technologists, land representatives, and district office customer clerks. Throughout the 1970s and 1980s, as the new job evaluation system was designed and implemented, there was a significant upward movement of jobs—Group 1 was essentially phased out, and the division between male and female jobs moved upward to Group 5. The internal hierarchy changed little, however, and the distinctions between clerical and technical streams, and between female and male work, were incorporated into the new job evaluation system that the union helped to design.

The Job Evaluation Task Force was a full-time committee constituted in the fall of 1974. It consisted of three representatives from the union, three from the company, and one consultant. The task force members were joined by three additional representatives, one each from the union, the company, and the consulting firm, to form a steering committee overseeing the progress of the task force. The entire membership of the task force and the steering committee was male. This gender imbalance was soon raised as a problem by some women members. The following exchange between members seeking women's representation on the task force and the president of the OTEU illustrates that the gendered nature of job evaluation remained invisible to those charged with designing the new job evaluation system. As one female member wrote to the president:

> All of the appointees are male in spite of the fact that the routine office work of [the company] is done almost exclusively by female union members and that fully 46% of union members are women. This represents a serious imbalance in the makeup of the Task Force. I suggest that an addition (or two) is in order to rectify this oversight.[87]

In response, both OTEU and BC Hydro representatives agreed that 'the best available people were selected' and 'sex was not a factor'. Further, the task force consultant suggested that although it was too late to consider adding additional members, women should know that 'any interested party or group could ask and arrange an audience with the task force to outline their specific concerns'.[88] Two months later a group of 40 women sent a petition protesting 'the injustice of having no female representation on the Job Evaluation Task Force' and asking 'how much longer is this discrimination to be tolerated?'[89] This time, stung by the charge of discrimination, the president's response centred on issues of process that eschewed any responsibility for outcomes:

> The union requested the Executive Council on two occasions to submit names of employees who would be willing to take on this onerous task on our behalf. There were approximately eleven female Councillors at that time. As a result of those appeals, there

was not one female member who responded to our invitation, and the Union therefore formed the committee from the available employees who were willing to act on your behalf. On this basis, I would hope that you would recognize that there was no discrimination at any time and, in fact, such could not exist in the absence of any female candidates.[90]

As if to underline that the responsibility for the absence of women on the task force rested squarely with female members, the president added: 'Personally I would welcome the day when more of our members, and that includes the female members, become interested and *active* in the affairs of the Union.'[91] Chastened by the president's response, 34 of the original petitioners sent apologies for their failure to find out the facts and expressed 'regret [for] any unpleasantness the petition caused'.[92]

The issue of gender representation was not raised again. Over the next four years an entirely male Job Evaluation Task Force, with union members drawn from the upper end of the technical hierarchy, designed and tested the new job evaluation system. As two people who were involved in different phases of this process commented:

You're talking about the high-level end of jobs and all male-dominated, no women representative. There was no woman in a Group 4 job, for example, sitting on this task force for job evaluation. . . . So when they were going through the testing that you go through in a new system, let's define what this word means and all the rest of it, that's one thing; but when they're going through where to emphasize the weightings on these jobs. The weightings are going to come out with a bias . . . because of who they are and where they are at [in the job hierarchy], and there is no real sense of exposure or understanding for the Group 3 or 4 positions.[93]

There is nothing inherently fair or unfair about any job evaluation plan, it seems to me. Much more important is the corporate culture. The corporate culture is most important and I wouldn't have called the corporate culture very advanced from a feminist point of view. It is very much engineering-oriented and there are very few women engineers. There are almost no women electrical engineers. So what we do have is a company run by 60-year-old engineers. . . . The plan was implemented, you see, by a steering committee who were all men. The pressure points, as they perceived it, were male jobs . . . things like technological jobs, technologists and technicians, the engineering and transmission,

transmission design technologists, some of the engineering para-professionals, if you like. A number of those were their pressure points, and almost no women involved in those. At a later point [women's] jobs such as word processing and data entry became pressure points, but those were not jobs that were throwing out people who are going to be willing, ready and able to lead union job evaluation efforts.[94]

Thus, the personal experiences of technical men dominated the task force so that skills involved in such jobs, and not those skills practised by women, were well articulated at the design stage. In addition, non-union community standards of remuneration also affected the views of union representatives. As always, male office workers sought to compare themselves favourably with other men, whether skilled blue-collar workers in other unions or engineers higher up the office hierarchy in the utility company, while clearly differentiating themselves from female co-workers. Indeed, as one former member of the task force remembered, some union representatives argued for two separate job evaluation systems:

> I can remember some of the people on the committee saying, 'Well, really we should have two job evaluation systems, one for the technologists who are able to argue their relativity with the IBEW, and then we won't have the women's jobs carting those down.' It didn't sound quite right to me . . . but there were still people on the task force, even from the union side, who quite strongly believed that the women's jobs were keeping their jobs down. [95]

Moreover, there is no indication that members of the task force sought to resolve this problem of 'carting down' the value of men's jobs by attempting to raise the value of women's jobs.

The new job evaluation system was an updated version of the factor point plan implemented in 1945, a 13-group hierarchy with considerably more points for responsibility (decision-making) and education, and fewer for difficulty (the complexity of the job) or working conditions (see Table 12). Forty-eight non-office jobs, most of which were traditionally men's jobs, remained outside the formal job evaluation system. Only eight non-office jobs were traditionally women's jobs, all in the cafeteria. Those eight cafeteria jobs, plus one men's job—fire prevention equipment server leader—were the only non-office salaries set at a rate *lower* than if subject to the new job evaluation scheme (see Table 13). The amount lower than job evaluation ranged from 3 per cent less for fire prevention leaders to a whopping 37 per cent less for cooks and cafeteria leaders. In contrast, all other traditional men's non-office jobs resulted in salaries higher than job evaluation produced: the largest increase was for meter readers, with a 26 per cent premium over job evaluation. Forty-two per cent of non-office men were meter readers (Table 13).[96] The rationale for negotiating higher salaries for men's non-office jobs was clear enough and had long been accepted by the union; these were jobs that paid better in blue-collar unions or in the community at large. It is more difficult to explain how the OTEU could agree to pay female cafeteria workers 11–37 per cent less than job evaluation suggested they merit when participation in job evaluation provided the opportunity to re-evaluate this practice.

In addition to the continued exclusion of non-office jobs from job evaluation, a number of job-related factors were explicitly excluded from consideration. These exclusions included the following: physical effort, manual dexterity, mental stress, productivity, character or personality of incumbent, appearance, shift work, maturity, sex, level of independence or supervision received, monotony, boredom, or frustration.[97] Reweighting job evaluation in this way was certainly gendered, but in complex ways. Many of the factors excluded from consideration affected women more than men; women's jobs were more restrictive in regard to appearance and personality, relied on particular forms of dexterity, and were often more routinized, stressful, and boring. The increased emphasis on education and responsibility favoured male technical jobs at the upper end of the office hierarchy. In the lower and middle levels it favoured upgrading women, whose levels of education and communication skills had been devalued in the old system; at the same time, men's jobs that did not require such skills were downgraded. The task force 'played' with the weighting of factors until it achieved a '60 per cent fit' between the old and new job evaluation systems, with 20 per cent of jobs moving up, 20 per cent down, and 60 per cent remaining the same.[98] To increase union buy-in the salaries of those who were downgraded were protected or blue circled.

Overall, the task force attempted to tie job evaluation more clearly to the values of the company:

> What does the Company do? Why is it there? And what are they prepared to pay for? And one of the things that was really brought up was customer service. And certainly the lower-level customer service jobs all substantially moved up, which were all mostly female-dominated. This gave some problems because there were

Table 12
Comparison of Office Job Evaluation Plans, 1945 and 1981

Factor Groupings, 1945		Weighting, 1945
Knowledge & skills		40.8%
Education	22.4	
Experience	18.4	
Difficulty		27.7%
Complexity & judgement	14.5	
Initiative	13.2	
Responsibility		23.7%
Errors	11.85	
Contacts	11.85	
Working Cenditions		7.8%
Working conditions	4.1	
Physical demand	3.7	
Total:		100%

Factor Groupings, 1981		Weighting, 1981
Knowledge & skills		43.7%
Education	23.8	
Experience	19.9	
Difficulty		17.9%*
Analysis	6.0	
Creativity	6.0	
Judgement	6.0	
Responsibility		31.8%
Decisions	19.9	
Communications	11.9	
Working conditions		6.6%
Total:		100%

*The total for difficulty was recorded as 17.9% even though adding its three component parts equals 18%.

SOURCE: Report of the Job Evaluation Task Force, 31 Mar. 1981, Appendix H2.

Table 13
Non-Office Jobs in the 1981 Job Evaluation Plan

Job Title	No. of Incumbents	Salary Difference under Job Evaluation
Survey PSO	13	– 17%
Print machine op. clerk	1	– 9%
Rodman	1	– 9%
Sr. instrumentman	10	– 1%
Jr. instrumentman	14	– 1%
Instrumentman	14	– 1%
Chainman	38	– 10%
Survey party chief	7	– 1%
Layout artist	2	(not recorded)*
Records clerk	1	– 2%
Records & M/F clerk	5	– 9%
Timekeeper	1	– 3%
Tobacco & sundries clerk	1	– 13%
Chart changer 2	1	(under appeal)
Receiver shipping clerk 1	3	– 17%
Receiver shipper	1	– 7%
Chart changer 1	1	(under appeal)
Utility messenger	1	– 10%
Messenger driver	1	– 12%
Messenger	4	– 1%
Senior mail clerk	8	– 2%
Meter reader	21	– 26%
Meter reader B	44	– 26%
District meter reader	90	– 26%
Pole U/D clerk	10	– 7%
Assistant steward	1	– 10%
Waitress	9	+ 11%
Kitchen helper dishwasher	1	+ 14%
Cafeteria leader	1	+ 37%
Pastry cook	1	+ 21%
Cook HO	2	+ 36%
Cook EDR	1	+ 37%
Salad maker	1	+13%
Sandwich maker	1	+ 13%
Security guard 2	13	– 9%
Security guard 1	11	– 3%

Table 13 *(continued)*

Job Title	No. of Incumbents	Salary Difference under Job Evaluation
Typesetter	1	(not recorded)
Drafting trainee	16	(under negotiation)
Bindery operator	2	(not recorded)
Lithograph operator 1	4	(not recorded)
Lithograph operator 2	2	(not recorded)
Process photographer	3	(not recorded)
Fire prev. equip. server	3	− 3%
Fire prev. equip. s. leader	1	+ 3%
Clearing inspector	7	− 9%
Senior clearing inspector	2	− 9%
Mail truck driver	5	− 2%
Attendant clerk	1	− 8%
Total	382	

Note: The third column in this table represents the change in maximum salary if the non-office jobs were remunerated under job evaluation. A negative value (which occurs for all but one traditionally male job) indicates a higher salary due to non-office designation, whereas a positive value (which occurs in all of the traditionally female non-office jobs) indicates a lower salary due to non-office designation.

*Rate differences that were not recorded by the Job Evaluation Task Force pertained to jobs in printing and made reference to another collective agreement. Though the information is incomplete it is unlikely that these jobs (historically organized in blue-collar unions) would have been higher under job evaluation.

SOURCE: Report of the Job Evaluation Task Force, 31 Mar. 1981, Appendix 1, Non-Office Jobs.

office jobs and field jobs doing somewhat similar stuff, collections and, you know, talking about people's problems in billing, errors and that kind of stuff. And what happened was the higher-level [female] clerical office job moved up to the same level as a lower-level [male] field job. A lot of people weren't terribly pleased about that. . . . Basically the field job [had been] looked upon as having more technical expertise and it really wasn't there, it wasn't really technical expertise [so these jobs came down in evaluation].[99]

Group 1 was essentially eliminated. In the predominantly female jobs, Groups 2 through 5, at least 40 per cent in each group moved up, while between 9 and 13 per cent moved down. The groups with the largest percentage of downward reclassification were Groups 7 (24 per cent), 8 (37 per cent), and 9 (25 per cent), all men's occupations and mostly in the lower and middle levels of the technical hierarchy. Those in the top end of the technical hierarchy were more likely to remain stable; for example, in Group 10, 11 per cent of jobs moved up to Groups 11 and 12, while 11 per cent of jobs moved down to Groups 8 and 9.[100] As one former member of the task force explained:

> The plan had a technical bias because differences between factor degrees in formal education was 40 points, whereas all the other factors were 25 points. So it was very heavily weighted to examine education. So that recognizes technologists and technicians, which still are typically male. And the same bias is in engineering.[101]

Thus the new job evaluation system simultaneously raised and recognized the value of some women's skills, adjusted the bottom of the male hierarchy slightly downward, and further valorized technical jobs at the upper end. Moreover, in spite of the realignment of job evaluation, the gendered distribution of women and men in the office changed little. In 1981, 83 per cent of women remained in Groups 1 through 6 (fully half in Groups 2–4), compared to 14 per cent of men (Table 14).

It was not the mandate of the Job Evaluation Task Force to design a gender-neutral job evaluation system. As we can see from the exchange over the lack of female representation on the task force, its members did not recognize the gendered nature of job evaluation at the time, though many came to recognize it later on.[102] For the most part, the OTEU's role in job evaluation reasserted the privileged position of men in the office union and valorized the technical office worker it had helped to create. Moreover, it did so at a time when others were beginning to question gender biases inherent in job evaluation systems.

In other respects, however, the new job evaluation system accomplished its aims. It was an open and transparent system that had resulted from union-management consensus. Job evaluation included an appeal procedure in which the union was fully involved as a member of the Joint Evaluation Monitoring and Appeals Committee.[103] Unlike the task force that created the job evaluation system, this committee included women representatives from both union and management sides of the partnership.[104] It is unclear whether more gender

Table 14
Distribution of Office Workers, by Job Group and Sex, 1981

Job Group	Women	Men	All Employees	% Women
Non-office*	71	339	410	17%
Group 1	4	0	4	100%
Group 2	55	4	59	93%
Group 3	157	7	164	96%
Group 4	667	25	692	96%
Group 5	340	41	381	89%
Group 6	224	185	490	55%
Subtotal	1,447	262	1,709	85%
Group 7	96	162	258	37%
Group 8	68	223	291	23%
Group 9	33	343	376	9%
Group 10	23	326	349	7%
Group 11	8	122	130	6%
Group 12	5	81	86	6%
Group 13	2	7	9	22%
Subtotal	235	1,264	1,499	16%
Total	1,753	1,865	3,618	48%

*Non-office jobs are organized within the OTEU but classified as non-office jobs and excluded from job evaluation.

SOURCE: Employee Counts, 31 Mar. 1981. Supplied by BC Hydro.

balance affected the long appeals process to any degree, since the structure of the job evaluation system was not open to appeal, but it at least brought to the table members with experience in female clerical jobs who were more likely to appreciate the complexity involved in the performance of such tasks.

As the new job evaluation system was put into place in 1981 the OTEU took advantage of the timing to demand that the company finally resolve the remnants of the historic female differential, which had been hidden when the separate and lower female wage scale was eliminated in the late 1960s. In contract negotiations later that year BC Hydro finally agreed to a demand the union had on the bargaining table for over a decade: systematic rationalized pay scales in Groups 1–12 to eliminate the relatively lower salaries in Groups 1–4. The new pay system was the same in each job group: a 9 per cent gap between one group and the next, and a 17 per cent increase within each group as members progressed through five length-of-service increases. The result was higher increases for women in Groups 1–4 and lower increases in Groups 5–10.[105] Finally, the female differential was eliminated and women achieved the four-decade goal of 'equal pay for equal job evaluation'. Perhaps ironically, outside the union negotiating committees for whom the historical record remained salient from one contract to the next, few members in 1981 remembered the dual wage scales, and fewer still understood how discrimination against women had been buried in a skewed pay system. Petitions protesting the agreement were circulated by many of those in Groups 5 through 10, complaining that 'family heads' were being discriminated against with a lower wage increase.[106] Perhaps more ironic in terms of gender equity, an important part of hiding the female differential was the removal of all men's jobs below Group 5 and reclassification to non-office status to avoid further comparisons between lower-level male and female jobs. Rather than challenge this practice the OTEU entrenched it in the new job evaluation system, leaving non-office jobs exempt from job evaluation so some men's jobs (but not women's non-office jobs) could be remunerated at higher rates of pay.

After devoting nearly a decade to developing a new job evaluation system and handling hundreds of appeals, BC Hydro restructured the job evaluation system in 1986, five years after its implementation. Though a model system of management-union co-operation, the job evaluation system was complex and expensive to maintain, a cost borne by both parties. Moreover, from the company's point of view, the union had gained considerable power, and it soon sought to reassert corporate control over job evaluation.[107] The new factor point job evaluation plan, with individual job evaluations for each position and a complicated appeals committee, was dismantled in favour of a 'job family' or 'whole job classification' system that grouped similar jobs into a series of families. The 13 job groups were maintained within these families, and the 1981 job evaluation system remained the basis for the creation of the new, simplified classifications. Thus, although the job evaluation system was altered yet again, it changed in form rather than substance. The gender biases built into the joint union-management job evaluation system continued in a new form, with union involvement, and thus the ability to reconfigure the system from within was completely eliminated.[108] In some ways the new system of job families, with new clerical, service, and technical families, made the separate career ladders for men and women even more transparent.[109]

Negotiating Masculinity

The postwar office was transformed through automation, computerization, and educational credentialization. The creation of skilled technical office workers was part of this transformation at BC Hydro. A conventional reading of the growth of technical jobs might point to increasing levels of skill and advanced education required to perform more complex tasks. From this perspective the changing organization of the office is itself a product of broader technological change. It must be remembered, however, that technology is developed within a social context and its application is mediated by cultural assumptions and power relations. Redefining office work at BC Hydro was shaped by a technocratic engineering culture that valorized applied science and engineering technology. In this environment it is not surprising that corporate management, composed largely of professional engineers, defined technical expertise as tasks related to support work for engineers and valued these tasks more highly than other clerical skills.

Management did not unilaterally restructure office work at the utility company. Workers negotiated the definition of technical skills through collective bargaining. In this sense the growth of technical office work formed part of the politics of skill among workers themselves. Considerable union energy and resources went into negotiating separate technical and clerical streams of office work. These practices included union negotiation of job evaluation, the value of various kinds of office work, and who might have access to particular jobs; special attention to the negotiation of end rates for dozens of men's non-office jobs; preoccupation with increasing the technical component of OTEU jobs through negotiation over engineers- and technologists-in-training and attempts to change labour law; the union's own representation of clerical work as increasingly homogeneous and non-specialized; and, not least of all, the change in the OTEU's name to signal the importance of technical office work within the union.

Job evaluation was the most important venue through which the union redefined office work. The OEA began to shape job evaluation in the mid-1940s when it demanded a restructured system that defined Group 4 as the floor for men's work and the ceiling for women's work. In the 1970s the OTEU won the right to become a full partner in designing and monitoring a new job evaluation system. As has been pointed out in other contexts, job evaluation rationalizes gendered assumptions and power relations about the value of jobs while transforming them into abstract gender-neutral language.[110]

The job evaluation system the union helped to develop and implement in the 1970s and 1980s was no less gendered than its predecessor from the 1940s, though gender shaped job evaluation in more complex ways. More emphasis on formal educational qualifications, decision-making, and communications and less on working conditions combined to raise the value of some women's work, lower the value of men's work at the bottom end of men's office hierarchy, and raise the value of male technical jobs at the top of the hierarchy. In contrast to the immediate postwar years, when male breadwinner rights were paramount, the hierarchical valuing of job skills made no reference to gender. Instead, masculine privilege was reinscribed in job evaluation in two ways: (1) through the valorization of technical work as an apparently gender-neutral assessment of skill; and (2) through the exclusion of non-office jobs from job evaluation to facilitate higher levels of remuneration for men's (but not women's) non-office work.

Contrary to assumptions embedded in job evaluation systems, notions of technical skill at the utility company were never gender-neutral. The environment changed for all office workers in the post-war period as new forms of technology became standard office equipment—from electric typewriters, automated billing machines, and calculators to computers, sophisticated software applications, and Internet browsers. Yet we have not seen all office workers transformed into technical workers of various kinds. Instead, the definition of technical skills is bound up with gender divisions in the office. Women's operation of technology in the office has seldom been considered technical in any sense.

The creation of the technical office worker at BC Hydro can, in fact, be read through the negotiation of masculinities. As we saw in Chapter 3, one side of this process was tied to working-class conceptions of masculinity embodied in physical labour and breadwinner wages. Wage comparisons between white-collar and blue-collar union men in the company were one facet of negotiating masculinity in working-class terms. At the same time, white-collar workers could strive to have their skills recognized in ways similar to those of middle-class professionals. Over time, the latter became a key union strategy embodied in redefining men's clerical work as technical work associated with engineers. In so doing, technical white-collar men were further separated from white-collar women and from blue-collar men.

Just what did this technical skill consist of? The first level of technical experience was identified with work in the field, familiarity with technical language and job sites, and clerical support for engineers. In reality, field experience was usually limited to reading meters outside or delivering parts to construction sites; technical language was defined to be any sphere men might be more likely than women to be socialized within, such as automotive or construction terminology (but not domestic technology with which women might be more familiar); and support work for engineers seemed only to imbue male occupants with technical experience. Nevertheless, a combination of field experience, familiarity with technical language, and/or clerical support for engineers established the requirements for entry to the bottom rungs of the technical career ladder. In essence, then, masculinity determined access to the bottom rungs of the technical job hierarchy, and familiarity with construction sites, particular forms of technology, or access to outdoor work was part of performing masculinity.

The technical career ladder in the office was really a preferential system of training and promotions for men. Some of this training was formal, including short specialized courses run by the company and, later on, courses at technical institutes. However, much of this training was informal mentoring on the job:

> If you were working on the job, and you came in there and say you came in there to work in my department, and you and I worked together over a period of years, you'd be doing some of my work for me during that period of time. And we'd be talking about the job and you'd be asking me questions, and we'd be going out and looking at jobs together and I'd be talking to you about what we look for and that type of thing. There's a point at which you can just do the job.[111]

The informal nature of these training networks involved workplace friendships, as men passed on job-related knowledge to other men lower down the technical hierarchy. On-the-job mentoring remained an important part of workplace culture that excluded women. Few women were in jobs where such mentoring was likely to occur. The expectation that it was up to workers to pursue mentoring relationships through constant questions and offers to take on the tasks of male co-workers was less well understood by women; and those women who did try to behave 'like men' might find that equally problematic.[112] Gendered mentoring opportunities were a key factor in translating men's clerical support for engineers into demonstrations of technical experience that provided promotion to the bottom rungs of the technical ladder.

The creation of technical and clerical workers in the office was all part of 'doing gender' at the utility company. The gendered career ladders found at BC Hydro were not unusual compared to other North American workplaces. What is notable in this case is the ability to examine how masculine and feminine jobs were produced and reproduced as part of collective bargaining, immersed between working-class and professional middle-class constructions of masculinity. Of course, not all men were the 'right kind' of men. Racialized minorities did not gain access to the company until relatively recently. Moreover, there is no reason to assume that the cultural demands of appearing heterosexual were any less important for successful performance of masculinities on the job at the utility company than elsewhere in the postwar decades. White heterosexual masculinities were normalized among working-class and middle-class men.

Postwar restructuring of office work was not limited to constructing technical work while mediating masculinities; it also involved challenging gender inequality. By the 1960s women had become an enduring presence in the Canadian labour market. Women were embarking on long-term careers at BC Hydro and elsewhere while remaining in the office after marriage and child-bearing. On the one hand, the union negotiated the homogenization of women's clerical work, in contrast to men's specialized technical positions. Yet, it also fought against gender discrimination on many different fronts, including discrimination in pay rates and job evaluation. For example, the union aggressively pursued job evaluation grievances on behalf of women when the feminization of clerical jobs resulted in downgrading job evaluation, when job content was manipulated to manufacture gender difference where none existed, or when women's educational qualifications were ignored.

These struggles for women's equality were pursued within union traditions of equality as 'sameness', with a male body used as the appropriate measuring stick. Inequality was only visible when women's treatment differed from men's (as in the manipulation of job evaluation or unequal pay in the female differential). Gender inequality was not visible when identical treatment disadvantaged women relative to men (as in seniority provisions), or when it was buried in organizational systems that the union itself helped to create (as in job evaluation). Thus, although the OTEU was committed to equality for women and men, in practice the union simultaneously challenged and reproduced gender inequality as it negotiated changes at the office.

When some women began to raise issues of gender representation on the Job Evaluation Task Force in the mid-1970s they began the process of developing a new gendered consciousness in the union. These women helped to make the privileging of their male co-workers' experiences and needs visible for the first time since breadwinner discourses were common in the forties and fifties. They raised concerns about how the absence of women from the task force might result in a failure to understand what women do in their office jobs. Having helped to segregate women's work in particular kinds of clerical support positions, union leaders and the men on the task force never imagined that they did not understand the skills these jobs entailed, or that they were in any way biased in regard to their evaluation of such jobs. The response of union and management to complaints by women indicated a blindness towards, rather than a conscious attempt to ensure, masculine privilege. None the less, the decisions of the task force further entrenched gender inequities in the office.

As the women's movement began to reshape politics in the 1970s and 1980s more women began to challenge the masculine culture within unions and to raise new 'women's issues' at the bargaining table, including profound critiques of job evaluation. In the OTEU this process of political feminization was embedded in a union culture invested in a technical hierarchy of skill inscribed with meanings of masculinity within an engineering corporate culture. The contradictions inherent in the attempt to feminize union culture and practices in this context form the subject of the next chapter.

5

Can Feminism Be Union Made?

*I think the men took the Women's Committee very
personally and very negatively. 'Why do we need a
Women's Committee?' Or, most of the time it was
the name: the Women's Committee. 'Why don't you
call it something else?'*[1]

Challenging Masculine Privilege

Women were a strong presence in the OTEU from its inception at the
end of World War II. Until fairly recently, however, union leadership
was dominated by men, especially men in the higher technical positions, and union policies and priorities were shaped largely through
men's experiences. Masculine privilege was explicit in the postwar
years, as the union appealed to the responsibilities of breadwinners as
the basis for men's right to better jobs and higher wages. These arguments receded over time, replaced by neutral language about equality
and workers' rights. By then, however, masculinist assumptions were
normalized elements of bargaining strategies, contract provisions,
and the organization of the office. When union women began to raise
issues of gender equality in the 1970s, therefore, they posed a fundamental challenge to the union.

Embedded in union traditions were conceptions of equality with
which feminist politics often came into conflict. Within the union
equality was understood as identical treatment of all individuals, or
sameness, a notion embedded in liberal political theory. Abstract
notions of disembodied individuals obscured the substantive

inequalities experienced by women and racialized minorities. As Anne Phillips has argued:

> Political equality is not guaranteed by the equal right to vote, nor gender neutrality by the abstractions of the liberal individual. Abstract individualism imposes a unitary conception of human needs and concerns, and this serves to marginalize those groups who may differ from the dominant norm. The needs of women then appear as a 'special case' (though women make up half the population).[2]

In fact, as we have seen, the disembodied worker on whose behalf the union bargained, and developed traditions to serve, was actually *embodied* in the White male. Raising issues and demands that differed from this position, therefore, was perceived either as divisive and contrary to union solidarity or as special interests that were secondary to traditional union practices.

From a liberal perspective, then, equality implied sameness and as such it was counterposed against any accommodation of 'difference'. Yet many union women came to reject this position and demanded both equality and acknowledgement of gender differences. To do otherwise was to limit desires for equality to those situations in which women could emulate men's lives. Most women's life circumstances did not emulate men's, as societal norms and power relations combined in a double day of domestic and paid labour for increasing numbers of women. As Cynthia Cockburn has argued in the British context, trade union feminists began to redefine what real equality might mean: 'What we are seeking is not in fact *equality*, but *equivalence*, not *sameness* for individual women and men, but *parity* for women as a sex.'[3] Perhaps not surprisingly, demands for women's rights often came into conflict with established notions of equality among union members.[4]

Feminist politics in the OTEU should be put in the context of broader trends in North America. The second wave of the contemporary women's movement emerged in the late 1960s alongside trends towards smaller families, higher levels of education among women, longer-term labour force participation among women, and political movements for civil rights and post-colonial liberation struggles. In this context popular ideas about gender equality dispersed across North America and elsewhere. In the Canadian context the *Report of the Royal Commission on the Status of Women* in 1971, for the first time, presented information on the multiple ways that Canadian women were disadvantaged and helped to bring feminist concerns into public consciousness. With the support of the OTEU two women members prepared a brief for the royal commission on the situation of female office workers at BC Hydro. This brief, written in 1968, highlighted the ghettoization of women in the lower ranks of clerical work as well as the injustice of the female differential.[5] The brief focused on gender discrimination by the company. Soon, as we saw in Chapter 4, a feminist critique of union practices also began to develop. Feminist trade unionists in the OTEU challenged masculinist traditions, largely through the Women's Committee. The Women's Committee, formed in the late 1970s, played a central role in organizing women activists and provided a forum to develop strategies for change. Not surprisingly, the Women's Committee became a lightning rod for controversy, a target of resistance to change as much as a vehicle for change.

Whether women union activists' challenges to masculine privilege should be referred to as feminist has been a subject of some debate among women within the labour movement.[6] Certainly many union women who struggle for gender equality do not call themselves feminists. This is at least partly because, outside of some academic circles, the term 'feminist' is often pejorative. As one activist commented about the labour movement in British Columbia: 'The BC labour movement is terribly conservative on women's issues anyway. That's not just a problem in the OTEU. If you look at the BC labour movement compared with the Ontario labour movement, it is death to be called a feminist, political suicide.'[7] What is clear is that some union women, and some men who support them, have developed a *gendered analysis* sensitive to the different experiences of, and power relations between, women and men. A gendered analysis questions how union traditions, strategies, and practices might affect women and men in different ways, given the unequal social locations, opportunities, and constraints affecting men and women.[8] When a gendered analysis is tied to broader goals advancing the position of women we may refer to such positions as *feminist* in political terms. In this study, then, the term 'feminist' is used to reflect assessment of members' actions in advancing gender equality and does not necessarily suggest self-defined political identities.

Making Gender Visible

When the OEA was certified as a union in 1944 women formed a slim majority of office workers. Preferential hiring and promotions after the war soon increased the number of men and by 1949 women constituted 42 per cent of union members (see Table 6). As the utility company expanded over the next three decades the proportion of women grew. In 1981, 48 per cent of union members were women (see Table 14); by 1991 this had increased to 55 per cent (see Table 2). Although women had always formed a large and visible presence within the union, as their numbers grew so, too, did their political presence within the OTEU.

The increasing feminization of the office corresponded to changes in women's labour force participation across North America. In Canada the labour force participation rate of women doubled between 1961 (29.5 per cent) and 1991 (59.6 per cent).[9] By the 1990s women comprised 45 per cent of the paid labour force in Canada, and their patterns of labour force tenure increasingly resembled those of their male co-workers.[10] For most women marriage had long since ceased to mark departure from paid employment and motherhood corresponded with relatively brief periods of maternity leave rather than a prolonged departure from the labour force. By 1990 more than half (53.5 per cent) of all Canadian women with children under the age of three were employed in the labour force.[11] Yet among those working full time (three-quarters of all women in the labour force), women still earned just over two-thirds (67.6 per cent) of men's earnings and continued to do the bulk of unpaid but essential labour in the household.[12] Moreover, women continued to work in a limited range of jobs concentrated in clerical and service occupations.[13] Perhaps not surprisingly, the additional responsibilities and continued economic disadvantages faced by women contributed to the diffusion of feminist ideas and politics intent on improving the status of women in every sphere of social life.

The emergence of feminist politics began in the OTEU in the mid-1970s. At the same time that more women were embarking on long-term careers at BC Hydro the representation of women in elected union office was actually declining. As Table 15 shows women's representation declined on both the governing Executive Board and on the larger Executive Council of the OTEU during the 1960s and 1970s, a trend that was reversed in the mid-1980s. In the union's first 30 years there was seldom more than one woman on the Executive Board and she was almost always the recording secretary. As the size of the Executive Board increased, from only four members through the 1950s to between eight and 12 members in the 1970s and 1980s, female representation became more problematic. As a proportion of the Executive Board, women dropped from 25 per cent in the 1950s to an average of about 15 per cent in the sixties and seventies.

Table 15
Elected Union Representatives, by Sex, Executive Board
and Executive Council, 1949–1993

	Executive Board		
Year	Men	Women	% Women
1949	3	1	25%
1952	3	1	25%
1954	3	1	25%
1957	4	1	20%
1960	6	1	14%
1963	8	1	11%
1966	7	1	12%
1969	6	2	25%
1971	5	3	37%
1974	7	1	12%
1976	8	2	20%
1978	11	1	8%
1981	10	3	23%
1984	7	5	42%
1987	6	6	50%
1990	7	7	50%
1993	9	7	44%

	Executive Council		
Year	Men	Women	% Women
1949	16	12	43%
1952	14	13	48%
1954	14	11	44%
1957	20	9	31%
1960	32	8	20%
1963	34	13	28%
1966	40	10	20%
1969	38	13	25%
1971	44	10	19%
1974	44	10	19%
1976	47	11	19%
1981	48	18	27%
1984	46	20	30%
1987	34	23	40%
1990	36	25	41%
1993	48	38	44%

SOURCE: Executive Council Minutes, 1949–93.

Representation on the larger Executive Council showed similar trends, dropping from over 40 per cent female in the 1950s to about 20 per cent in the 1960s and 1970s.

It may be that the time constraints of the double day, as more female members were wives and mothers by the 1970s, affected women's level of union activism and their ability to stand for elected office. At the same time, one might also surmise that the shift to longer-term careers might have increased women's interest in union affairs. Whatever the impact of demographic changes on women's propensity for union activism, the decreasing representation of women corresponded with trends within the OTEU that militated against the recruitment of women. These trends included changes in the constitution, the increasing bureaucratization of the union, and the shift to gender-neutral language and assumptions.

One of the electoral mechanisms that increased women's representation on the Executive Council in the early years was tying some positions to particular jobs and the gender of the incumbent. In 1957, for example, 18 of the 29 positions on Council specified the gender of eligible members: 11 positions specified men and seven specified women. In 1958 this was reduced to eight positions (four for each sex), reduced further to six positions (three for each sex) in 1967, and eliminated completely in 1976.[14] These constitutional changes corresponded with the expansion of the OTEU as it organized office workers outside of BC Hydro. By 1966 the OTEU encompassed over 3,000 members covered under six collective agreements; about two-thirds of the membership were at BC Hydro.[15] To reflect the increasing diversity of the membership, councillors were specified by specific employers. Councillors from BC Hydro were specified by geographical region of employment or large divisions within the company, not by specific job titles. Overall, women faired less well as the union sought to reflect other elements of its increasing size and diversity.

As the union grew in size, so did union bureaucracy. The OTEU hired more business representatives to service the membership. This additional layer of union staff mediated between the membership and elected union officers and management, tending to decrease the need for activism among the rank and file. Business representatives were always men. In the mid-1970s, for example, the OTEU had nine business representatives working full time. Most of these men were recruited from the technical stream at BC Hydro.[16] These union staff shared little in common with most women members and were unlikely to form many mentoring relationships that might encourage women's activism. As one observer commented:

Women members' grievances were treated with less seriousness, as having less importance than men's grievances. And the women were talked down to, and they were talked out of grievances. . . . Women's experience at work was completely different than men's experience at work, and these [male] reps had come out of the company but their experience wasn't the same as the women's. So, in part, they didn't understand what these women were saying. It had not been like that when they were there, so these women must be exaggerating, making it up, being emotional, all these things that fit stereotypes anyway.[17]

A common complaint of women in clerical jobs, for example, involved demands to perform menial tasks and personal service for superiors, tasks that were unrelated to the requirements of the job. Men were rarely expected to perform personal service like making coffee for others or picking up the boss's laundry or gifts for his wife. The male business representatives simply did not understand why women might find such tasks demeaning and thus did not see how this might be a serious union issue. The following exchange in the late 1970s, for example, illustrates the repercussions of this gendered experience. A woman queried whether the standard phrase in her job description to 'perform related duties as assigned, such items of a minor nature which do not affect the value of the job' meant that she had to 'make coffee for 30 men'. The response of the business representative handling the complaint showed a failure to understand an experience that was then common for women in the office: 'Making coffee or going to the bank etc. are minor duties and she could do them because while she is doing these things she isn't doing other things. She seemed satisfied with this explanation.'[18] Aside from the paternalism of his response, there was an evident failure to realize that demand for 'duties of a personal nature' was linked to the subservience of women in the office. To many men this issue seemed trivial; to many women it exemplified their subordinate status and lack of respect. Indeed, a few years later one of the first issues raised at the negotiating table by the Women's Committee was to abolish the need to perform 'duties of a personal nature'.

In addition to constitutional changes and the development of a masculine union bureaucracy, shifting discourses of gender neutrality affected perceptions about the need for gender-balanced representation. The profoundly gendered and racialized nature of the office and individuals' experiences throughout the utility company had been obscured by gender-neutral language and the principle of equality as sameness. Those in leadership positions within the union did not appreciate how masculinity shaped the utility company or the culture of the union, and thus failed to recognize the consequences for democratic representation of members. As one activist commented, to a considerable degree the union was part of a technocratic corporate culture at BC Hydro:

> The union came out of the company, and it's a very conservative culture in the company—male-dominated, technicians, technologists, engineers, anybody with an engineering, technical qualification is god, you know. It's a very, very conservative environment, and so the leadership of the union came out of that, is part of that.[19]

One need not impugn the intentions of union leaders, who no doubt sought to represent their members in an equal manner. Indeed, as we have seen, the OTEU confronted discrimination wherever it was observed. But systematic differentiation that resulted in better jobs and career prospects and higher pay for men was simply not recognized as a form of discrimination. Discrimination was understood as a largely individual phenomenon, demonstrated by failure to receive identical treatment, for example, the existence of the female differential, denying promotions in situations of identical qualifications, manipulating job evaluation to create gender difference where none existed, or failure to provide equal conditions for women on the job.[20] The OTEU pursued all such grievances. By treating equality as an individual phenomenon associated with identical treatment, however, the burden was on individual members to demonstrate that they were treated unequally. Conditions that might affect whole groups on the basis of gender or other criteria, and thus remedies that might require more systemic solutions, were not identified as union issues.

Like most unions the OTEU followed events in other unions and in the larger provincial, national, and international labour movement. The release of the *Report of the Royal Commission on the Status of Women* in 1971 motivated some in the labour movement to begin to examine more closely the situation of women workers. In British Columbia, the BC Federation of Labour held its first Conference on Women's Rights and formed a Committee on Women's Rights in 1971. The following year the Women's Rights Conference was identified as an 'educational seminar' for women.[21] It focused on the history of the labour movement, the organization of trade unions, public speaking, and parliamentary procedures so that women might more effectively participate within unions. In line with these developments the OTEU formed a Women's Committee comprised of seven women who were members of the Executive Board and Council to act as delegates to the BC Federation of Labour's women's conferences.[22] It is not clear what other duties, if any, this first Women's Committee performed, but the Women's Committee was not reconstituted after the 1974 elections that brought a new president, Fred Trotter, to power. The former chair of the Women's Committee urged the new Executive Board to consider 'the tremendous beneficial aspects of forming, organizing, and implementing' a Women's Committee, but no such committee was struck.[23]

In the community at large, management was also becoming more aware of gender equity issues. In 1977 BC Hydro sought union co-operation for a new policy to promote equal career opportunities 'to ensure that both men and women are given equal consideration for any job vacancy or competition for which they are qualified'.[24] For its part, the OTEU took this as another opportunity to castigate management about ongoing pay discrimination.

> It has been a matter of policy of the Local to support equal opportunity for both men and women and we do not intend to vary that position and will therefore co-operate with programs toward this end. . . . We would hope that the company, as a result of this new approach, will be more receptive to removing the discriminatory wage policy which presently exists under the salary scales.[25]

With increasing feminist activity in other parts of the labour movement and growing demand from some women in the OTEU, a Women's Committee was formed in 1978 that would have a major impact on union politics. Established as a special committee by Trotter, its mandate was 'to inform the rank and file female membership about the benefits of union membership and what can be achieved through collective bargaining and to involve them in the policies and procedures of the union.'[26] The chair of the committee and its members were appointed by the president, committee minutes were distributed to the Executive Board, and regular reports were made to Executive Council.

The Women's Committee quickly became the centre of feminist activism in the union as it rapidly expanded its membership. From six members at its first meeting in the summer of 1978, it grew to 25 members by the following year.[27] Members came from several companies organized in the local by that time.[28] Committee members were scattered throughout the province but meetings were largely confined to the greater Vancouver area. Thus, extensive mailing lists and a newsletter were developed to keep members from other regions informed about events and issues of concern to women.[29] The Women's Committee developed five objectives that were approved by Executive Council in the fall of 1980:

1) Increase the participation of women members in Local activities and in committees and as members of elected bodies of the union.
2) Inform all present and new members of the Local about the existence, aims and activities of the Women's Committee.
3) Encourage individual members within each bargaining unit to join the Committee and/or submit their recommendations to the Committee.
4) Campaign for the acceptance and support of union officials and representatives, for the aims and programs of the Women's Committee.
5) Encourage women in the various bargaining units to press for favourable contract clauses and review existing clauses for discrimination.[30]

Some of the issues the Women's Committee identified for action can be considered old issues that the union had long tried to redress. Resolution of the historical remnants of the female differential, restructured and hidden in 1969, was the most obvious of these. Beyond long-established issues of gender inequality, however, women began to raise new 'women's issues' within the union. These included women's representation among union staff and in elected union office, and bargaining demands around sexual harassment, day care, job-sharing, flex-time, pay equity, broader human rights protection, family leave, paternity leave, and reproductive health issues. Many new women's issues reflected the burden of domestic responsibilities and child care falling largely on women's shoulders, with remedies that might be useful for fathers as well as mothers. Other issues related more directly to the history of systemic gender discrimination in the labour market, from low pay to sexual harassment. Still other issues pursued by the Women's Committee, in the OTEU and in other unions, encompassed equity concerns for women and men of colour, lesbians and gays, and persons with disabilities.

Over the next decade or so some women's issues gained broad support as valid union issues; others did not. As the Women's Committee became a vocal and effective forum for change it also became a lightning rod for resistance to change. By its very existence the committee challenged business-as-usual by making gender differences more visible within the workplace and by pointing to the need for systemic remedies. In so doing the Women's Committee challenged established union traditions. First, it challenged the division between workplace issues and family and social relations that could not be left outside the office door. Second, it challenged explanations for gender differences that were grounded in individual choices divorced from the structural relations that shape opportunities and constraints. And third, it challenged the notion of a disembodied worker for whom equality could be attained through identical treatment for everyone. In general, the greater the challenge to union traditions, the greater the resistance to particular women's issues.

It was clear that women would have to organize themselves if they sought to attain the strategic positions from which to create change in union practices and working conditions in the office, and the organization of the Women's Committee was an important part of this process. Among the first issues pursued by feminist activists was the dearth of female representation on the Executive Board and Executive Council and as business representatives and members of important union committees. In its first year the Women's Committee lobbied for equal representation for women on the Joint Evaluation Monitoring and Appeals Committee to monitor the new job evaluation system (see Chapter 4), for the appointment of female business representatives, and for a committee member to be appointed to the staff selection committee. It also collected research to identify issues for collective bargaining.[31] The committee met with business representatives to share information, including statistics on the distribution of men and women in the office, and thereby educate their paid negotiators about the importance of women's issues. As one member remembered, however, education was not enough. Women had to be where decisions were being made: 'It is important to have women on your negotiating committee and all that to get your women's issues pushed through; otherwise, they are throwaway issues.'[32] In a very short time the Women's Committee helped to get women activists into some of these important decision-making positions.

The Women's Committee had considerable early success, but it was watched closely by the president and Executive Board. The governing Executive Board included only one female member in 1978, and she also chaired the Women's Committee. The committee's most immediate success was to encourage women to run for elected office and OTEU staff positions. In July of 1979 an activist on the Women's Committee became the first woman hired in a non-clerical position by the OTEU; she was hired as a communications officer and later worked as a business representative. Three women won election to the Executive Board in the 1981 elections, all of whom were activists on the Women's Committee.[33] The following year two of these activists were hired as business representatives.[34] In the 1984 elections five women who had at some time been activists on the Women's Committee, including the new president of the local (Anne Harvey), were elected to the Executive Board.[35] As Table 15 shows, in just six years women had reached near parity on the Executive Board (42 per cent), increased their presence on Council (30 per cent), and helped elect the first woman president of the OTEU. By the end of the decade 50 per cent of the Executive Board and 40 per cent of councillors were women.

At the same time, some gains were already being made at the bargaining table. A member of the Women's Committee was appointed to the BC Hydro bargaining committees in 1979 and again in 1981. At the bargaining table the Women's Committee first focused on an extended maternity leave provision, which was successfully negotiated into the 1979 collective agreement.[36] It identified two issues that made it to the bargaining table in 1981: day care and a 'no personal duties' clause. Nothing was won on day care, but management agreed to non-binding action on 'personal duties': 'A memo from senior management was written to ensure managers were not expecting their staff to perform such duties. An article in *Speaking Out* [the Women's Committee newsletter] conveyed that to members.'[37] Over the next decade many new women's issues were identified for the bargaining table, but progress was slower than expected. Getting women into strategic decision-making positions did not mean that more substantive change would automatically follow. Many union members, particularly men, opposed the Women's Committee and its initiatives. Before considering some of the central conflicts over specific issues we need to consider the general climate within which the Women's Committee operated.

Those who were active on the Women's Committee in its early years remembered a generally unsupportive climate within the union:

> Well, you could feel the Council go 'Oh God' whenever there was a Women's Committee report. . . . They knew we were a group that was always going to report, that always had something to say, and maybe they would have to think about it, because whatever it was we were asking for, a change to the by-laws to allow for day care or something, you could feel, if not hear, this collective 'Oh God, the Women's Committee report, Oh God', because they knew there was going to be something they'd have to listen to.[38]

It was always an uphill climb. And when we'd go to the Executive Council meetings what we found is if you take an issue to the Executive Board, then the Executive Board would sort of pre-warn the Council. Then the issue would come up, some of the men on the Executive Board would then rally some of the men on the Executive Council as an opposition to the issues that we would be trying to bring forward. So by the time we took our issue to the Executive Council they were there ready to speak against it.[39]

A lot of good issues came out of the Women's Committee but it was always viewed very negatively by the men. . . . I think the Women's Committee was really a burr in everybody's saddle. Number one, it was the Women's Committee, it sounded like an exclusive club and it was always viewed as the women are in the back room and they're plotting to overthrow this union.[40]

It was not uncommon for opponents to try to neutralize the Women's Committee by seeking to change its name and its focus:

One guy on the Board would stand up every meeting and say, 'Why do we need a Women's Committee here?' Almost every meeting. And then, 'I believe we think there should be a man on the committee.' 'We think it should be called the Human Rights Committee.' 'We don't need a Women's Committee.'[41]

There were several times that they would try to change the name of the Women's Committee, to abolish the Women's Committee.[42]

I think the men took the Women's Committee very personally and very negatively. 'Why do we need a Women's Committee?' Or most of the time it was the name: the Women's Committee. 'Why don't you call it something else?'[43]

Activists were conscious of how feminist issues could be buried by other concerns and thus resisted revamping the committee under a human rights rubric.[44] Visibility was important to advance women's issues; visibility was a two-edged sword, however, that intensified opposition.

The degree of resistance to the Women's Committee made progress time-consuming and demanded new organizational skills among its members. Women activists took courses on Robert's Rules of Order, developed assertiveness-training seminars, and co-ordinated their strategies prior to Board and Council meetings. These initiatives helped them operate more effectively in the bureaucratic masculine culture of union meetings and contract negotiations that made them constantly aware of their status as outsiders.

> When you start out and you've got these men that have been around a very long time, and some of them are good speakers . . . there was this intimidation factor. And that was one of the things that the Women's Committee thought about. The more women that came in, some of them took, deliberately took, public speaking and things like that to try and improve how we feel ourselves, but also how we would be perceived by other people as more confident.[45]

> I took a course on Robert's Rules of Order just for survival on the Executive Council for the issues that were there. Because it took such a lot of work to get the issues there, and it didn't seem right that by a technicality they could get rid of your committee, or do this or do that just because they didn't like what you were trying to do.[46]

> Through the Women's Committee we identified one of our needs to be assertiveness training because you needed those skills to stick with the issues. So we developed an assertiveness-training course and put that forward for weekends and we did that around the province.[47]

> The union was very male-dominated and I think it's just one of those things that happens in unions. Through my involvement in the Women's Committee I got to meet more women and saw that I wasn't the only woman who wanted to do things in the union. There were other women in that committee who not only wanted to do things but who certainly could do them with a great deal more flare and intelligence than a lot of the elected people who were there, both male and female. That definitely influenced my decision to run [for office], the fact that there were plenty of good, strong, intelligent, dedicated women who were running for positions. . . . I guess you could call it the 'new girls' network'. We sort of discovered each other and realized, hey, I am not alone. I have sisters here. And we wanted to do things. We wanted to change the union for the better and show that, yes, women can do these jobs, too.[48]

These strategies helped develop a new women's support network and the skills and confidence to operate effectively within the union. As the Women's Committee became a stronger presence, resistance also grew. In particular, relations between the Women's Committee and the Executive Board and the president, Fred Trotter, who had been in office since 1974, worsened in the early 1980s, and Trotter imposed new restrictions on the committee's activities in 1983. As a result of 'political division between male and female members' the Women's Committee was instructed to cease holding information sessions for women, which it had been conducting across the province. It was ordered to restrict its assertiveness-training workshops to job stewards and councillors rather than to the general membership. Furthermore, the Women's Committee was pressured to alter the content of its assertiveness-training program, which the president argued 'gave the impression of being put on by women for women'. The committee was instructed to exclude the 'Women's Bill of Rights' or alter the language to 'member-person' rather than 'women'. Finally, 'due to negative connotations' the name of the program was changed to 'Asserting Your Rights in and out of the Workplace'.[49]

Two specific issues had raised the ire of many members in and out of elected union office. These were attempts to get sexual harassment language on the bargaining table and a women-only membership survey. The Women's Committee identified sexual harassment language as a priority and developed a 'Policy Paper on Personal and Sexual Harassment' in 1981. The policy paper included definitions of harassment and a complaint procedure to be bargained at the negotiating table. The Executive Council flatly refused to approve the policy paper. Women's Committee activists were unable to convince their union brothers, and no doubt some of their union sisters, that sexual harassment was a serious issue to be addressed in bargaining.[50] As one activist commented, on issues like sexual harassment gender really mattered:

> Women's committees are very important in getting that sort of thing brought to the forefront in their unions because nobody knows what it's like unless you are a woman. You don't know what sexual harassment is. You don't know some of the things that happen in the workplace in women's jobs because they wouldn't happen to a man.[51]

In an attempt to gain support for the issue of sexual harassment the Women's Committee developed a survey on personal harassment and administered it to union members in March 1982. The results, reported to the Executive Board and Executive Council, identified six forms of personal harassment, with sexual harassment the most common problem. The results of this survey were never conveyed to the membership because 'the President has a concern about survey statistics.'[52] Two years later, when the Women's Committee attempted to update the still unreleased information, the president 'confiscated' the new surveys and 'disallowed' distribution of a Women's Committee newsletter communicating the results.[53] As one activist commented, resistance to bargaining a sexual harassment policy was based not only on the failure of many men to understand this issue, but also on the fear that it might be used against innocent union men: 'I had real fights with the bargaining committee about the clause, because the men were afraid of innocent men getting charged, and we went through all of those issues.'[54] Sexual harassment was one of the first items added to the bargaining agenda after Anne Harvey was elected president in 1984.

Even more contentious than the issue of sexual harassment, a debate that was largely confined to elected union representatives since survey results were kept from the broader membership, was the decision to conduct a women-only membership survey. In the spring of 1980 the Women's Committee distributed a Women Members' Questionnaire throughout the union. Over 1,200 women completed the questionnaire; more than 600 of these women were from BC Hydro, constituting 35 per cent of women members at the utility company.[55] Women were asked to do two things: (1) indicate whether an item should be addressed in collective bargaining; (2) rank the top five items in order of importance. Thirteen issues were identified in the survey: family leave, educational leave, child care, adoption and improved maternity/paternity leave, flexible starting times, sexual harassment protection, the right to refuse 'duties of a personal nature', security for shift workers, reduced workweek, improved vacations, career paths and on-the-job training, phased retirement, and job-sharing.

The results for BC Hydro are found in Table 16. Nine of the issues identified by the Women's Committee were deemed by a majority of women to merit attention at the bargaining table. Of the four issues that received less than 50 per cent support in regard to collective bargaining, two of these were ranked fourth (child care) and sixth (sexual harassment) in terms of importance. This suggests that although fewer women thought these were worthy of bringing to the bargaining table, those who did so identified these issues as very important. The two most important issues identified in the survey were shorter hours (a four-day workweek) and the need for career paths and on-the-job training for women. Support for shorter hours (ranked first), child care (ranked fourth), family leave (ranked sixth), flexible time (73 per cent support), adoption/maternity/paternity leave (52 per cent support), and job-sharing (52 per cent support) reflected the difficulty

Table 16
Results of Women Members' Questionnaire, 1980

Issue	% Desiring Attention in Collective Bargaining	Ranked in Order of Importance
4-day workweek	70%	1
Career paths and on-the-job training	78%	2
Educational leave	67%	3
Child care	less than 50%	4
Family leave	62%	5
Sexual harassment	less than 50%	6
Flex time	73%	unranked
Improved vacation	67%	unranked
Adoption/maternity-paternity leave	52%	unranked
Job-sharing	52%	unranked
Phased retirement	52%	unranked
Duties of a personal nature	less than 50%	unranked
Security for shift workers	less than 50%	unranked

Note: Percentages less than 50% were not recorded. These results refer to women at BC Hydro and do not include responses from women in other parts of the local.

SOURCE: Women's Committee Files, Report on the Women Members' Questionnaire, 1980.

many women have negotiating the double demands of the workplace and the household. Career paths and on-the-job training (ranked second) and educational leave (ranked third) related more directly to the ghettoization of women in the bottom of the occupational hierarchy and to their exclusion from technical career ladders at BC Hydro.

The Women Members' Questionnaire was an important barometer that helped the Women's Committee gauge the degree of support for potential bargaining issues and provide leverage within bargaining committees. Quite unintentionally, it also demonstrated the depth of opposition to the committee's existence, *among both men and women*. In many respects members' comments about the questionnaire were more illuminating than the survey results. Seventeen pages of comments with over 200 individual excerpts were compiled to summarize members' comments about the survey. Many of these comments came from job stewards, who were asked to circulate the questionnaire; some supported the survey, but many others were upset about the exclusion of men. The following comments by male job stewards illustrate these latter sentiments:

The women in my area don't care about any of the items and don't wish to fill out the survey.

I will distribute them but I'm striking out any reference to male or female.

The girls in my area are quite happy with things the way they are and so they didn't bother to answer the questionnaire.

Though I agree there have been obvious reasons for concern, I disagree that separate items, as shown in the recently circulated questionnaire, form a base for bargaining. What's good for one contract-wise should be good for all. If the union does not ensure that all are protected, then the union should be made to answer. What is evolving is not the answer.

I don't believe the best interests of the Local are served by circulating this bulletin. It may in fact be a violation of Section 7 of the Labour Code.

Thrown disgustedly into wastepaper basket.

This questionnaire shows reverse discrimination—if 'equality' is what it's all about, this should be addressed to EVERYONE and women will have the opportunity to be counted, on an equal basis.

The latest bulletin has caused a lot of unrest among my members and I think it is about time that you [the president] and the Executive Board took another look at the necessity of having a Women's Committee. I personally feel it should be disbanded as soon as possible.[56]

Some female job stewards held similar views, questioning the appropriateness of gender-specific surveys and committees:

Some of the females here, myself included, feel this questionnaire should not have been sent to 'women members only'. Almost all questions apply to males as well. As far as the Committee for women, this is in itself discrimination—against men.

We believe all members are represented by the union and there is not a need to single females out.

The reaction was one of instant disapproval on the part of the men and doubt on the part of the women as to the ambiguity and usefulness of the questionnaire.

Why are women being singled out for the questionnaire, if the results of this survey are to be submitted as suggestions for future agreements all members should have a voice. My views are adequately represented now and a women's group asking for special provisions for child care, maternity leave etc. is discrimination against women and men who are childless.

We are trying to stop the company from dealing with us in a different way to men. This is a giant step backward. Please don't pursue this further. I think this is a mistake. We want equality, not special 'for women only' concessions.[57]

Among other points of tension, some of the above comments by job stewards pointed to persistent tensions between different definitions of 'equality' as sameness versus difference.

Nearly two-thirds of OTEU women did not fill out the questionnaire. Failure to co-operate may well have been an expression of the ultimate form of disapproval. On the other hand, it should be remembered that large surveys rarely have a high response rate without repeated follow-ups, which the Women's Committee did not do. Moreover, as some of the comments above suggested, some women were prevented from taking part in the survey. Other women certainly faced a climate of open disapproval from some co-workers, so that lack of compliance may have been a path of least resistance. Several women commented on the resistance they faced from male co-workers:

Our questionnaires have been sabotaged by the male members on our floor and do not correctly represent a male or female point of view. I suggest a more diplomatic approach prior to attempting any other fact finding endeavours. It seems the male population borders on hysteria.

As I was handing out the questionnaire to the women in our office one of the men asked what it was. While in the middle of trying to explain the literature and Women's Committee, I was told, 'that's bullshit, what the hell do you have a Women's Committee for?' I tried again to explain. He felt that we belong to one union and therefore should not need a separate committee for women. Obviously, men are not aware of the special areas with which many working women have to concern themselves.

The councillor on our floor has refused to distribute the survey but we don't think he should be allowed to deny us the right to fill it in. Can you please send me more copies.[58]

The survey helped the Women's Committee set priorities for bargaining issues. As a direct result of the survey some women sought more information on specific issues, suggested other things the committee should look at, and asked to be added to the committee's mailing list. Some men, too, expressed support for the work of the Women's Committee and asked to see the results of the survey. A summary of the results was published in the union's newsletter later that year. To a considerable extent, then, the survey helped raise the profile of the Women's Committee and broadened its support. But it did so in a climate in which support and resistance went hand in hand among both men and women. Higher visibility brought with it more opposition. In the months following the distribution of the women-only survey the president ruled that all future surveys must be approved in advance by the Executive Board, not just the president, who had approved the survey in question. As occurred whenever tensions rose between the Women's Committee and the Executive, the president and several business representatives attended the next regular meetings of the Women's Committee.[59] The Women's Committee never did another survey aimed only at women members. Moreover, when the Women's Committee later surveyed members about personal harassment, as we have already seen, the Executive Board contained the controversy by simply refusing to distribute the information to the broader membership.

There is no question that in the early 1980s the Women's Committee constituted a significant challenge to masculinist traditions in the union. It made gendering visible as a union issue for the first time since the 1950s. However, the Women's Committee succeeded in making only some aspects of gendering visible—women's demands for special provisions—without successfully challenging assumptions that traditional union practices were gender-neutral. Opposition to the Women's Committee, feminist ideas, and women's issues could, therefore, be cast as a defence of democracy premised on identical treatment for all and special rights for none. Such arguments are particularly salient in a union context, the survival of which is premised on the collective solidarity of workers. It was difficult for women activists to challenge the normalization of masculine privilege without threatening the solidarity of the union. Thus, although in a fairly short period of time the Women's Committee helped to feminize the leadership of the OTEU, opposition to feminist politics remained strong.

Feminizing the Union

In 1984, 40 years after the union was first certified, the first woman president was elected to head the OTEU. Anne Harvey had worked as a publications editor at BC Hydro for two years, a fairly senior Group 9 job. She was a former activist on the Women's Committee and the first woman hired as non-clerical union staff when she became communications officer in 1979. By the time of her election five years later she had also worked as an OTEU business representative and so had a fairly high profile in the union. Without a long history with BC Hydro, and without experience in the male technical streams, the new president was an outsider in the union bureaucracy in many respects beyond her gender. She challenged a president who had been in office for 10 years in the immediate aftermath of a long, costly, and unpopular strike (see Chapter 6).[60] The 1984 election exposed serious divisions within the OTEU that would shape union politics for the next decade. These tensions included divisions over political philosophy, the meaning of union democracy, leadership style, responsibility for the disastrous strike of 1983–4,[61] and, in often less explicit ways, gender. Women's issues were not explicitly raised during the election campaign but the presence of a woman candidate in a masculine culture meant gender was nevertheless part of the subtext of the election and subsequent political divisions. In its female form gender was always visible; men remained normative and apparently ungendered union members. One consequence of this, regardless of the policies pursued, was the perception that women received preferential consideration.

> One of the things that was used as a slanderous remark against her [the president] was 'all she's interested in is women's issues.'[62]

> The conflicts in the union were based on different union philosophies and feminism all rolled into one, I would say. I would characterize her [the president] as a feminist, and somebody who looks upon trade unions as social movements, and who believes very strongly in membership control of the union. And I think that the

people who were in the opposing political camp disagreed with all of those philosophies. They thought that the union's main purpose was to service the collective agreement and to negotiate a contract. It shouldn't be involved in other things. . . . I think it was a philosophical difference about what unions are supposed to be, [but] it was made into 'she is a raving feminist.'[63]

The 1984 election saw four other women elected to the Executive Board, and 20 women elected to Executive Council. In fact, 1984 marked a trend towards gender equality in elected office, reversing the downward slide of the 1960s and 1970s. The following election, in 1987, brought female representation to 50 per cent on the Board and 40 per cent on Council (see Table 15). In terms of gender representation, then, the union underwent a process of feminization in the 1980s. Opposition to the Women's Committee did not seem to spill over automatically into a rejection of female candidates. All of the women elected to the Executive Board in 1984 and 1987 had some previous involvement with the Women's Committee, though their level of activism around women's issues varied enormously.[64] It was never the case, moreover, that the majority of women on the Executive Board or Executive Council supported the new president, let alone endorsed feminist union politics. In fact, the majority of the Executive Board, both male and female, were aligned with her predecessor and actively opposed Anne Harvey's presidency. A truce of sorts was established midway in her first term in office. By her second term in office, after re-election in 1987,[65] some former strong allies from the Women's Committee were also opposed to Harvey's presidency and actively worked to defeat her in 1990. Divisions among the union leadership were very complex and were often open and bitter during this time; these political divisions were affected by, but were certainly not reducible to, gender politics.[66]

Most union members were unaware that the Women's Committee had been a launching ground for new female activists.[67] For example, activists from the Women's Committee did not play a high-profile role in the 1984 election. Behind the scenes, however, connections forged in the Women's Committee were critical for planning and even funding Harvey's bid for the presidency.[68] At least initially, some of the new president's strongest supporters were members of the Women's Committee who expected her to support women's issues. Although she identified as a feminist, however, women's issues were never an explicit part of the new president's agenda. The decision to 'soft soap' women's issues was intended to broaden support for change and head off opposition aimed at the Women's Committee. As one activist commented:

> She campaigned on administration that delivers and leadership that listens, that was the theme. . . . Because you can't just take women's issues because it would cause a split, so you had to have sensitivity. We talked about all of that, you know, we were going to do things for women and that, but we couldn't put it out there in the forefront because people would be threatened. Men would be threatened. It's the usual thing that women do, they try to soft soap things a lot of times, because they are afraid of the repercussions. But the reality is, as you get longer in the tooth, it doesn't matter how much you soft soap. The reaction is still there, so you might as well just take it head on.[69]

In a process that had begun under the previous executive, more women were hired as business representatives. At the same time, and in contrast to the perceptions of many critics, less was accomplished in efforts to bargain women's issues than might have been expected. In part this was due to large-scale corporate restructuring that demanded considerable and immediate attention (see Chapter 6).[70] The Women's Committee remained an independent force in the mid-1980s and continued to pursue issues aimed at improving the position of women. Initially, the Women's Committee worked with the support of the president but soon was often in opposition. More often than not the Women's Committee remained at odds with the Executive Board and Executive Council, where the climate for feminist politics remained generally unsupportive, perhaps more so since it was linked to general criticisms about Anne Harvey's leadership. At the same time, members of the Women's Committee were on the BC Hydro bargaining committees in every set of negotiations and did help to negotiate a number of women's issues in the late 1980s. Still, progress on women's issues was slow. Corporate restructuring absorbed considerable union energy and tended to place women's issues more squarely in the ranks of secondary bargaining issues peripheral to the main interests of the membership.

Following the 1984 election the Women's Committee quickly reinstated its assertiveness-training courses, dusted off its 'Policy Paper on Sexual Harassment' to try again for Executive Council approval, and published a newsletter outlining the results of the 1980 Women Members' Questionnaire.[71] The committee persuaded Executive Council to adopt a new policy reimbursing child-care expenses during union meetings and workshops, and sponsored a conference on women in the workforce and a workshop on women and stress.[72] The Women's Committee identified several issues that made it to the bargaining table in the 1986 negotiations: sexual harassment, family leave, and protection for pregnant women using video display terminals (VDTs). Of these three, movement occurred on only one issue, sexual harassment. The sexual harassment policy designed by the Women's Committee in 1982 was endorsed by BC Hydro, which agreed to communicate the policy to managers. Union negotiators believed the company had agreed to include the policy in the contract as a letter of understanding. Management denied this was its commitment. In the end, language on sexual harassment was not incorporated into the collective agreement until 1991.[73]

The Women's Committee proposed a number of other issues that were rejected by the bargaining committee, including affirmative action, job-sharing, and paternity leave.[74] The first of these, affirmative action, would never gain support as a union bargaining demand. In fact, the OTEU actively resisted affirmative action strategies some years later (see Chapter 6). Resistance to measures that might address systemic disadvantages facing women or other groups prevented the Women's Committee from addressing 'career paths and on-the-job training', even though in 1980 women ranked it second in overall importance with the single largest percentage of support (78 per cent) as a bargaining issue (Table 16). Thus, the most defining characteristic of gendered work at BC Hydro—segregated clerical and technical career ladders—remained unchallenged.

The Women's Committee was active on a number of fronts during Harvey's second term in office (1987–90). The committee sought greater autonomy and petitioned to become a standing committee rather than a special committee convened at the discretion of the president.[75] This was not successful; instead, conflicts occurred with the president over budget, priorities, and the appointment of the committee chair.[76] Unlike conflicts with the previous president, which were located more generally in opposition to new feminist ideas, conflict with President Harvey in the late 1980s was linked to leadership style, personalities, priorities, and methods, not to feminist goals *per se*, though at times conflict was just as intense. Still, the Women's Committee accomplished a number of policy objectives in the late 1980s. It developed a sexual harassment program for union members; developed gender-balanced hiring criteria for the union (plus or minus 10 per cent of gender representation, with gender parity preference among equally qualified candidates); conducted a survey on child-care needs; once again targeted the need to perform 'duties of a personal nature'; and drafted the OTEU's first report on pay equity.[77]

Contract negotiations in 1989 were undertaken by a bargaining team with more gender-balanced representation than at any time in the past; five of 12 members were women, and all had been involved with the Women's Committee at some time in the past. With the end of corporate restructuring women's issues, for the first time, were well represented in bargaining demands. This inevitably led some critics to complain that the union was only interested in women's issues.[78] Issues on the bargaining table included family leave, protection for pregnant women using VDTs (both on the previous agenda), job-sharing and paternity leave (both rejected by the previous bargaining committee), and protection from discrimination on the basis of sexual orientation (for the first time). Two of these issues were won in 1989. Women using VDTs won the right to reassignment during pregnancy and a job-sharing policy was ratified.[79] The provision for job-sharing had been advanced most strongly by management and the provision was weak from the perspective of OTEU members. For its part, the union maintained a degree of resistance to anything other than full-time regular employment. Although job-sharing was added to the collective agreement, union consent was required for each job-sharing arrangement; as a result it was difficult for union members to access this provision and few job-sharing arrangements have resulted.[80]

Although the Women's Committee remained active during the 1980s and achieved a number of initiatives, its impact on union culture was more limited than one might have expected, especially given its early influence in attaining gender-balanced union representation. With the election in 1990 of a new president, Ron Tuckwood, an activist who had long been in opposition to the previous president, the Women's Committee became largely inactive. It continued to exist but would no longer play the same role researching bargaining issues and pressing for their inclusion at the negotiating table. The Women's Committee met infrequently in the first half of the 1990s and maintained a very low profile.[81] Moreover, it became a matter of some controversy that, for the first time, the Women's Committee now included a man among its members.[82]

None the less, a decade of activism among union feminists appeared to have a lasting impact on the OTEU. The number of women elected to union office during the 1990s maintained approximate gender parity. As well, over time some women's issues gained wider acceptance in the OTEU and in the labour movement generally. In the 1991 contract negotiations, in spite of a nearly invisible Women's

Committee, a significant number of women's issues were won. A sexual harassment policy was finally included in the collective agreement. A decade after the Women's Committee first tried to get it on the bargaining table a 'no personal service' clause was finally negotiated. In addition, paternity leave, protection on the basis of sexual orientation and family status, and a commitment to investigate the issue of pay equity were all won in 1991.[83]

We might conclude that to a considerable degree union issues, and not only elected representatives, had been feminized during the 1980s. Thus, even in the absence of organized feminist pressure, women's issues could be added to the collective agreement. Yet, the inclusion of particular issues did not indicate that opposition to union feminism had disappeared. Resistance remained into the 1990s and contributed to the very low profile of the Women's Committee. As one committee member commented:

> So there's a lot of flak. We have to be really careful as far as what the Women's Committee does because we have a lot of men in the union that really get incensed about it. So, basically, what we're doing now is not rock the boat as much as possible as far as the Women's Committee is concerned. . . . The president sets up the parameters of what the committee can do, and then anything we want to do has to be approved by the Board and then, in turn, by the Council. So we have a lot of stipulations put on us.[84]

Union politics had been feminized enough to support special needs identified by women—if these could easily be added to the existing framework of the collective agreement. Where feminist activism posed a more fundamental challenge to masculinist traditions, resistance within the OTEU remained strong.

Negotiating Gender:
From Workers' Rights to Women's Issues

During the 1980s feminist activists brought gender issues to the attention of OTEU members. This focus on gender centred squarely on women: ways in which women workers faced discrimination, or special needs women had in the workplace. In this discourse the male was the absent point of comparison, the disembodied worker who had no special needs and thereby got no special treatment. There were no 'men's issues' as a counterpoint to newly defined 'women's issues'. The implicit counterpoint was broader notions of 'workers' rights' that had developed over a century of labour history in Canada. By the

1970s these rights had long been assumed to be gender-neutral. Equally important, workers' rights and women's issues remained separate—the one did not imply the other. Women, it seemed, were a special case among workers. The OTEU might try to *accommodate* women's issues, but it had a *duty to ensure* adequate representation of workers' rights.

Gendering was not more prevalent in union practices in the 1980s than it had been previously; rather, it was simply made more visible than it had been since the postwar years. Gender relations, with particular notions of masculinity and femininity, were always part of collective bargaining. For the most part, as we saw in Chapters 3 and 4, issues of masculinity formed the core of collective bargaining practices. In often contradictory ways the OTEU negotiated the place of the technical office worker in relation to blue-collar crafts*men*, male engineers, a technocratic corporate culture, and women clerical workers. Although the language of collective bargaining had long since abandoned a breadwinner discourse, replaced by a disembodied worker and notions of workers' rights rather than breadwinner rights, masculine privilege did not disappear. The shift to a gender-neutral discourse did not alter the material effects of gendering processes.

One reading of gender politics in the 1980s is to see a shifting balance of power within the union as women began to organize collectively through the Women's Committee. In this sense feminization can be seen as a gradual process of incremental change, with setbacks to be expected along the way. The OTEU was much further along this road to feminization in the 1990s than a decade before. Certainly the number of women's issues bargained into the collective agreement would support this view. Real gains for women have been made. Indeed, by the 1990s many women's issues become an accepted part of bargaining in the OTEU, as in the labour movement generally. Thus, women's issues continued to be bargained even in the absence of a viable Women's Committee. At least in part, this was because women also attained a level of gender-balanced representation in the union, a trend that is unlikely to be reversed.

Another reading of these events points to the limits of feminist activism in a masculine union culture and the difficulty of creating more substantive change. Here the appearance of gender neutrality that obscures the reality of masculine privilege constitutes a significant barrier for change. Substantive change requires a fundamental rethinking of union traditions, not just the incremental addition of women's issues at the bargaining table. This implies engendering all union members and assessing bargaining strategies and existing contract language in terms of their substantive effects. This is difficult to do so long as women's issues stand apart as separate, assumed to be the only issues that are gendered. By definition such special needs remain secondary to more universal workers' rights; and where the two come into conflict the latter will more than likely prevail.

These two ways of reading gender politics in the OTEU are in fact two sides of the same process. Those women's issues that were bargained into the collective agreement are ones that can be defined as meeting some special needs to accommodate women: maternity/paternity/adoption leave, protection from VDTs while pregnant, job-sharing, no 'personal duties', a sexual harassment policy, and protection on the basis of sexual orientation. Even though some of these measures, in particular paternity leave, job-sharing, and sexual orientation protection, certainly apply to men, these are still special provisions that do not fundamentally influence the way the office is organized. Of those measures that were bargained, only sexual harassment policy challenged masculine culture in the office, and it is no coincidence that it constituted a major site of conflict between union leaders and the Women's Committee in the early 1980s. Other women's issues that posed a more fundamental challenge to business-as-usual, such as affirmative action, career paths, and on-the-job training for women, were never endorsed as legitimate bargaining issues. Even pay equity, which was commonplace in the labour movement by the 1990s, was picked up quite late by the OTEU and then massaged in such a way as to maintain the gendered wage hierarchy in the office (see Chapter 6). Incremental change could accommodate women's special needs precisely because their accommodation did not require rethinking traditional union practices.

A third reading of this process focuses on shifting definitions of 'equality' and 'solidarity'. Feminist notions of equality challenged union traditions of equality as identical treatment for everyone regardless of substantive outcomes. From this traditional perspective demands for special women's issues were open to charges of seeking preferential treatment for women. In fact, resistance to feminist demands were often couched in terms of upholding the principle of equality for everyone. Trade union feminists were unable to challenge this notion of equality without at the same time threatening solidarity within the union. Under these circumstances, decisions to 'soft soap' gender issues and drop the most contentious of these were pragmatic political decisions. Women were unlikely to make significant gains in the office if their union could not withstand the internal political divisions that ensued.

Gendering processes within the union provided another vantage point from which to consider equality. As union activists and leaders, women faced difficulties that their male counterparts did not. Just as women were marked as a special case of workers, and women's issues were marked as the only bargaining issues to have gender-specific consequences, so, too, were women union leaders marked as the only ones whose politics might be influenced by their gender. Charges of being preoccupied with women's issues were used to discredit women, and even unrelated policy disagreements were more likely to be inscribed within a gendered subtext. Moreover, union culture was not supportive for women activists and they required special efforts to learn survival skills and teach such skills to other women.

Visibility was double-edged for feminist activists. Through the Women's Committee gendering was once again identified as an explicit part of collective bargaining. Negotiation over women's issues blurred boundaries between public and private space, workplace and family relations, and individual choice and structural constraints. Processes of gendering in the office, the union, and in broader social relations were *problematized* rather than taken for granted as the normal order of things. In so doing, union feminists made some of the consequences of gendering visible to union members. Gender issues were interpreted in a fairly homogeneous form, however, reflecting the dominance of White women in the union and in the Women's Committee.[85] The racialized nature of gender relations remained invisible. Nor was the Women's Committee strong enough to disturb the underpinnings of masculine privilege embedded in union traditions and in the organization of the office at BC Hydro. Nevertheless, the Women's Committee was effective enough to elicit considerable opposition within the union.

For the most part, however, the Women's Committee did not systematically evaluate the foundations of the collective agreement and traditional union practices. As we shall see in Chapter 6, neither members of the Women's Committee nor anyone else used a gendered lens to scrutinize bargaining strategies that provided greater protection for senior White men during corporate restructuring in the 1980s and 1990s. For most members of the Women's Committee, too, women's issues were special needs that could be tacked onto the existing collective agreement without disrupting the union's main business. In the following chapter we will explore the consequences of this approach during a recent period of massive corporate restructuring.

6

Restructuring, Resistance, and the Politics of Equity

I know quite a few men that really want promotions, though, and they feel quite bitter about it. . . . The [employment equity] program is very unfair. They sort of say, if you're not female, and if you're not Oriental, forget about it.[1]

The New Reality

The 1980s marked a period of dramatic change for office workers at BC Hydro. Under the twin influences of neo-liberal economic policies adopted by both federal and provincial levels of government and corporate demands for restructuring, downsizing, and flexibility, office workers saw their conditions of work deteriorate. Job security and expected career mobility evaporated in the midst of massive lay-offs and the casualization of the workforce. Regressive labour legislation and conservative fiscal policies underlay demands on public-sector workers for increased productivity and flexibility, while placing labour firmly on the defensive.

Paradoxically, these trends coincided with the feminization of the union and new demands for gender equality, and, for the first time in the Canadian context, employment equity programs. Employment equity legislation was implemented to improve the employment prospects of four designated groups: women, visible minorities, Aboriginal peoples, and persons with disabilities. Canadian employment equity legislation has few teeth and does not technically apply to utility companies in British Columbia. But employment equity legislation served as a broader incentive to set voluntary targets for employment equity groups, and many large companies did so.[2] In British Columbia, and particularly in its largest urban centre where most workers at BC Hydro were concentrated, the 1980s brought major demographic changes through immigration. By 1991 just under one in four people in greater Vancouver was a person of colour, not including those of Aboriginal descent.[3] The workforce at BC Hydro was becoming more diverse and issues of race/ethnicity joined gender and disability to inform debate and policies about equity.

Employment equity policies adopted by BC Hydro in the early 1990s were in some respects more image than substance, but still there was a feeling among many White union members that the tables had turned against them, particularly against White men. Suffering the loss of career mobility due to corporate downsizing and new forms of flexibility and casualization, men no longer possessed the career prospects most expected when they were hired; neither did most workers in the office. Notwithstanding the real decline in men's career mobility, the OTEU's response to restructuring in the 1980s and 1990s reinforced racialized-masculine privilege. Union strategies towards employment security, seniority, bumping and recall provisions, temporary work, contracting out, and other measures, including resistance to employment equity policies, reinforced existing hierarchies in the office. Resistance to employment equity turned on defending the rights of White men, but this was not so for other union strategies. The union sought to protect all members from the effects of corporate restructuring, but the uneven impact of union strategies was largely invisible to OTEU negotiating committees. Whether intentional or not, as the union confronted the new realities of the eighties and nineties, its goals and bargaining strategies remained firmly embedded in the racialized-masculine culture within which its traditions had been forged.

Restructuring Office Work

The early 1980s were marked by a major economic recession in Canada, which had particularly severe consequences in British Columbia. Massive restructuring in the forestry industry, the engine of the provincial economy, produced official unemployment rates that hovered around 16 per cent by 1984.[4] Experimenting with neoliberal economic policies, the provincial government took advantage of the recession and escalating levels of unemployment to push through an unpopular restraint program. A sweeping package of 26 separate legislative bills was introduced in 1983 to cut back the civil service and the welfare state and reduce the rights of public-sector workers, organized labour, and community and advocacy groups. Opposition to the restraint agenda crystallized in the Solidarity Coalition, uniting labour with social and community groups. The Solidarity Coalition organized the largest demonstrations witnessed in the history of British Columbia and took the province to the brink of a general strike.[5]

Office workers at BC Hydro were embroiled in these events in two ways: first, in resisting government legislation as active participants of Operation Solidarity, the labour arm of the Solidarity Coalition; and second, in resisting corporate restructuring and downsizing at BC Hydro. These two came together in a long and costly strike over the winter of 1983–4. The strike was a watershed, marking the shift from steady employment to massive lay-offs, followed by casualization, contracting out, and privatization; from contract gains to concession bargaining; from labour militancy to rank-and-file demoralization; and from uncontested union elections to deep divisions over union leadership. Throughout the 1980s, then, the OTEU struggled to protect its members hard-won rights in the face of aggressive management concession demands and internal controversies.

Workers at BC Hydro had benefited from the prolonged postwar economic expansion and enjoyed decades of job security found in few other industries. Men who began working in the office in the fifties, sixties, and seventies anticipated a lifelong career with the company, considerable mobility up the office job hierarchy, better wages than mostly non-union colleagues in other offices, and a secure retirement. The recession of the early 1980s shook that foundation, and by mid-decade it was clear that this security would never return.

> I guess everybody looked at going and working at the company from high school graduation to the grave. And that happened for many years, and it changed.[6]

> And you know, the philosophy was that you get a job here and you get on regular, you perform satisfactorily, and there's no serious problems, and you've got a job here for the rest of your life. . . . That really was the way it was, but that's not the case now.[7]

The first lay-offs at BC Hydro began in the summer of 1982. The recession in forestry and mining, combined with escalating interest rates, produced corporate losses and withdrawal from further hydro development projects. The first lay-offs involved 10 per cent of the workforce, concentrated mostly in the engineering sections linked to the construction of dams. Over 100 office workers also received lay-off notices by the end of the year.[8]

In the midst of difficult contract negotiations the following November, with management seeking the first concession contract in decades, OTEU workers, alongside their blue-collar co-workers in the IBEW, struck BC Hydro as part of Operation Solidarity. Operation Solidarity walk-outs ended within a week with controversial hand-shakes between the leaders of the BC Federation of Labour and the International Woodworkers of America representing the forestry workers, and the Premier of the province.[9] But the strike at BC Hydro lasted for three months, until February 1984, and ended with the company winning concessions from the unions.[10] In his address to members at the contract ratification vote, which the bargaining committee recommended against, President Trotter summed up the union's position as follows:

> For the first time since 1962 [when BC Electric was nationalized to form BC Hydro] you have faced an employer out to kick the hell out of you. The company, we admit, has attained a settlement on their terms, if accepted. They have won the battle today under the circumstances of the times. However, I do not concede that they have won the war.[11]

Concessions in the 1983–4 strike were a prelude to aggressive corporate restructuring over the next several years. In the summer of 1984, just months after the strike ended, the company began a program of massive lay-offs. By the end of the year staff had been cut by one-quarter; of the 2,500 utility workers laid off, over 1,000 were OTEU members. By the end of the following year the workforce was down by over one-third, or 3,400 employees.[12] The engineering sections were hit first as the company withdrew from development of power projects. By the fall of 1984, 40 per cent of the engineering division, including hundreds of technicians and support staff in the OTEU, had been laid off. The lay-offs soon spread throughout the company, including large numbers of middle management.[13] When the dust settled the union had lost one-quarter of its members at BC Hydro.

With the workforce drastically reduced BC Hydro embarked on strategies of work intensification and increased flexibility. The number of temporary employees and contracted-out work mushroomed. BC Hydro won concessions on flexible hours of work, experiments with empowered work teams, multi-task job descriptions, and home-work. In addition, the company privatized several corporate units.[14]

For the rest of the decade office workers were buffeted by the effects of these various restructuring initiatives.

It is worth recounting successive management negotiating positions over the next decade to illustrate the extent and direction of corporate demands for flexibility and attempts to minimize union power in the office. Aggressive concession bargaining began in 1983 and contributed to the strike that year. Management demanded two major concessions that would shape bargaining for the next decade. First, a longer workweek, with an increase from a 35-hour week to a 37.5-hour week, was sought. A 35-hour week was won in 1974 with a scheme that provided members with one day off every two weeks, or 17 days off in all; management sought to end this program, referred to as reduced-work-week-leave (RWWL).[15] Second, management sought concessions on flexible hours, requiring employees in some divisions (at first restricted to safety and energy conservation) to work straight time shifts anytime between 6:00 a.m. and 10:00 p.m.[16] BC Hydro won this concession. As a business representative commented, 'To ask people to work any hours between 6:00 a.m. and 10:00 p.m. as determined by the employer without any premiums [additional pay] is to turn the clock back 20 years.'[17] Thereafter, attempts to extend flexible shifts and increase hours of work became a standard part of management bargaining.

In the next round of negotiations, in 1986, BC Hydro's demands for increased flexibility and cost savings continued. As the union predicted, the foothold in the area of shift work without compensation was expanded: the company sought to expand flexible hours to include a broad range of jobs in customer service.[18] This was not accomplished, but BC Hydro did achieve its main cost-cutting proposal that year: the job evaluation plan that had been jointly designed, implemented, and monitored with the OTEU was replaced. Expecting to save $300,000 a year, the corporation implemented a streamlined system of job families that would allow more managerial flexibility, and *no union participation*, in job evaluation.[19]

Concession bargaining was even more apparent in the next set of negotiations, in 1989. Still seeking to extend flexible hours into customer service and increase the workweek by buying out employees' reduced-work-week-leave, management also sought to breach bargaining units by placing redundant management and professional staff in OTEU positions and by bargaining completely separate new agreements in its recently privatized subsidiaries.[20] By 1989 the post lay-off demoralization among union members had softened and strategic strike action prevented major concessions.[21] Still, BC Hydro won the expansion of flexible shifts to a wide range of jobs in customer service, including up to six weekends a year.[22]

Demands for flexibility were widened again in the 1991 negotiations. BC Hydro sought to double the number of weekends available for flexible work scheduling (from six to 12), initiate split shifts (three days on, one day off, two days on), and initiate flexible starting times for all employees between 6:00 a.m. and 10:00 a.m., Monday through Saturday, at management's discretion. In addition, the company sought a longer workweek (to 37.5 hours) through a voluntary buy-out of RWWL days, the initiation of work teams with bonuses (or empowerment projects), and experiments with homework.[23] In exchange for a wage increase management won most of these concessions, with the exception of split shifts, no bonuses for work teams, and the number of weekends expanded to 10 rather than 12.[24]

The 1993 collective agreement (which was the last to be negotiated at the time of writing[25]) contained a new set of concession demands that focused on internal flexibility for hiring and promotions. BC Hydro adopted an employment equity policy to increase opportunities for women, visible minorities, Aboriginal men and women, and people with disabilities. Employment equity goals were linked to a number of management demands regarding flexibility in hiring, training, and promotions. Specifically, BC Hydro sought to reduce seniority rights for promotion and training opportunities and establish preferential hiring of external over internal candidates for all jobs in Groups 1–5. Job flexibility was sought by new restrictions on the right to compete for lateral transfers and promotions, to require the supervisor's approval during the first 12 months in a job; eliminate the requirements to post temporary job openings if spanning less than one year or for jobs below Group 6; eliminate seniority for temporary employees; and allow employees to transfer from management or IBEW into OTEU positions.[26] In addition, a weak form of pay equity was proposed in advance of provincial legislation then expected imminently.[27] Strategic strike action again staved off some of these concessions, including employment equity provisions. Management did attain its pay equity proposal, rather than the more extensive union proposal, restrictions on the ability to seek lateral transfers and promotions, the right to place non-union members into OTEU jobs, and weaker seniority rights with the new language on job vacancies.[28]

The combination of lay-offs and the cumulative effects of a decade of concessions on flexible hours, work intensification, and the casualization of the workforce transformed the office for all employees at BC Hydro. But in significant ways restructuring was a racialized-gendered process with complex and uneven outcomes. In some respects the situation of OTEU men was most adversely affected. Unlike women, men enjoyed considerable career opportunities through the 1970s and mobility into the higher levels of the office job hierarchy was almost considered a right. With the lay-offs in 1984 career mobility for men ended abruptly. The number of jobs declined by one-quarter, with the heaviest losses in engineering support work: 'Clerical work was affected less [by the lay-offs]. They still needed the clericals. They were getting rid of the higher groups. . . . They were phasing out people like the engineers, the technologists-in-training, [and] the apprenticeship programs were stopped in the IBEW.'[29]

Men and women who were laid off had no recourse but to bump down the job ladder to try to maintain employment. Temporary postings and contracting out removed more jobs from the purview of regular union members.

> There's no way a regular person would go out on one of those [temporary] jobs because you lose everything.[30]

> Almost every job is bulletined as temporary . . . I think that is definitely a step for the worse because full-time regular employees won't bulletin for a job that may only last six months or a year or two years because then they don't know where they're going from there; maybe laid off.[31]

Most regular workers were unwilling to risk their seniority by bidding on temporary jobs. Other office work was contracted out at both the bottom and upper ends of the office hierarchy, from cafeteria work to specialized technical projects.[32] The results were blocked mobility for everyone and downward mobility or unemployment for many. The number of men in the union dropped dramatically, from 1,865 to 1,177 between 1981 and 1991, a decrease of 37 per cent. The number of women dropped less sharply, from 1,753 to 1,434, or 18 per cent, altering the gender balance in the union (see Tables 2 and 14).

Men also experienced more downward mobility than did women. Sixty-one per cent of men were in Groups 7–12 in 1991, compared to 68 per cent a decade earlier. Conversely, the proportion of men in Group 6 and below nearly doubled in the same time period, from 14 to 26 per cent. Women did not experience the same levels of downward mobility. Eighty-three per cent had been in jobs in Groups 6 and below in 1981, and 79 per cent remained so a decade later. The number of women in the top half of the job hierarchy actually grew from 13 per cent to 19 per cent.[33]

The last decade had witnessed new mobility for women that had not existed previously, with a handful of women entering traditional male jobs like meter reading, surveying, drafting, and customer accounts representatives. None the less, women's mobility remained much more limited than did men's. There were more than four times as many women as men in the bottom half of the job hierarchy, and more than twice as many men as women in the top half (see Table 2). Almost all (88 per cent) of the men below Group 7 were employed in Groups 5 and 6, compared to 62 per cent of similarly situated women. And even among those women who moved beyond the glass ceiling, more than half (55 per cent) of those above Group 6 were employed in Group 7. In comparison, only 15 per cent of comparable men were restricted to Group 7 jobs.[34] The average female salary was only 77 per cent of men's average salary in 1991.[35] Moreover, recession and restructuring occurred just as women were beginning to make the first inroads into previously male jobs in the office, so growth in women's career mobility that might have been expected was effectively blocked.

Overall, restructuring reinforced decades of traditional gender segregation in the office. Young union members, of both genders, had the least seniority and lost their jobs first. Not surprisingly, the few women who were beginning to breach male enclaves in the better paying technical and non-office fields were younger women. In jobs that many men could bump into, these women were the first to be laid off and the last to be recalled. In some cases women laid off from technical jobs were hired into clerical positions even if they had no previous clerical experience; these clerical positions could then prove difficult to escape.[36] There are no hard data to document the number of workers of colour in the office. But previous hiring patterns favouring White men and women and the relatively recent demographic shifts through changing immigration patterns suggest that workers of colour, more likely to be younger and with less seniority, were disproportionately affected by the lay-offs and restructuring of the 1980s.

Promotion possibilities at BC Hydro had always been gendered, tied to technical training through support work for engineers and doing one's time in small communities throughout the province (see Chapter 4). Recall and bumping provisions following lay-offs exacerbated this gender dynamic. Men, particularly White men, were more likely to have greater seniority and experience in sought-after jobs. In addition, men were more likely to have appropriate skills to be considered for any retraining opportunities and greater geographical mobility to uproot families and move around the province. Even bidding on

other clerical jobs could be difficult for women whose family responsibilities, and the greater reticence of husbands to follow wives than
the reverse, were more likely to impede promotion prospects and the
likelihood of holding onto a job in the event of lay-off.

It is perhaps not surprising that the casualization of the workforce
affected women, and especially women of colour, much more than
men.[37]

All these temporaries were being brought in. They were all
younger people. They were all mostly female. The people that
were coming in at the higher rate of pay were usually from outside
hires with degrees that were coming in at the Group 9, 10, and 11
jobs and they were mostly male.[38]

If we consider only regular employees, in 1991 the number of women
and men in the office union was almost identical (961 women and
924 men). The difference lay in the distribution of the temporary
workforce. In 1981 only 10 per cent of all union members were temporary; by 1991 this number had ballooned to 28 per cent, and two-
thirds of all temporary workers were women. In 1991, 35 per cent of
all female union members (473) were temporary, compared to just 21
per cent (253) of men.[39] At the same time, some of these temporary
workers became a preferred source for training and promotions in
light of their greater youth and educational qualifications:

With the temporaries, it's just created a whole influx of different
problems. From problems in job selections, problems in not making them regular employees so their employee status is not correct,
giving them the training because they're young and they are
promotable and they're marketable. The senior employees are
being overlooked for promotional opportunities because they're
considered too [old]—'Why should we waste the training on you?
You're going to be gone in a few years anyway.'[40]

In addition, the continuous trend towards greater unilateral managerial control over hours of work, starting times, weekend work, and
shift work had particular implications for parents trying to juggle
household and work responsibilities. In most Canadian households
women continued to bear the brunt of these family responsibilities
and were potentially more adversely affected by management's flexible work scheduling.

It is clear that downsizing and the construction of a flexible workforce had uneven consequences for different groups of union members. Yet, perceptions of these trends were somewhat distorted by the

greater sense, and indeed the greater reality, of entitlement long experienced by White men. Their perceptions of entitlement exacerbated the sense of grievance felt by many White men in the OTEU. The union, drawing on established union traditions in defence of seniority, job hierarchies, skilled positions, and regular full-time work, fought a rearguard action to protect its members' rights in the face of aggressive restructuring. OTEU activists paid little or no attention to the differential impact company policies—and their own strategies—were having on workers. In the context of the history of racialized-masculinist union culture these strategies of resistance also provided unequal protection for women, members of racialized minorities, and younger members in ways that were usually both unintentional and largely unrecognized.

Strategies of Resistance: Reinscribing Privilege

When the new reality of restructuring began in the early 1980s the OTEU, much like the rest of organized labour, was caught by surprise. These were the first lay-offs in decades and the union had woefully inadequate provisions relating to lay-offs, recall, and bumping procedures that less stable work environments usually made a priority. Lay-offs occurred on the basis of inverse seniority within very narrowly defined divisions of the company. Bumping rights only applied within these divisions, and only *for jobs a member had previously held within that division*. Recall was based on seniority for the specific job an employee had lost; but for all other positions recall was based on an employee's past record of *ability and seniority*. In addition, bumping and recall were *not* region-specific and might require members to move anywhere in the province. In this context seniority, the traditional basis for establishing job security in Canada, did not provide much security for senior workers facing lay-offs, and this soon became the union's chief bargaining issue.[41]

The first round of collective bargaining following the first round of lay-offs was in 1983. The OTEU sought to strengthen seniority by widening the bumping and recall provisions to include divisions of former employment within a member's current geographical area. In this first concession agreement, and following a long strike, the OTEU only managed to extend bumping rights in a very limited manner. Recall and bumping could occur in jobs determined to be *within the same job hierarchy* by the job evaluation department. As a business agent explained at the contract ratification vote, province-wide recall and bumping remained in place:

There is very limited access provided under Article 8 for employees to bump into previous divisions where they worked. We tried
to get [the company] to provide that people would be able wherever possible to bump at their headquarters or to headquarters
which wouldn't require a change of residence wherever possible.
We did not succeed.[42]

Large-scale lay-offs began just after the strike ended and, as discussed above, produced uneven effects on members. In the next
round of negotiations, in 1986, the OTEU continued to seek broader
seniority rights for bumping and recall but ceased to pay attention to
obstacles presented by relocation. A seniority system that operated
within job hierarchies prevented competition between those in men's
and women's jobs; on the other hand, women breaching these gender
barriers were particularly vulnerable to being laid off. For many
women, however, the issue of relocation was often most central to the
ability to exercise their recall or bumping rights.

The OTEU tabled demands to enhance seniority rights for bumping
and recall within designated job hierarchies by basing access on
seniority and 'sufficient ability to perform the job' or the ability to do
so 'within a reasonable period of training and orientation'. Demands
were no longer tied to current geographical location but instead to
providing moving expenses incurred as a consequence of bumping or
recall to another region.[43] What the OTEU won in this contract was
more modest but it did enhance seniority rights. Bumping and recall
procedures were extended to those in equal or lower job groups in a
designated hierarchy; selection was based on an individual's past
record of ability and seniority; and there would be no compensation
for moving expenses.[44]

With the threat of further lay-offs over, the OTEU's concerns later in
the decade turned to different forms of employment security: protection against contracting out, protecting the integrity of bargaining
unit work, stemming the growth of a temporary workforce, and maintaining equivalent provisions for workers in newly privatized companies.[45] In 1989 the union won a master collective agreement covering
the privatized subsidiaries and a form of employment security within
BC Hydro: 'regular employees were protected against layoff caused
by shortage of work, contracting-out, automation, new equipment,
new procedures, or reorganization, *provided they agreed to accept
retraining or relocation.*'[46] Job security now depended on the ability
to retrain or relocate. As discussed above, relocation possibilities
were shaped by the nature of gender relations in the wider society.

Similarly, retraining opportunities at BC Hydro were embedded in technical job hierarchies segregated from female clerical jobs. Women rarely attained the appropriate qualifications considered suitable for job training.

Employment security applied to regular workers but did not prevent further casualization as new jobs opened up. As we have already seen, the number of temporary workers soon escalated, as did the practice of contracting out. This process was also gendered. Temporary job postings appeared more at the lower end of the job hierarchy, while contracting out appeared more at the upper end.[47] In its bargaining in 1991 the union's main concern was to enhance employment security and the career mobility of more senior members. The OTEU sought to ban contracting out, prevent other utility workers from performing OTEU work, limit the use of temporary workers, and attain new language for promotions based on 'seniority and sufficient ability to perform the job, in that order'.[48] With an ageing membership[49] suspended on the corporate career ladder for nearly a decade, it was not surprising that the OTEU identified the preservation of skilled work in the top half of the job hierarchy as central to its demands on contracting out and promotions based on seniority.[50] However, this effectively meant the union prioritized the protection of men's jobs and promotion prospects. The provision won continued to have the same gendered consequences as previous language that tied bumping and recall to relocation and retraining.

> A regular employee shall not be laid off as a direct result of the employer contracting out work presently performed by the employee unless the employee is given the following options:
> 1) to exercise his/her bumping rights;
> 2) to accept a placement opportunity;
> 3) to accept training
> and declines all three.[51]

In a significant victory the OTEU also won preference for 'regular employees with the ability and highest seniority, in that order' in job competitions involving temporary employees or external hires.[52]

Temporary workers were a particular problem for the union, creating a two-tiered system among OTEU members that could threaten union solidarity. In an effort to reduce contracting out the OTEU signed an agreement providing new seniority rights and fringe benefits, such as dental and pension plans, for temporary workers in exchange for the ability to hire 'long-term' temporary employees.[53] By the following year it became clear BC Hydro's use of temporaries was 'excessive' from the union's point of view. Thus, the OTEU sought the above 1991 contract language favouring regular over temporary members in job competitions. In exchange, however, the OTEU accepted a new definition of 'temporary': anyone on a contract for less than three years (an increase from one year), with temporary positions to become regular if extended beyond three years.[54] This extension of temporary employment had gendered implications, too:

> The women are lower grouped so it's a double whammy. You're temporary and you're lower grouped. And because you're doing clerical work, the management don't know the value of your work, so you're more likely to keep being temporary. . . . The men who are going into temporary positions tend to get one- or two-year temporaries, because they're technical jobs. . . . So [women] have more instability.[55]

Viewed as interchangeable workers whose turnover was not considered problematic, women were less likely to become regularized because they were less likely to get longer contracts in the first place. With recognized skills, and though less likely to be in temporary positions at all, men could more readily transform longer contracts into regular positions.

Contracting out, incursions on bargaining unit work, enhancing seniority in job competitions, and regularizing temporary positions were all elements of contract negotiations again in 1993. No improvements were won on any of these issues, in spite of strike action, and, as noted above, BC Hydro won important concessions that weakened the ability to protect bargaining unit work and restricted internal competitions for jobs.[56] In light of these concessions and failure to win key union demands, the bargaining team recommended against ratification of the 1993 contract. After 19 months of negotiations, 18 weeks of selective strike action, and two sets of mediation, the contract was ratified with a margin of just six votes (50.14 per cent).[57]

Over the previous decade conditions of work had changed dramatically for office workers at BC Hydro. Gone were secure jobs with men's expected career mobility up the job ladder. Grievances over job insecurity and lack of career mobility shaped union demands and strategic responses to new concessions demanded by the company. As we have seen, the racialized-gendered process of corporate restructuring was reinforced by many of the union's own strategies that, intentionally or not, often privileged the position of senior White men. By the early 1990s these union demands began to crystallize around notions of fairness to union members. Fairness was assumed

Picketing BC Hydro, 1994. (OTEU 378 News, Sept.-Oct. 1994: 11a.)

to mean the same thing for all union members. Challenging the company's interpretation of what constituted employment equity, the union made employment equity demands of its own. Some of the union's equity demands, such as pay equity, were concerned with improving the situation of lower-paid women. Other demands, such as for equity through improved seniority rights, reinforced the status quo in the office.

Resisting/Redefining Employment Equity

BC Hydro developed an employment equity policy in 1991 with a new human resources strategy called 'Building Team 2000'.[58] The focus of the new policy was threefold: to lower the age of the workforce since 'only 6% of our workforce was below 30 years of age'; to promote women into management positions and into the blue-collar trades because 'only 4% of senior professional and managerial positions were held by women' in 1988; and to respond to demographic changes in the 'cultural/ethnic composition . . . of the workforce entrants'.[59] An employment equity policy was designed to prepare BC Hydro for the labour force realities of the next century.

> To meet the challenge of a general shortage of skilled people from traditional sources of supply, we will look at new sources for qualified people. Women and other target groups, such as the

disabled, are becoming an increasingly important source of the labour force supply.

To reach this objective we will:

- emphasize increased hiring, promotion and education of women and other target groups.
- work with educational facilities in a Partners in Education program, to ensure those institutions are aware of our needs and offer appropriate courses/programs.
- review hiring, promotion and compensation policies and work practices to ensure that they are as bias-free as possible.
- invest in necessary support systems and work/family issues such as access to day care, elder care, specialized equipment, etc.[60]

There is little doubt that an employment equity policy was needed. By the company's own account, out of some 6,000 employees[61] in 1991 it employed only 28 people with disabilities; only 12 women in all of the blue-collar trades, which numbered over 2,000 employees; and a total of 'six native hires during the fiscal year', and these were apparently temporary positions.[62] And by 1991 the number of women in management positions had doubled to 8 per cent, at least 'partially attributable to the introduction of a new management job evaluation program'.[63] As one manager remembered, the number of women in management did not actually increase very much.

They made all the personnel people managers, and 80 per cent of those of course were female to start with. They used to be called just supervisors, or exempt staff, they weren't managers. So they increased by about 40 or 50 female staff into the management ranks by changing the designation of women's jobs. [But] most of them aren't really managers.[64]

BC Hydro made clear in its communications to management that employment equity did not mean adopting measures of affirmative action.

Employment equity is NOT reverse discrimination. Ideally, our vision is to have a workplace that is representative of ALL groups of our population, at all levels. We are not advocating preferential hiring of women or any other target group. We want to ensure that everyone is aware of the opportunities/skills required and that where appropriate, we support the training and development needed to compete equally for future opportunities. Quotas have NOT been set but our corporate key performance indicators (targets)

Production department clerks. (*OTEU 378 News*, Nov.-Dec. 1991: 4.)

allow us to measure our progress as is the case with our other strategic business initiatives. INDIVIDUAL SELECTION DECISIONS ARE BASED ON QUALIFICATIONS AND POTENTIAL.[65]

The employment equity policy adopted was in line with 'soft' targets and reinforcement of the merit principle embodied in Canadian legislation rather than the 'harder' quotas and more proactive

Customer accounts representative, cashier, and credit clerk. (*OTEU 378 News*, Nov.-Dec. 1991: 4.)

traditions of affirmative action found in the United States. The promise of significant change through 'soft' employment equity targets almost always fell far short of its goals.

There was considerable divergence between the perceptions of many OTEU members that employment equity policies profoundly shaped hiring and promotion decisions and the views of others that little had changed:

> The company talks about equity of employment and access and there's always the caveat, if you qualify. Well, how do you qualify? I went to an equity meeting involving managers and we're talking about Aboriginal people, the disabled people, they're taking about women, going on and on, but the bottom line was 'if they qualify'. . . . They don't want anyone to be unqualified but they are not prepared to give that extra [help] for those persons.[66]

Aboriginal men and women and those with disabilities were the most disadvantaged but appeared to benefit the least from employment equity policies. The presence of one blind receptionist in the office, who was laid off after one year, was apparently considered quite extraordinary.[67] Aboriginal office workers were even scarcer: 'We've got people from many different races [in the union], but not a single

Service technicians. (*OTEU 378 News*, Nov.-Dec. 1991: 5.)

Native Indian. Well there's something wrong there.'[68] At the same time, as Vancouver became increasingly multi-ethnic during the 1980s and 1990s, the office became much more ethnically diverse. This new diversity was not found equally at all levels of the office hierarchy: 'There were some Chinese Canadians that were in some of the technical jobs, but you know, the lack of visible minorities in the senior positions is quite noticeable.'[69]

BC Hydro's employment equity policy focused predominantly on getting more women into management positions and, with much less success, into the entirely male blue-collar trades organized under the IBEW. As one former business representative reflected:

Employment equity was non-existent [for OTEU members]. For example, efforts to get women who had worked in clerical positions in the engineering side of the company to be given the opportunity to have access to on-the-job training programs. The engineering hierarchy basically was a training hierarchy, where you started, you came in at the bottom and did some very basic technical things. And then you moved up, it was a natural progression. And men who were engineering clerks could get into this bottom hierarchy engineering job very easily. Women who worked as clerks in the same area, who did very much the same work, couldn't [get in]. . . . I would be very pleased if they really did develop programs that would allow women to move more easily into the technical stream. I did not see any evidence of any recognition of the necessity for that when I was there. [Outside of management] what they were concentrating on was trying to get women to climb [utility] poles to earn more money, and those of the women that I knew had no interest whatsoever in becoming a lineman.[70]

The segregation of male and female jobs within the office was neither identified by management as a particular problem of employment equity nor much affected by the new equity policies. There was no attempt to build job ladders between the clerical and technical job hierarchies, for example, yet this constituted the single most important barrier to gender equality within the office.

Those women who had access to career mobility in the 1980s and 1990s were those with higher educational qualifications. Few women ever worked their way up the office hierarchy the way men had done until recently. Perceptions did not always tally with this reality. Though some members might believe women were favoured over men in the 1990s, for the most part promotion opportunities reflected the superior qualifications of the women in question.

Because of their policy on hiring women, she's probably better off than being a man right now. . . . There have been quite a few promotions that have been women moving up. Well, the thing is, they were brought in from outside, and I don't really think that the people available were extremely qualified. They were basically qualified but not extremely well qualified. And the women that were brought in both had CGAs and MBAs. Whereas the men that were qualified only had their CGAs.[71]

I think that the company is trying to put women in management now, which they didn't before. We have hired, in the marketing area, the last three marketing specialists have been young women. Now they do have university degrees. But I would say five years ago, if it was the same situation they would've been male, or at least two males and one female, instead of three young women.[72]

Questions were raised about the degree to which the corporate culture of BC Hydro, dominated by the masculine technocratic culture of engineering, was really amenable to restructuring along the lines suggested by employment equity goals. After all, the existing management made decisions about hiring and promotions; they were instructed to hire first and foremost on *their perceptions* of an individual's 'qualifications and potential'. The culture that valorized technical knowledge associated with engineering and promoted to management ranks through technical office hierarchies and doing one's time in the hinterland was not, in itself, reconsidered. In fact, 'a mobile and flexible workforce' developed through 'recruit[ing] workers who are willing to relocate' was a central objective of 'Building Team 2000'.[73] These expectations of a record of flexible relocation pose a problem for women's advancement into senior management. One female manager commented that the dual assumptions that relocation was essential for management experience and that married women won't relocate prevented women from even being considered for most senior positions.[74]

Others characterized the company's employment equity policy as 'tokenism'. For example, one former manager commented that the corporate engineering culture prevented much significant change. He argued:

> The reason for that is that the company is very much run by engineers. And the way these things naturally happen is, you don't do this for women, women come in and force things to change. But, there are no women decision-makers, or very few. And there are not likely to be for a long, long time until they start at the bottom of the engineering school. . . . The engineers don't want to be 'male chauvinist pigs', and I don't use that term, they're just trained and educated to be. . . . Engineers spend so much time learning engineering, which is a tough course, that they don't have time to learn to be human beings.[75]

Indeed, another manager argued that corporate culture had changed little: 'we still accept mediocrity in men more than we accept mediocrity in women at the higher level.'[76]

For senior management, employment equity could be demonstrated by an increase in numbers alone rather than by some more intangible change in corporate culture. A few more women in traditionally male terrain were highly visible, providing an aura of greater change than had really occurred. One business representative recalled a high-level meeting with senior management where this point was brought home to her:

> We were talking about employment equity and the styles of women, and they were bragging about the fact that they [now] had all these women managers, and they could name every one of them. And I said, 'It just proves my point', and they didn't even understand what I was taking about.[77]

In contrast, from the perspective of most union leaders, and no doubt the bulk of the membership, issues of employment equity and change in the workplace were more far-reaching than the company's employment equity policy suggested. As one union activist commented:

> I think it's easier for men to get ahead than women. Women seem to have to have all of the qualifications, where they'll take the guy and say, 'Well, he can work up to it.' And I think it's probably still that way to some extent. It depends on the area. In some areas they almost go overboard the other way, where they'll take a woman over a qualified man, even though she may not be qualified, because they have this quota they have to meet now. You know, their employment equity. They have all these fancy words so they have to hire the cripple and the minority person and the woman, and it's almost hard if you're sitting there as a guy to get ahead. The other interesting thing that's happened through the lay-offs in the eighties, they lost all the younger people. All the younger workforce went out the door. And they're in a situation now where there's a lot of people who are in their forties to fifties and within 20 years they're all going to be gone. So it's fairly easy now for the young. They're almost hiring younger people off the street and bouncing them ahead of this group of 40- to 50-year-olds that are sitting there, that have been with the company for 20 or 25 years. And they're moving these younger people ahead into management jobs and into other [union] jobs with higher qualifications.[78]

These observations, made by a White male activist in his fifties, capture the contradictory impact of a decade of corporate restructuring and equity politics. Largely as a result of women's organizing within the OTEU and feminist influence throughout the labour movement, there was a broad acknowledgement that in the past women were not treated equitably in the office. For many, however, this issue was poorly understood. Moreover, as the above quotation illustrates, women's inequality was often acknowledged with one breath and denied with the next as new equity demands stood in conflict with men's traditional career expectations.

Acknowledgement of systemic employment inequities was less often extended to other equity groups, such as those with disabilities or members of racialized minorities. With the lay-offs in the early 1980s wiping out most younger employees and recourse to large numbers of temporaries in subsequent years, members of colour were still concentrated among the younger, least senior, and casualized workforce. In spite of this, visibility to White workers shaped perceptions that men and women of colour were receiving preferential treatment.

> I know quite a few men that really want promotions, though, and they feel quite bitter about it. . . . The [employment equity] program is very unfair. They sort of say, if you're not female, and if you're not Oriental, forget about it.[79]

> Traditionally a lot of Asian people have gone into accounting so we have lots and lots of Asian people [in accounting], and at the supervisory level. And there were comments raised along the way that maybe these promotions were filling quotas.[80]

While the office was clearly much more diverse in ethnic origin than a decade before, it remained the case that some racialized groups were less likely than others to be hired for office work: 'You don't see too many Black people around here . . . [and] there's not a lot of East Indian people.'[81] And although popular belief might be that women of colour were especially advantaged in the era of employment equity, the glass ceiling appeared no less impervious. Perceptions of competence and fairness in the hiring process were mediated within the gendered hierarchy in the office.

> It seems if you're a man and you're a minority you get treated more equally than a woman who's a minority. . . . A woman's a woman. They're good for typing, clerical stuff. It's like they're born with these skills or something. . . . But to get out of these jobs is next to impossible. To get above pay Group 6 is next to impossible.[82]

OTEU members' perceptions about differential mobility opportunities were more accurate in relation to the increasing generation gap between older members who survived the mass lay-offs of the early 1980s—most now well above 40 years of age with decades of job experience but few formal educational credentials—and younger members, often first hired as temporary or contract workers, with university degrees and diplomas from technical institutes.

> The company has a new initiative to hire people under 30 years of age, much stronger educational requirements. A lot more consultants being brought in to do interesting specialized tasks, and so they're brought in with the qualifications, and perhaps the other people aren't given the opportunity to move up any more.[83]

As one activist commented, after the lay-offs the demand for educational credentials increased so much that he would no longer be able to attain his present job.

> They tell you if you want to have this job, you've got to go take this university course at night school. You might be somebody that's been working at the company for 15 years. Came out of high school, had all the formal education that you needed to get a job at that point, and have worked your way through the various hierarchies at the company, and have performed at a certain level. . . . So you've achieved some degree of technical expertise in some situations internally, and you've learned it on the job. . . . But it's rare in most cases now that you'd get the consideration that would get you into the next job. It's the only way I got it. I didn't get it because I've got a formal education. I don't have a formal education. I got my job because I was willing to move. . . . And quite frankly, if you were coming into it as an entry-level job you'd need your BCIT certificate, at a minimum.[84]

The senior workers who worked their way up the job hierarchy were predominantly White men located within traditional gendered career paths. In contrast, the junior members were more ethnically diverse, including many women with advanced educational qualifications in competition for traditional men's jobs in management and elsewhere. These trends—the increasing demand for educational credentials, the gap in educational qualifications between generations of workers, and the presence of a more ethnically diverse workforce, again, particularly among younger workers—combined to undercut the expectations of career mobility held by senior White men and the perception that other groups were the recipients of favouritism.

At the heart of equity concerns for the union, then, was frustration over blocked career mobility, and White men experienced the greatest loss of expected career mobility. From the perspective of men *expecting* promotions, the promotion of anyone who might be a member of an equity group was suspected to be based on attributes other than job qualifications. Thus, although the majority of OTEU members were part of employment equity groups, since women alone constituted 55 per cent of members, employment equity policies were identified by the union as 'unfair' to union members.

As a union newspaper article on the fear of reverse discrimination suggested, employment equity should be redefined around fairness for all members, not special measures targeted towards designated equity groups: 'The union vision of employment equity means *fairness for all workers*. Employment equity means *eliminating favouritism* and other tools used for discriminatory behaviour.'[85] And what is the fairest way to eliminate favouritism? To ensure that seniority is protected in hiring, promotion, and training opportunities:

'Seniority is not discriminatory; everyone earns it in the same manner. Using [employment equity] programs to undermine seniority by favouring some groups is attacking fairness in the workplace.'[86] The OTEU also suggested that better integration of people with disabilities could be attained by giving priority to 'union members returning from long term disability leave'. To address the generation gap in educational qualifications, the union said, there should be a 'clear mechanism for determining work experience equivalents with paper qualifications'.[87]

> Unions have always struggled for workplaces free of discrimination. Workers should be hired and promoted without irrelevant factors such as race, creed, colour, sexual-orientation or political beliefs being considered. . . . Our goal should be to protect the majority interest whether we are bargaining language about employment equity or pay equity.[88]

Given the nature of union representation in Canada, with closed-shop bargaining units in which everyone covered by a contract must belong to the union, it is not surprising that OTEU interpretation of equity in employment considered only existing union members. In this sense the union's gaze was expected to be inward-looking. Defining employment equity policies as unfair to the majority of workers, however, when in fact a majority of members belonged to the targeted equity groups, did not represent the interests of the majority. The OTEU endorsed its traditional position of formal equality embodied in identical treatment anchored in seniority. In so doing it privileged men over women, White workers over workers of colour, and senior members over more junior members, while ignoring issues of substantive inequality among its own membership.

At the same time, the union had every reason to be wary of employment equity programs unilaterally implemented by BC Hydro. As the recent history of restructuring, downsizing, and demands for ever-increasing flexibility had shown, the company sought to weaken the union. Seniority rights were a key part of union control that had not, until then, been subject to management concession demands. Indeed, strengthening seniority had figured at the centre of union demands throughout the 1980s and 1990s, and members had proved willing to exchange more flexibility in hours for better seniority provisions. When BC Hydro translated its employment equity policy into specific concession demands in the 1993 contract negotiations, therefore, the OTEU responded by denouncing these initiatives as an attack on hard-won seniority rights: 'Make no mistake, resolution of employment equity issues will be very difficult, given the implications for our existing Union membership, and their rights to jobs and promotions based on their "seniority and ability".'[89]

BC Hydro identified employment equity as a 'centre-piece proposal' in negotiations, concentrating on what it saw as impediments to achieving equity. Its two key proposals were (1) preferential hiring of external over internal candidates for all jobs below Group 6 (mostly women's jobs); and (2) weakening seniority rights to facilitate promotion and training among targeted groups.[90] In a bargaining update to members, the union negotiating committee warned:

> The Employer wants to implement an 'affirmative action' or 'employment equity' program to provide preferential treatment for people with disabilities, visible minorities, women and aboriginal people with respect to 'employment and development' opportunities, subject to 'qualifications' but without regard to seniority. This demand by the Employer has huge implications in terms of the training and career advancement prospects for our existing union members. . . . The Employer wants to abridge the career development and job security prospects for existing bargaining unit members in order to achieve its 'employment equity' target. . . . [It] wants to have the right to hire external candidates for job vacancies rated at job Group 5 and below on a preferential basis, that is, ahead of internal candidates who are union members.[91]

The union's position pitted existing members against unknown external applicants with higher qualifications, and clearly this was one element of the company's intent to hire younger employees. But in characterizing 'soft' targets of employment equity as the 'hard' quotas of affirmative action, already vilified in popular media from the United States, the union did more than protect existing members' right to compete for jobs below Group 6. It identified all employment equity policies as an attack on union members, making it impossible to develop internal policies to begin to break down entrenched gendered divisions in the office. Instead, members were reminded of the need to 'safeguard ourselves against attack by an employer determined to achieve employment equity through an "affirmative action" campaign'.[92]

At the same time the OTEU developed its own package of broader demands that it labelled employment equity and tabled these demands in negotiations. Some of these demands were attempts to win back earlier concessions; others were linked to more flexibility for workers tied to family and health issues.

4. Employment Equity
   4.1 Hours of Work—remove cash option for RWWL [reduced workweek leave], limit flex hours
   4.2 Voluntary versus Mandatory Overtime
   4.3 Family Leave—bereavement leave, family care leave
   4.4 Leaves of Absence—entitlement, call back/return from LOA [leave of absence]
   4.5 Occupational Health and Safety—employee fitness [health club], bus passes [lost more than a decade before when transit became a separate company][93]

Flexibility for family leaves and employee-defined, rather than management-dictated, flexible hours were family-friendly demands that might ease the double burden many women faced. However, none of the union's employment equity demands directly addressed internal equity issues for the four designated groups.

For a number of reasons the union's attempt to redefine employment equity on its own terms was not particularly successful. There was no obvious cohesion to this group of demands and no rationale was provided. Most issues were not clearly tied to any common-sense notion of equity since claims of fairness could apply to almost any union demand. Most union employment equity demands were not priorities for the membership. And finally, the OTEU's own coupling of employment equity with affirmative action made any union demands under its name suspect.

The attempt by the OTEU to redefine employment equity was in fact a missed opportunity. Some other unions have attempted innovative measures to protect members' hard-won seniority rights while promoting equity in the ranks (see Chapter 7). A union proposal might have turned employment equity inward so that its own members in the designated groups, after all, a majority of union members, might have first crack at promotions for which they were qualified, perhaps still based on a combination of seniority and ability. Bridges and cross-training between the clerical and technical ladders might have been proposed since this remains the greatest inequality in the office. Such a proposal might be fostered as part of the creation of equivalencies between experience and paper qualifications already suggested by the union. Finally, a more creative approach to seniority could be developed to allow a number of affirmative action positions while preventing the company from simply abrogating all seniority rights. Instead, the OTEU's position on employment equity was firmly grounded in resistance to a perceived attack on senior White men. In the process, the interests of the majority of its members were over-looked, and the union failed to develop a progressive program of employment equity that might better protect the interests of its members at BC Hydro.

The Politics of Pay Equity

If the OTEU's position on employment equity was reactive rather than proactive, the same cannot be said for its position on pay equity. Pay equity was initiated by the union and was on its bargaining agenda in 1991 and again in 1993. As we saw in Chapter 3, the OTEU's struggle for equal pay for women began in the late 1940s when it tried to abolish separate male and female pay scales and achieve 'equal pay for equal job evaluation'. Though the union pioneered the struggle for equal pay for women with its early redefinition from 'equal work' to 'equal value', masculinist assumptions shaped concerns about equal pay in the postwar decades. A more radical critique of the value of work and job evaluation systems emerged in the 1970s and 1980s. Defined in terms of comparable worth or pay equity, it provided a historical assessment of work and argued that work had been valued *because it was performed by men* and undervalued *because it was performed by women*. Thus, pay equity demanded both more gender-neutral comparisons of the tasks involved in male-dominated and female-dominated jobs and the recognition of previously taken-for-granted skills used in women's jobs.

In spite of its long struggle for equal pay for women at the utility company, spanning from 1949 to 1981, the OTEU was rather late to embrace these broader feminist demands for pay equity. When the OTEU put pay equity on its bargaining agenda in the early 1990s, moreover, its demands remained abstracted from the union's own role in this process at BC Hydro. This was particularly important since the job evaluation system jointly designed by union and management continued to form the basis of job evaluation in the office.[94] These contradictions were expressed in a union pay equity formula that limited comparisons to men's jobs outside the bargaining unit. The gender dynamics of union composition, and its history of helping to construct separate male technical and female clerical hierarchies, made it difficult for the OTEU to go beyond external points of comparison and tackle the internal hierarchy it had helped to create. On the other hand, pay equity demands allowed the union to raise long-standing grievances about the devaluation of all office work in comparison to their blue-collar co-workers in the IBEW, another important issue of gender equity that BC Hydro refused to address. In many respects, then, the union's pay equity demands brought it back to the conflict over skill and masculinity between white-collar and blue-collar men.

In the context of pay equity demands made throughout the public sector, the OTEU put pay equity on the table for the first time in negotiations in 1991. The union did not have a specific pay equity plan in mind when it tabled this demand. For the most part the membership did not understand the issue and there was no groundswell of support pushing it forward. Predictably, then, pay equity was not prioritized in 1991.[95] A pay equity formula was only developed by the bargaining committee as negotiations drew to a close. The bargaining committee 'got a formula together and that was a month before bargaining ended. Understand this, we've been preparing since December before, the formula was finally done in November, the bargaining ended in December. So nothing happened.'[96] There was no real movement on pay equity in that round of negotiations.[97] Pay equity was on the agenda again in 1993. This time the formula had been developed two years earlier, though little educational work had been done with the membership in the intervening period.[98] BC Hydro, anticipating imminent provincial legislation and instructed by its government-appointed Board of Directors to settle the issue, put forth its own pay equity plan.[99] The company proposed to establish pay equity through a more gender-neutral job evaluation plan with fewer pay groups and broader bands to bring the bottom and top in each band towards the middle.[100] From the company's perspective, appropriate comparisons to assess gender-neutral value were to be found within the office alone and might result in raising the bottom of the female clerical pay scales while lowering some of the less technical male jobs.

In contrast, the union adopted a more radical position that demanded company-wide comparisons between jobs held by white-collar women and blue-collar men that would, in the long run, increase the wages of OTEU women and men.

Your union's proposal for addressing pay equity includes:
1) Elimination of the Job Classification system.
2) Wage rates to be determined by direct negotiations.
3) Establishment of one pay rate, or end-rate, for each job with allowance for 'training rates' for some mutually-agreed higher grouped technical positions.[101]

This three-pronged strategy was devised to address the imbalance between the OTEU and the IBEW. The IBEW had never been subject to a job evaluation scheme, bargained specific wages for distinct jobs, and bargained end rates for jobs (that is, the rate everyone performing the job received, sometimes with a lower rate for apprentices). In contrast, the OTEU could only bargain increases tied to existing wage rates established within a complex job evaluation system. It was unable to negotiate the place of a job within the classification system or the wage of one type of job in relation to another. It could not, in other words, engage in direct negotiation over wage rates as did the IBEW. The only exception to this was negotiation over non-office jobs. Moreover, office workers' wages were subject to incremental increases over a five-year period before reaching the top rate. This was known as the 'steps on scale' and meant, in effect, that it took five years to reach the end rate for a job while the IBEW workers achieved it immediately.

> Our goal is to end discrimination and unfair practices of paying different amounts of money to perform the same bargaining unit work.[102]

> A lineman gets a lineman's rate; truck driver gets a truck driver's rates, and they get the end rate for the job. Office workers are so smart that we've rationalized ourselves into this malarkey about time in job and all of that. What we're really saying is, 'there's the end rate for the job, we'll let the company pay us less for the first five years.' Stupid. It's got to go.[103]

Both the inability to bargain directly over wage rates and the inability to bargain for an end rate, eliminating the 'steps on scale', were tied to the job evaluation system. The OTEU argued that job evaluation allowed management to underpay office workers.

> Job evaluation is controlled by management and doesn't fairly value jobs traditionally done by women. The reason blue collar workers' wages outstrip white collar workers' earnings is that they bargain salary rates for each job and can negotiate increases based on their work volume. . . . Bargaining pay rates for different jobs will stop the Company from manipulating the system in their favour.[104]

> I argue that job classification systems do nothing more than deflect office and technical workers' power. It's the power of the anger of their members, when the employer has to look them in the eye and say, 'You are not worth that money. Not some system says you're not worth that money, I'm telling you as the employer you're not worth that money.' It's a whole different dynamic, and the employers do that, [they say] 'It's the system.'[105]

The OTEU's strategy to achieve pay equity by abolishing job evaluation was based less on feminist critiques of gender biases built into evaluation systems[106] than it was on the belief that office workers had to begin to emulate their blue-collar counterparts if they were to win comparable wages for office workers. The desire to emulate the IBEW's bargaining style was coupled with these pay equity demands. Commenting on the different styles and effectiveness of blue-collar versus white-collar bargaining, one business representative argued:

> The way blue-collar workers negotiate, they walk in, they say, 'I want this much money.' And the employer says, pardon my language, 'F. off.' And the blue-collar worker then says, 'Yeah, well then we'll strike you.' And the employer says, 'Do it.' The blue-collar worker doesn't bluff, they do it, eh? And as a result of that approach, there's nothing sophisticated here, this is not saying, 'Why do you want this much?' and the blue-collar worker saying, 'Well because tada-tada-tada.' It's none of that. The real answer is because we want it. It's 'you got it, we want it.' We know that we're going to maximally have to hurt you, or scare you, to get the maximal out of you that you're going to give us, or that you can afford to give us.'. . . [With white-collar workers] you go to the bargaining table, and you say, 'Well, we want this much money.' And the employer says 'No.' You say, 'Well, aren't you even interested why we want it?' This is the white-collar bargaining, all right. I've done both, it's much different. You got to justify it.[107]

In coupling pay equity demands with a blue-collar style of negotiating the union, perhaps paradoxically, attempted to create a more confrontational, masculine style of bargaining and achieve pay equity at the same time. However, an equally powerful reason to link pay equity with the IBEW was the clear inequity between pay rates at the bottom of the blue-collar hierarchy and those in the OTEU:

> The current job evaluation system has 61% of members paid less than a janitor. . . . A janitor in the International Brotherhood of Electrical Workers earns $18.41 an hour which is the top of an office salary group 6.[108]

> The sweat and skill of our labour is worth at least as much as that of a janitor. . . . More than sixty percent of our Union Members, the vast majority of whom are women, make up to $7.50 an hour, or $15,000 a year, less than what management pays a janitor. . . . This is an outrageous pay inequity which must be fixed, NOW![109]

The union's pay equity proposal was to eliminate the bottom four pay groups altogether to bring the starting salary in the OTEU to a Group 5, equivalent to the bottom salary of the janitor in the IBEW.[110]

> The janitors are getting I believe $17.64 an hour now. They don't have any skill sets that are required to do their job. They do work some shift work, which is not a big deal. The company is getting into flexible hours and doing some shift work, and with three months' notice they can move somebody [in our union] onto shift work if they want to. And you get a clerical coming in, say, at a Group 4 rate or a Group 3 rate and they're making $10.00 an hour. They have to have typing skills. They have to have filing skills. They have to have some computer skills. They have to make sure that they've finished grade 12. The janitor doesn't have to have a grade 12 diploma. So the inequities are there, and that has to be addressed.[111]

> You have to have a bit of knowledge to be a janitor, you have to be able to read warning labels on dangerous products and stuff like that. You can't be a complete moron, but it doesn't really take an awful lot of training and you can do the job, you know. Our people, we grant, really need more than that. They have to be able to use software programs and stuff like that. But at least it's a starting point. We said okay, the minimum entry for this union office is going to be top of a Group 5.[112]

> How many skills do you have to bring to the janitor's jobs? Not to downgrade the janitor's job, but if that's the pay level that's considered for keeping the floors clean and keeping the place presentable, what about the clerical person who is putting out documents for the company? Aren't they at least equal?[113]

Very few members were below Group 4—only 2 per cent of women—so the proposal amounted to flattening the hierarchy by raising members in Group 4 to Group 5 (28 per cent of women and 5 per cent of men) and eliminating 'steps on scale' for everyone.[114] This new flattened hierarchy would place 55 per cent of women and 19 per cent of men in the entry-level salary group. Understandably, many women who had taken 15 or more years to work their way to the top of a Group 5 position were upset by this proposal:

> We're going to have lots of problems as far as pay equity is concerned. One, from long-term employees say, like myself, who've been there for x number of years. I've been at the top of my Group 5

rate for nine years now. Why should somebody come in off the street and make the top of a Group 5 just like I am, when it's taken me 16 years to get there?[115]

Using a system such as the one proposed to establish salary scales will result in a total end to incentive to broaden one's knowledge and experience to obtain higher-paying positions in the company. I, for one, will have a difficult time dealing with the fact that the position I now hold, and worked very hard to obtain, will receive the same wage as the first position I held in this office.[116]

The union's pay equity initiative was, of course, seen as a first step. In addition to drawing equivalencies between clerical and janitorial rates at the bottom of both pay scales, the OTEU hoped later to reassess the entire company job hierarchy:

We basically did two things. We compared the starting rate to the janitor. And then we looked at the engineering job groups and we said, okay, the engineering job hierarchy is a male-dominated hierarchy within the union, let's look at the skills that are necessary to do the jobs within that male hierarchy. Let's try and adapt them for all these other jobs. So that's basically what we did.[117]

In the process of comparing union jobs with other jobs the bargaining committee identified a few internal inequities between higher-end female clerical jobs and lower-end male technical positions within the OTEU. For the most part, however, inequities focused on comparison between technical OTEU jobs and IBEW and external trades and technical positions. These comparisons were meant to broaden pay equity to include undervalued men's jobs.

You'll get some male members that feel they're going to lose something because of [pay equity]. . . . And I've pointed out to a lot of men, it's your issue, too. It's not just a women's issue, it's a people issue. Because, the example I give them is that typing is not evaluated in the job evaluation system that's so sexist to start with. It's not evaluated. And I say 'You're doing typing, that's not evaluated in your job. Why do you feel this is a women's issue?'[118]

Well some people, I'm talking about the people at the higher end, they say, 'Listen, we believe that the problem has been resolved, okay, that we gave up money [in 1981].' And they did give up a considerable sum of money so that people in the lower salary groups could achieve the rationalization of their salary scales. 'And it's time that you deal with us, you deal with our concerns.'

And they are legitimate concerns. When they compare [their salaries] to other people doing the same job in other industries, they don't compare very favourably. . . . They could go to a private-sector employer and get a lot more money, and get the same benefits, and maybe better benefits even. . . . Pay equity is not only an issue for the people at the low end, there's people in the middle and the higher end that have a problem, [but] the majority of the problem is at the low end.[119]

On the one hand, approaching pay equity as a broad systemic problem that affected underpaid men as well as women was a useful strategy to gain support in a union with a large number of men. At the very least, all unions seeking pay equity have sought to ensure that men's wages do not drop as women's rise, an outcome often desired by employers. On the other hand, a strategy that did not fundamentally rethink the clerical/technical divisions in the office, and placed pay inequities between groups of men in the same package, tended to undercut the basic thrust of pay equity as an issue of historically undervaluing skills used in predominantly female work *on the basis of gender*. Under the OTEU's pay equity proposal the skill hierarchy in the office would remain largely intact:

We're hoping to do it in a two-tiered thing. Where at first you bring the bottom levels up and bring them into that level 5. And then you look at these people who are at a Group 5 rate [who] should either be at the Group 6 or the Group 7 rates, and move everything else up the hierarchy.[120]

The union ignored comparisons internal to its membership for important strategic reasons, but this, too, weakened pay equity arguments.

We use a janitor as our pay equity comparison as someone that's not in our union. It's safer to use it. . . . We decided to leave the meter readers [entry-level male position] out of this equation. . . . Do I agree a meter reader's overpaid? I'm not going to say that. But do I think that the secretary should be paid more than the meter reader? Yeah, I think so. But I mean the meter reader has to put up with some tough conditions. Well, no, the meter reader has it pretty easy. It's better to use the janitor and say that all those people should be paid the same.[121]

The use of janitors as the appropriate comparison for the majority of clerical workers, while strategically advantageous in the context of the company's pay practices, was problematic in other respects. First, janitors were expected to be phased out or contracted out fairly soon, eliminating ongoing wage comparisons. And second, clerical jobs in Groups 4 and 5 were admittedly considerably more skilled than janitorial work, so using this point lowered estimations of clerical skills.[122] To some degree, as one member commented, such comparisons maintained the notion that clerical work is, in fact, unskilled work.

> A comparison of a janitor's position and that of various different levels of office clerks etc. I find totally ludicrous. Not only are the physical differences apparent but the knowledge required as well as training and the various degrees of responsibility are so vast that to lump them together is demeaning to all those involved.[123]

As another member commented, these comparisons were themselves gender-biased:

> If you think that your new 'job level' alignment is going to eliminate the disparity of pay between men and women, you must be smoking something. Any nimrod can see that your proposed [new] job levels 1, 2, and 3 are jobs, by a very large margin, held by women. Job level 4 is probably about 50–50 and jobs 5 though 10 are mostly men. I suggest that all you have done is propose one 'unequal' (your reference) system, from a gender standpoint, with another, except that your proposal gives no credit or value for time spent on the job.[124]

In the end the OTEU was unsuccessful in budging the company from its position that pay equity must occur through a modified gender-neutral job evaluation system comparing only OTEU jobs. Thus it got no closer to bargaining specific wages, end rates, or parity with the IBEW. Nor did it manage to abolish the 'steps on scale', though these were reduced in number. The 1993 contract so narrowly accepted by union members set aside a maximum of 1 per cent of payroll to address pay inequities and adopt a 'pay equity job evaluation plan' based on that recently won by provincial government employees.[125]

> We won't have solved it, and it'll be particularly not solved because we'll have a continuation of some form of job classification. That in itself will mean the same thing will continue. Because it will allow the employers in positions of power within management, who will still be males, to do what? Manipulate the job classification system to keep the wages low.[126]

Having won a pay equity formula at the bargaining table, even if in a form the union leadership recognized as inadequate to address gender inequity in the office, the union would find it extremely difficult to bargain a better pay equity initiative in the future.

Without strong support from its membership the OTEU was in no position to prolong strategic strike action to achieve stronger pay equity measures. Such support was clearly lacking throughout the negotiations and, at least partly, was linked to the union's failure to undertake the necessary educational campaign.[127] In addition, the long-standing distaste for comparisons between white-collar workers and their blue-collar colleagues seemed to remain strong. But perhaps the most important factor undermining membership support for pay equity was the strong attachment to the legitimacy of the office hierarchy and its corresponding pay structure among the majority who had worked their way up the respective clerical and technical ladders over the decades.

> [We can't touch the hierarchy] like the 9 per cent difference in wage scales. 'Oh, you have to leave that, can't touch that.' You know why we have to leave that there? A lot of hard work to put that there.[128]

> There are people within the union that would say, oh yeah, you've got to keep that 9 per cent [spread between pay groups]. . . . You need that incentive to take the next higher job. I think you need to reduce the gap between the two jobs, like between these levels. I think 9 per cent is probably too far, and that will have the effect of straightening that line out. But I guess the trouble is at the top. I mean, I don't think you can do it in isolation of the income tax laws. Because as you get up you're paying more in income tax. So somehow you have to put that into the equation.[129]

> There is a logical increase in levels of responsibility, knowledge and training required as one progresses from one job to the next. One has only to read the individual job descriptions to confirm what I am saying. This is the very basis of the job re-evaluations that took years to complete, and resulted in job descriptions currently in place.[130]

It should be noted, too, that it was the women's clerical hierarchy that was to be abolished or at least severely truncated in the union's pay equity proposal. This was a continuation of the union's homogenization of clerical work. The technical hierarchy remained untouched, and was anticipated to undergo only minor adjustments even if all phases of the union's plan were ever implemented. In the end, most women had little to gain, and many perceived themselves losing relative to lesser-skilled women. Thus, in the end the union's arguments about pay equity failed to address the central issues of gender inequity *within* the union and failed to win much support even from its female members.

Little wonder, then, that the OTEU was unable to win more commitment from BC Hydro to resolve the pay inequities it had identified. The implementation of the pay equity plan was anticipated to eliminate classifications below Group 4 and provide small increases for clerical jobs in the bottom half of the office hierarchy.[131] It was unlikely to have a major effect in restructuring the gender divisions or corresponding pay differences embodied in five decades of evaluating and organizing office work at BC Hydro, let alone the historical inequities identified between the company's white-collar and blue-collar unions.

Fair to Whom, Equitable How?

The union's experience with the coexisting realities of downsizing, flexibility, and casualization, on the one hand, and increasing demands for equity, on the other, pointed to the difficulties inherent in attaining progressive redistribution of opportunities for higher jobs and incomes when conditions for all union members were declining. Had feminist politics and other equity demands not coincided with the new realities of declining opportunities, job insecurity, and flexible working conditions, chances are that challenges to racialized-masculinist traditions would have been less threatening to senior White men who already felt under attack. In the context of expanding opportunities, the entry of more women and people of colour into management and higher-level jobs within the office union might not have been perceived as access at the expense of opportunities for Euro-Canadian men. In the context of real wage gains, pay equity increases to raise women's salaries substantially closer to those enjoyed by men in the OTEU and in the IBEW might have gained broader support if those already better paid were not experiencing a relative decline in their incomes. Such was not the context of the 1980s and 1990s, however.

One reading of equity politics in the 1990s might focus on the effects of relative deprivation attributed to restructuring. Declining real wages and opportunities, particularly for those who survived the lay-offs of the 1980s and lacked the educational qualifications of more recent employees, produced blocked mobility that was acutely felt by more senior union members. Since men had previously possessed realistic expectations of considerable upward career mobility, they were likely to feel the most disadvantaged by the early 1990s and to perceive the promotion of anyone who might be a member of one of the four equity groups as unfair discrimination against themselves. Shaped by the politics of race in the United States, where affirmative action had come to be associated with 'reverse discrimination' against White men, and notwithstanding the ongoing predominance of White men throughout senior positions in the office and the management hierarchy, even the soft targets of corporate employment equity policies became suspect. In this context, and rather than attempt to redefine equity policies to address inequities faced by its members, which could undermine hard-won union rights, the union unilaterally asserted that fairness through seniority was necessary to maintain the status quo within the office.

Another reading of these events points to the pitfalls of developing strategies around workplace equity without a broader understanding of historical processes in the labour market. This leads to questions about whether a single standard of fairness can coexist with the recognition of historically based disadvantages in the office. For decades, being White and male had imparted a kind of unearned advantage[132] that was never considered when designing union strategies in the 1990s. Indeed, the idea that White men had made their way up the office hierarchy in a kind of affirmative action system for decades would likely be rejected by most union members. Were historical patterns better understood, contemporary efforts to increase equity might be seen against previous systems of inequity, rather than against a status quo perceived to operate through disembodied merit. Instead, acknowledging feminist insights about the gendered construction of skill and value in the workplace remained abstracted from the OTEU's understanding of its own history.

A third reading of these events places equity demands in the context of ongoing negotiations over masculinity at BC Hydro. Support for pay equity and other measures to eliminate discrimination against women was embedded in negotiating masculinity between white-collar and blue-collar men. When measures to promote gender equity threatened to move beyond these confines, equity conflicted with the expectations of men for upward career mobility and the union's priority of entrenching seniority rights. These contradictions were not easily resolved, so the OTEU advanced measures for a particular form of pay equity that sought parity with the IBEW while leaving the clerical/technical divisions in the office intact, and simultaneously resisted employment equity strategies that might help bridge that gap.

Not only were equity politics immersed in the negotiation of masculinity, these events were also located within the construction of 'Whiteness' as the dominant location from which union strategies were developed. Another reading of conflicts over equity, then, focuses on the notion of visibility inherent in processes of racialization. If support for gender equity was contradictory, support for other equity groups was non-existent. With so few Aboriginal or disabled men or women in the office these groups were largely invisible to union activists, posing neither an external threat to existing members nor an internal threat to the promotion prospects of senior White men. Men and women of colour, on the other hand, constituted in the eyes of White members a group whose hiring and promotion were highly visible. Corresponding with the generational/educational divisions in the membership, this group seemed favoured in the workplace. Favouritism was presumed by many White members to rest on racial/ethnic origin at least as much as on trends towards credential inflation that marked the periods before and after the major lay-offs. Unlike White women, then, who were acknowledged to have suffered some historical wrongs still reflected in clerical pay structures, women and men of colour were characterized only as the potential beneficiaries of reverse discrimination.

Finally, yet another reading of equity politics highlights the importance of systemic patterns that cannot be reduced to the motives of individuals. In general, OTEU strategies did not consciously advance the interests of White men. Responses to restructuring, downsizing, flexibility, and casualization exacerbated uneven effects on different groups of members in ways that went largely unobserved. Certainly these events cannot be explained as resulting from sexist or racist motives of individuals. Union traditions were premised on assumptions about identical impacts on neutral disembodied workers such that fairness and equity could mean one thing for all members: seniority. Most OTEU activists were not used to thinking about members as 'embodied', that is, located in diverse gender, racial/ethnic, sexual, ability relations and power structures in the broader society that might necessitate diverse approaches. Yet union traditions were in reality embodied in a particular type of worker—able-bodied, heterosexual White men—whose interests traditional union strategies continued to serve best.

The OTEU's response to the simultaneous demands of restructuring and equity illustrates historically grounded processes of racialized-gendering in the workplace and the difficulty of making these visible so as to dislodge rather than reaffirm racialized-masculine privilege.

Visibility, it seems, only occurred when gendering was seen to advantage women or when racialization was presumed to advantage people of colour; when, in other words, such processes were working *against usual expectations*. Through feminist organizing in the 1980s and 1990s and restructuring that shifted the gender balance of members, women had successfully challenged some of the gendered assumptions embedded in union traditions. Contradictory union strategies that embraced the need for greater gender equity while reaffirming masculine privilege were the result of these uneven processes of feminizing union politics. The same transformation had not really begun to occur on issues of racialization and was unlikely to occur anytime soon in the absence of a critical mass of men and women of colour in union leadership positions. By the mid-1990s, then, the legacy of five decades of union organizing, negotiation, and resistance in the office had produced a largely unrecognized and systemic racialized-masculinist union culture that, while not impervious to change, had proved extremely resilient, and was reinforced through a period of corporate restructuring.

7

Learning from the Past,
Re-visioning the Future

Engendering Labour's Past

Office workers at BC Hydro have negotiated their conditions of work for over half a century. A more conventional labour history, as in Chapter 2, might offer an assessment of the relative strengths and weaknesses of organizing drives, strikes, bargaining strategies, and accomplishments, understood in terms of the union's ability to expand its membership, negotiate strong collective agreements, and enforce these agreements in the workplace. However, most conventional labour history and industrial relations research have not engendered male subjects or expressed much interest in 'the experiences of women, as workers or as trade unionists'.[1] For most scholars, the racialized and gendered nature of the organization of work, unions, and collective bargaining remains unexamined, indeed unrecognized. As this study shows, however, the collective bargaining process is gendered: from the definition of priorities and strategies to its uneven effects on members, workers negotiated a racialized-gendered office hierarchy through the collective bargaining process. Systemic inequalities constituted both the context for and the end result of these negotiations.

Along with the terms and conditions of work, office workers negotiated definitions of masculinity and femininity, conceptions of skill and technical expertise, and the meanings of fairness, equality, and solidarity within the union. Together these interweaving strands reflected power relations among groups of workers as much as between workers and management. The organization of the union and the workplace was mediated through relations of class, gender, and racialized power and privilege inscribed in union traditions and meaning systems. Past practices became conventions enabling and limiting future possibilities, making a historical understanding critical for charting a different course for the future.

This chapter reviews these interrelated objects of negotiation that continue to reinscribe racialized-masculine privilege—masculinity/ femininity, technical know-how/skill, and equality/solidarity—and explores examples of alternative union strategies that might create a more equitable office in the future. While in the end union members must decide what is appropriate strategy in the contexts within which they find themselves, this need not be done in isolation. The racialized-gendered nature of bargaining strategies is not unique to the OEA/OTEU/OPEIU. Much can be learned from other union activists. Calls for a feminist labour agenda have grown in recent years in an effort to promote greater equity among workers and to revitalize the labour movement as a whole.[2] The future of organized labour rests on its ability to reformulate traditions that emerged from early twentieth-century struggles for the rights of White male breadwinners and to develop new strategies more suited to contemporary social and economic realities. Connecting the past with a more equitable future requires looking backward to re-emphasize past concerns with social justice issues, while looking forward to redefine more broadly what equality, democracy, and social justice might mean for working people in the twenty-first century.[3]

Masculine Privilege Revisited

Gender was central to the organization of the utility company's office. This was neither a natural product of the type of work performed nor the result of unilateral management decisions. The 'proper place' of women and men at the office was an explicit objective of collective bargaining; recast into neutral language, the gendered order then became normalized. Negotiations were mediated through historically contingent conceptions of femininity and masculinity embodied in White, heterosexual, able-bodied workers. White-collar masculinity was fiercely contested, under pressure from blue-collar working-class norms of physicality, strength, and toughness to which male office workers could not measure up and aspiring to equally unattainable middle-class professional norms associated with engineers. Considered in relation to blue-collar men at the company, white-collar men never attained the status or financial rewards they deemed appropriate. Considered in relation to women, however, office men did establish their masculinity and their superiority through preferential access to technical career ladders. In so doing, particular assumptions about masculinity and femininity were reinscribed in the occupational job hierarchy in the office.

In the postwar decades women's place in the office was negotiated largely from the perspective of male co-workers, with women playing a subordinate role on the Executive Council. By the 1970s this had changed and new visions of women's roles and rights emerged to challenge conventional practices. Feminist politics, especially through the Women's Committee, destabilized the gendered order at the office. Women began to play a more significant leadership role within the OTEU as elected representatives and paid union staff. By the end of the 1980s gender equity had been achieved on the governing Executive Board and a number of so-called 'women's issues' had been added to the union's bargaining agenda. These changes did not occur without resistance, and gender politics remained divisive. Women activists often felt marginalized in meetings dominated by men with more experience, superior numbers, and the ability to retain control of the agenda. Not unlike other unions, and even in the context of women forming a critical mass of members and elected officers, the prevalence of a masculine union culture remained a barrier for women's participation on equal grounds.[4] The informal and most often unstated agenda of and for the disembodied (i.e., male) worker helped to shape union meetings and collective bargaining, defining what made it to the bargaining table, what would be prioritized, and what would be dropped along the way. This was critical for understanding the secondary place of women's issues in spite of policy statements to the contrary.[5] Perhaps not surprisingly, then, although gains were made on some women's issues, little was accomplished by way of reducing gender divisions at the office.

The most obvious manifestation of gendering processes at the office is the occupational hierarchy at the utility company. Yet for all this, the way in which the structure of jobs remains an object of union negotiation—and thus involves workers' active participation—is still largely unrecognized, even by feminist activists. The occupational structure at the company constitutes a racialized-gendered hierarchy of work. Managerial positions and professional engineers are still overwhelmingly White and male, as are blue-collar workers. Within the office union women predominate, but men occupy the top half of office jobs (73 per cent) and non-office jobs (82 per cent) that serve as entry-level positions for technical career ladders. Though today office workers are ethnically and racially diverse, White women and men still dominate the top positions in the respective clerical and technical hierarchies.

How did this occupational hierarchy come about? Union strategies privileging White male breadwinners in the postwar years helped to develop a sharp gender division of labour and the creation of a technical job hierarchy reserved for White men. In the 1940s and 1950s men and women were understood to have different rights. Men's rights were enhanced by the prescribed familial roles of family head and primary breadwinner. Women's rights were circumscribed by marriage and motherhood, by assumptions about lesser monetary needs in comparison to men, and by limited opportunities for promotions. In the racialized climate of postwar Canada, White men enjoyed greater claims than other men to higher-paying jobs and career mobility. Such notions dissipated in the decades after the war, but by then material privilege was firmly inscribed in seniority rights and in the separation of clerical and technical work. Elements of masculine culture were redefined as technical experience required for entry into positions providing on-the-job training and career mobility. Non-office jobs, such as meter reading and laying out instruments and tools at construction sites, became redefined as technical expertise that women did not have and could not gain. Working outside reading meters became prior experience in the field. Delivering material to construction sites became required familiarity with construction terminology and processes. Presumed familiarity with automotive repairs became essential skills for jobs outside the main urban centres. And general clerical assistance for engineers imbued men with the technical expertise to be promoted. Over time, men's jobs proliferated into hundreds of different, specialized, skilled technical office positions; women's jobs were increasingly homogenized into a few dozen less skilled clerical job descriptions. The trend towards technical educational credentials reinforced this gendered process while providing new rationales for gender neutrality. At the same time, external technical credentials provided some men, including some men of colour, an alternative route up the office ladder.

The construction of gendered notions of technical skill was all part of 'doing gender' on the job embodied in successive union negotiations. It was expressed in disproportionate attention to wages in skilled technical positions and in non-office jobs that were bargaining separately, in the importance of wage comparisons between white-collar and blue-collar men employed at the company, and in the monitoring of promotion opportunities only within gendered job ladders. The gendered occupational hierarchy that workers negotiated in the postwar decades became a normalized part of the office, an organizational foundation for further negotiation rather than an object of fundamental renegotiation.

These distinctions between clerical and technical job hierarchies were further entrenched in the job evaluation system developed in partnership by the union and management. The absence of women from the job evaluation committee, and the timing of this initiative prior to pay equity demands challenging gender-neutral assumptions of skill measurement, further entrenched clerical/technical divisions. The job evaluation system jointly designed by labour and management in the late 1970s continued to underlie job evaluation at BC Hydro in the 1990s. In a masculine engineering culture that valorized certain forms of technical skills, clerical skills embodied in women's office work remained undervalued at least partly *because women perform the work*.[6] Indeed, the ghettoization of women's work and its definition as low-skilled were inseparable. In a process that has also been observed elsewhere,[7] job evaluation was an important method of deflecting demands for higher women's wages with pay rates justified on the basis of a technical job evaluation process.[8]

The gendered wage gap was part and parcel of the gendered occupational structure of BC Hydro. These two dimensions cannot easily be separated because one's pay was premised on one's location within the job hierarchy. To some extent the correlation of wages and job grouping is transparent: a Group 5 job is judged to require less responsibility, skill, formal education, and/or effort than a Group 10 position and the incumbent thereby earns less money. In fact, the union negotiates salaries. The gap between one job group and the next may be small or large; the distribution of wage differentials is not a product of job evaluation *per se*. When the job evaluation system was implemented in 1981 the OTEU negotiated a 9 per cent wage gap between each job group. Although the wage differential between groups could certainly be narrowed, the OTEU accepted this 'traditional' wage gap as an appropriate measure of the value of skill differentials. Narrowing this gap was not raised at the bargaining table. Wage increases have been fairly modest since the early 1980s,[9] but even so, bargaining percentage increases reinforced the wage gap between higher- and lower-paid workers and contradicted union demands for pay equity.[10]

The pay equity strategy adopted by the union in the early 1990s also had contradictory implications for narrowing the gendered wage gap. As we have seen, comparing clerical jobs with janitors in the IBEW had some advantages, illuminating the widening gap between blue-collar and white-collar workers at the company, but it simultaneously reinforced the notion that women's clerical positions were not really very skilled. In fact, the homogenization of women's jobs was extended by lumping all jobs in Groups 2 through 5 into a single pay classification while maintaining the male technical hierarchy, even promising to negotiate it upward at a later date, and leaving men's non-office jobs out of the equation altogether. Though perhaps a useful strategy for gaining membership support, this weakened arguments for pay equity made on the grounds of gender discrimination. Instead, pay equity initiatives reflected the union's focus on parity between blue-collar and white-collar men at BC Hydro at least as much as the desire to raise the low level of women's pay. As such, feminist critiques of the construction of skill were very selectively applied and promised to leave in place the gendered order in the office.

One of the most important bargaining priorities the OTEU pursued was strengthening seniority rights. This, too, entrenched a racialized-gendered hierarchy in the office. With seniority advanced by the union as the unilateral basis for promotions, lay-offs, and bumping and recall rights during restructuring, long-term employees were favoured over more recent employees regardless of substantive issues of equity within the company.[11] Women with a history of work interruptions linked to family responsibilities and limited recent access to men's jobs, workers of colour only hired within the last decade or so, and younger employees with higher educational qualifications than their older co-workers were all disadvantaged by the implementation of straight seniority. Yet the tradition of seniority as an absolute good, indeed, as a barometer of fairness, as the union argued in its struggles over employment equity, entrenched patterns of job segregation. This trend was deepened by preference for regular workers over contingent or part-time, temporary, and casual workers, the vast majority of whom were women and included many workers of colour. At the same time, the union recognized that failure to integrate contingent workers into union rights and benefits threatened to undermine the overall viability and strength of the union by creating a two-tier membership.[12]

In numerous ways bargaining practices were embedded in union traditions that reproduced a racialized-gendered occupational hierarchy in the office, with sharp distinctions between clerical and technical jobs and notions of skill, upholding gendered, racialized, generational, and full-time regular access to career ladders, promotions, and on-the-job training. The result, of course, was large wage differentials between women and men. And, *however unintentional*, it privileged senior White men in the office, even as workers sought simultaneously to uphold union principles of fairness and equality.

The contradiction between the union's principles of fairness and equality and the inequitable result of many traditional bargaining strategies underscores the systemic nature of the racialized-gendered organization of work and collective bargaining. Embedded in traditional union notions of fairness and equality is an individual worker who arrives at work unencumbered by other responsibilities to family or community and whose competence is judged on individual performance alone. As critics have pointed out, this notion of formal equality is located in liberal theory, envisioning a society peopled by disembodied individuals; in reality, this 'equality' is embodied in the dominant social position of White, heterosexual, able-bodied men.[13] Although unions adopt a more radical notion of equality rooted in collective social justice when considering demands for the rights of workers as a whole—so workers have the right to organize collectively in trade unions and negotiate on a more equal footing with more powerful employers—most unions adopt liberal individualist notions of equality when considering equity among their own members.

The OTEU's commitment to equality was grounded in this formal notion of liberal individualism. The union fought on behalf of individual members who might be unjustly denied a promotion, improperly evaluated in job evaluation, paid less for equally evaluated work, or unfairly reprimanded or fired. Bargaining strategies were developed with this liberal concept of equality in mind. Thus, seniority could be conceived as a general good because everyone acquires seniority in exactly the same way, by putting their time in on the job. Pay differentials and job hierarchies could be supported because these reflect differences in skills that individuals worked hard to develop. Fairness could be assured by promotion based on seniority from among candidates with the minimum qualifications to perform the job. So long as one holds to this formal notion of equality, then, fairness is rooted in treating everyone exactly the same way with the expectation that equitable outcomes will surely follow.

In a union context this attachment to liberal notions of equality and fairness is strengthened by traditions of solidarity that demand divisions among workers be paved over to strengthen one's position at the bargaining table. Traditions of solidarity are based on assumptions of homogeneity. Workers who have different life experiences from the majority, or interests in conflict with those expressed by dominant groups within the union, can find it difficult to raise issues reflecting substantive inequities they might face. In the OTEU, as elsewhere in the labour movement, the desire for solidarity often led to charges that feminist activists were divisive or putting special interests before collective interests. Emphasis on solidarity, when combined with a liberal conception of equality, can provide the appearance of fairness while producing quite different results. As Cynthia Cockburn observed in the British context, union responses to equity issues also involve resistance to changing the status quo:

> The union's ambivalence to sex and 'race' equality is in part the result of the individualist approach to equality of opportunity pre- ferred by employers, in contrast to the collectivist traditions of the labour movement. Often, however, the ambivalence of the unions has to be read as a negative male response to women's activism.[14]

Workers do not arrive at the company gates, or anywhere else, as detached individuals with equal opportunities and constraints shaping their lives. Substantive inequalities, therefore, are not remedied by processes of formal equality that treat everyone in exactly the same manner. On the contrary, identical treatment often reproduces sys- temic inequities and dominant power relations. The development of alternative union strategies can be enhanced by considering how other union activists have begun to reconsider definitions of equality, soli- darity, and union democracy in more inclusive ways. As Anne Phillips has noted, 'What distinguishes a radical perspective on democracy is not its expectation of future homogeneity and consensus, but its com- mitment to a politics of solidarity, challenge and change.'[15]

Feminizing Union Culture

Some activists and scholars have begun to ask how feminizing union culture might lead to the redefinition of union practices and more equitable workplaces. In purely demographic terms the labour force has already been feminized, with women constituting 45 per cent of the Canadian labour force and 41 per cent of union members.[16] More- over, economic restructuring is producing more non-standard forms of employment historically associated with women, such as part-time, temporary, contract, minimum wage, and non-unionized work, a phe- nomenon described in terms of the feminization of labour.[17] With the growth of a contingent workforce among men and women and the decline of work in sectors historically central to the labour movement, with downsizing in the industrial, resource, and public sectors, it is clear that the labour movement must redirect its organizing efforts.

> If unions cannot organize in the private service sector, in small workplaces and among part-time workers, women and different ethnic groups, the decline in union membership will continue. . . .

There needs to be what has been called 'a fourth wave' of union-ization, equivalent to the industrial organizing of the 1930s, or the public sector unionization of the 1960s, but this time in the private service sector.[18]

A new wave of organizing likely depends on redefining the labour movement to make it more attractive to and representative of women, racialized minorities, and those in non-standard forms of employ-ment. The growth of feminist activism is an important dimension of this reorientation. In fact, it has been argued that 'the future of trade unions depends to a great extent on the flowering of feminism within its ranks.'[19] As Linda Briskin and Patricia McDermott suggest, a feminist vision means more than attracting new members who were traditionally excluded or marginalized in unions; feminism 'offers a point of reference for a re-visioning of the labour movement'.[20]

Re-visioning unions might begin with strategies to feminize union culture, not just in terms of numbers, but perhaps more importantly in terms of day-to-day practices in the workplace and at the bargain-ing table. This study has identified ways in which masculine domi-nance is embedded in the traditions, strategies, priorities, and outcomes of union organization and collective bargaining. Union culture in the office, like the corporate culture within which it oper-ates, remains racialized and masculinist in spite of the increasing diversity of its membership and formal commitments to equity. These contradictions suggest that feminizing the culture of unions will be a long-term project.

Letting women in is the first step in changing union culture, and one that has largely been accomplished in the OPEIU. For some time now women, who have always constituted a critical mass of member-ship, enjoy approximately equal representation as elected officials and union staff. However, it is less true that members of colour have been let in. The first person of colour to sit on the Executive Board was elected as secretary-treasurer in 1996.[21] Moreover, while women play a significant role in the union, a combination of masculine union cul-ture and unequal responsibilities in most households makes it more difficult for women to participate on equal terms. 'The big problem for women is the priority on their time. Women do not own their time.' [22]

> It's hard to get women to come to any of the meetings, and then they go home and have children they have to tend to. They have families, they can't get to meetings. And we don't, for instance, provide things like [on-site] day care so that they can come. . . . But you can put in for child-care expenses.[23]

This is not just a problem for activists—it affects union staff positions as well. Union work has been characterized as 'greedy work' that is all-consuming—demanding long hours (50–60 hours a week), weekend and evening work, and travel that makes it difficult to balance family responsibilities with work.[24] For both staff positions and activists, trade union activity is 'organized around a model of a male worker whose identity is largely located in paid work'.[25] These conditions of overwork are not healthy for men or women and contribute to a 'high incidence of stress-related illness, alcoholism and premature death'.[26] Changing this culture of 'greedy work' and recognizing and accommodating members' lives outside the office—through shorter hours, meetings during the working day, and on-site child care, for example—are in the interests of everyone in the labour movement.

Heterosexual male bonding and positioning, including aggressive and intimidating political styles, considerable alcohol consumption, and sexual banter and propositions, are often part of union activities in ways that are uncomfortable for many women.[27] The dominance of particular forms of masculinity in these contexts can be equally discomforting and exclusionary for gays and lesbians and members of cultural minorities. Sexual, racial, and homophobic harassment has become a workplace issue, but little attempt has been made to deal with it in the union movement itself.[28] These issues did not receive a high profile in the OPEIU. Moreover, contradictions persist between union policies and daily practices. The union bargained language on sexual harassment, for example, but pin-ups continued to appear in some technical/engineering sections of the utility company and crude jokes circulated about women running for office.[29] Changing the culture of the union requires dealing more directly and consistently with these issues of climate and harassment between members.

There is some indication that women have a different way of working within unions that might in itself have a beneficial effect on union organizing. Some studies have argued that women staff tend to have different priorities from men, focusing more on mentoring women, prioritizing equity issues, and promoting family-friendly initiatives.[30] Not only are women representatives more likely to support women's issues, many have a different style that is less hierarchical and authoritarian and geared more towards empowering members. Jane Stinson and Penni Richmond, for example, argue that this difference is related to women's own life experience:

A feminist alternative approach for union activity involves democratizing and humanizing unions as well as shifting the emphasis from business unionism to social unionism. Democratization is pushed forward by the greater importance many women attach to the process of how things are done rather than to the (patriarchal) emphasis on results. Women's experience of being excluded or undervalued may explain the greater importance we attach to reaching out to involve others, to being inclusive, and to gaining and sharing knowledge and developing women's skills and confidence.[31]

Clearly, this is not true for all women, any more than a single construct of masculinity encompasses all men; but many women, especially feminist activists, value a more socially integrated form of organizing. In this sense, feminist union organizing can be considered a resource to revitalize and strengthen both women's place in unions and the whole labour movement.

Aspects of this culture [of femininity] which are specially relevant to trade unionism are: the importance placed on affective rather than instrumental relationships; the emphasis on accommodation rather than confrontation; the priority accorded to social over purely economic factors; the connection made between home, employment and community; the acceptance of diversity and the belief that everyone's voice should be heard; a dislike of formality, hierarchy and top-down decision making and a belief in informality and the importance of grass-roots' opinion.[32]

As in most unions, this process of feminizing union culture and politics has been uneven and slow in the OPEIU. Women are present and vocal but feminist activists and the Women's Committee kept a lower profile in the 1990s than a decade before. In fact, it is a matter of some controversy that in the 1990s the Women's Committee was no longer composed solely of women.[33] Although in the long run feminizing union culture might be a boon to union organizing, especially since women dominate in the service sector, which is presently largely unorganized, in the short run it will likely involve power struggles over the meaning of union democracy.

Two notions underlie union traditions of democracy: collective solidarity of workers and fairness and equality among workers. As Rosemary Warskett has argued, notions of solidarity developed in conjunction with a defensive and aggressive business unionism that excluded women, immigrants, Aboriginal peoples, and those in marginal types of work.[34] Business unionism reflected the highly legalistic and bureaucratic labour legislation that shaped postwar unionization in Canada.[35] Traditions of solidarity, then, have not coincided with promoting equality among all workers. Broader conceptions of solidarity might recognize diversity and hierarchical power relations among workers and help to put in place new mechanisms to represent that diversity while challenging internal inequities. Warskett indicates that 'if unity is to be reconciled with equality, the differences within the labour movement and the working class need to be recognized and taken into account, rather than subordinated in the name of greater solidarity.'[36]

New ways of understanding solidarity involve two simultaneous movements: (1) addressing forms of inequality among union members, including sexism, racism, and homophobia; (2) broadening the vision of union issues from the workplace to the community, and thus from business unionism to social unionism. A return to social unionism requires reconnecting the labour movement to other progressive social movements and reconfiguring union issues to politicize the links between the workplace and home and the broader community.[37] The growth of union feminism is one indication that this process is already under way.

The shift to social unionism, and thus broader concerns with notions of social justice, also involves redefining concepts of equality. The distinction between concepts of formal equality and substantive equality is crucial here. As discussed above, formal equality refers to the dominant conceptualization in Western liberal thought focusing on equal treatment of disembodied individuals.[38] In the workplace, for example, formal equality is typically manifest in principles of equal opportunity.

> To give an (only slightly exaggerated) example. Let us say that a rule of equality of opportunity would entitle a qualified single-parent female lawyer with young children to be hired to work in a law firm from seven in the morning until nine at night, six days a week, with possible access to a partnership after ten years of full-time consecutive service, on the same basis as the men.[39]

Such approaches do not acknowledge social differences and power relations that often prevent people from competing on equal grounds in the first place. In contrast, notions of substantive equality focus more on the outcomes desired. This suggests, as in the example cited above, that equal opportunity is meaningless in a context where the rules of the game operate so as to favour some social groups over others—in this example, favouring those (mostly men) who do not have heavy domestic obligations that prevent such long hours at work.

Equality among union members can be facilitated by shifting beyond formal to substantive issues of equality of outcomes. In this way, demands for measures to accommodate differences related to historically grounded inequalities—such as special measures to promote women and/or workers of colour to jobs from which they have traditionally been excluded—can be understood as strengthening rather than threatening principles of equality and fairness. Where women and/or workers of colour form a minority, concern with substantive equality has also led to reconsidering basic democratic structures and processes. A simple majority vote in elections reinforces control by members of dominant groups, while a racialized-masculine union culture shapes opportunities to run for union office. Thus, alternative democratic structures are gaining favour in some sectors of the labour movement in Europe and North America. These include establishing a designated number of reserved seats on committees and executives for underrepresented groups, or more radical forms of proportionality, where special provisions are made for representation on decision-making bodies in accordance with an underrepresented group's proportion in the membership.[40] These new forms of representative democracy have also included strengthening forms of separate organizing, such as women's committees and human rights committees, by integrating these structures into decision-making processes.[41] To be effective such committees must strike a balance between autonomy and integration into union governance, thus avoiding marginalization on the one hand and co-optation on the other hand.[42]

In the context of the OPEIU, women asserted their numbers to attain significant representation by the 1990s. The same cannot be said for members of colour, who remain almost invisible in leadership positions. Reserved seats and proportionality are mechanisms that might strengthen the representation of members of colour. Similarly, forming and adequately resourcing an anti-racist caucus and/or a human rights committee and integrating it, alongside a more autonomous Women's Committee, into decision-making structures might produce a broader democratic structure among office workers. As some activists have pointed out, separate organizing remains as critical for workers of colour as it has been for raising women's issues at the bargaining table.[43] None of these modifications to democratic structures has been considered to date. The importance of questions of democratic representation does not rest on numbers alone; representation relates directly to issues of substantive equality. Creating institutional structures that better reflect the diversity of union membership will facilitate the articulation of a fuller range of issues, interests, and needs among workers. Such divergent, even conflicting, interests need not be seen as a threat to union solidarity. On the contrary, inclusive democratic processes facilitate more effective participation in establishing union goals, strategies, and priorities. In this sense, then, solidarity can actually be strengthened through diversity.[44]

Reformulating democratic structures and conceptions of equality and solidarity is both controversial and important if unions hope to ameliorate rather than perpetuate structural inequities in the workplace. At the same time, some long-cherished traditions of collective bargaining might be reassessed, including traditional approaches to seniority, wage structures, and access to work. The contemporary configuration of these traditional approaches evolved in a period when the rights of full-time, White, male breadwinners formed the uncontested core of union demands. Not surprisingly, the traditions that emerged continue to serve these workers best.

Seniority rights form one of the central tenets of collective bargaining in North America. Indeed, seniority has been called the 'soul' of collective bargaining agreements.[45] In the OPEIU seniority has figured centrally in language related to lay-offs, recall, bumping, promotions, salary scales, and entitlement to benefits. Seniority rights have been identified as a quintessential test of fairness, affecting all members in exactly the same manner. In the struggle over employment equity, as we saw, seniority was counterposed to preferential hiring or promotions on any other grounds regardless of recognized historical inequities faced by women, visible minorities, Aboriginal people, and those with disabilities. The OPEIU is not alone in its defence of seniority as a central union principle. Moreover, there are good reasons why seniority has become a beacon of workers' rights in attempts to lessen arbitrary or unfair management practices: 'Instead of the employer determining who should be promoted, transferred or laid off, it is decided according to the number of years of employment that workers have with that employer.'[46] Most Canadian unions have seniority clauses for lay-offs and job postings, and a near majority have seniority clauses for promotions and transfers.[47] In terms of equity, however, the way seniority is presently embodied in many collective agreements is 'harmful to women [and racialized minorities] and reinforce[s] their inferior position in the labour force'.[48]

Although seniority rights are central to organized labour in North America, this is not so in most other union jurisdictions. To understand why seniority became so important to North American workers it should be recalled that the modern labour relations system in the United States and Canada developed directly out of unrest during the Great Depression and associated industrial union organizing during the 1930s and 1940s. Job security, especially for older men, was central to industrial labour militancy and seniority became a key union demand. The Wagner Act in the United States (1935) and PC 1003 in Canada (1944) institutionalized this key worker demand in an effort to achieve industrial peace.[49] Thereafter, seniority rights were bargained in a variety of contexts by unions in every industrial sector. Within the North American labour movement, then, seniority came to be defined as an unqualified principle to ensure fairness for working people.

As American trade unionist Fred Gaboury has argued, however, workers should support the principle of seniority while recognizing that current systems of seniority can be discriminatory:

> The principle of seniority—that all workers be treated on an equal basis subject to collectively agreed upon standards and that workers have a vested interest in their jobs in direct proportion to their years in a given shop or industry—is a basic building block of class-struggle trade unionism. . . . But workers and their friends in the community—and this is especially true of white male trade unionists—must be clear on another question: *There are discriminatory seniority systems. . . .* No seniority clause is the result of divine inspiration; any can be changed. It is not un-American or anti-union to advocate modification of seniority systems so that special steps may be taken to protect the hard-won gains toward fair employment practices.[50]

So long as equality is understood in formal terms, seniority provisions can be considered fair when everyone acquires seniority, and thus preferential access to jobs, in the same way. When substantive equality is invoked, however, we must consider the effect of seniority on different groups of workers. Women seldom benefit as much as men from seniority rights. Unequal domestic responsibilities result in less continuous employment patterns and more part-time and temporary work, so women accumulate less seniority. Seniority units typically reproduce gender-segregated work patterns, with lower-level jobs contained in narrower seniority units; therefore, women have a more limited range of jobs upon which to exercise seniority rights, further entrenching segregation. Moreover, seniority rules revolve around LIFO (last in, first out) principles, penalizing women and workers of colour who have only recently gained access to more sought-after jobs. Thus, even when policies of employment equity or affirmation action have been implemented to redress discrimination in hiring and promotion, these measures are typically undone during the first round of lay-offs. Particularly during periods of economic restructuring, seniority systems operate to protect those already most privileged in the workplace and inhibit the movement towards greater equality among workers.[51] As we have seen, seniority had such unequal effects during restructuring at BC Hydro. Moreover, with seniority rights presently embedded in language on lay-offs, bumping, recall, and promotions it is difficult to foresee much change in the racialized-gendered organization of the office in the near future.

As a result some critics have called for modified systems of seniority to maintain protection of workers' hard-won rights to job security while accommodating the need for special provisions to promote greater equity in the workplace. Some unions are struggling to find ways to negotiate seniority provisions that accommodate progressive forms of employment equity rather than cast seniority rights and employment equity as incompatible. Such provisions in collective agreements in Canada are at present extremely rare. As Julie White points out, employers most often resist affirmative action initiatives that threaten to delimit managerial prerogatives over hiring and promotions. At the same time, few unions have seriously bargained for such measures.[52]

Several potential models to modify seniority have been suggested, depending on the configuration of the workplace, but those that might be appropriate include: (1) general suspension of seniority rules for certain underrepresented groups (so that the few Aboriginal workers or women in technical positions are not the first to be laid off or the last to be considered for promotions); (2) mechanisms to assign constructive seniority (such as assigning groups previously excluded from certain work the average seniority in that unit); (3) special adjustments to seniority (for example, continuing to accrue seniority during particular absences, such as maternity leave or family leave); and (4) prospective adjustments to seniority (so that members of underrepresented groups might have preferential seniority over other employees hired after a designated date).[53] The modification of seniority rights on these or other models involves redefining seniority from an absolute principle of fairness in which all special accommodations are identified as unfair and indeed discriminatory (hence, the popularity of the notion of employment equity as reverse discrimination) and developing a conception of seniority rights compatible with the goals of substantive equality. In this way the general principle of seniority can be maintained while acceptable employment equity provisions are negotiated also to address the racialized-gendered order in the office.

Proactive strategies involving adjustments to seniority provisions and usual career ladders are perhaps most urgently required to bridge the clerical/technical divisions in the office. On this issue other unions have negotiated provisions that might provide a model for the OPEIU. An agreement between the Communications and Electrical Workers and Bell Canada, for example, provided six months' technical training with full pay for women in clerical and operator positions. This in-house training was accepted in lieu of a community college diploma in electronics and seniority in jobs in the technical hierarchy for positions as technicians, suspending the regular provisions for up to 200 women each year.[54] A similar strategy might provide in-house training and bridges for a designated number of women employees at BC Hydro each year, while for the rest, usual seniority and qualifications apply. In this way some progress might be made towards desegregating the occupational structure while also protecting promotion opportunities for men in the technical hierarchy.

In addition to modifying seniority systems to address issues of substantive equality among members, other strategies have been proposed to reconfigure the concept of solidarity around work and wages. As economic trends increase the gap between 'good jobs' and 'bad jobs'[55] unions are struggling to address issues of access to better jobs. This has resulted in a variety of proposals under the rubric of solidarity of work. Unionization of the contingent workforce (i.e., part-time, short-term contract work) to provide them the same protections as full-time regular union members might be a first step.[56] New approaches to skill certification and training, portable beyond a specific workplace, can be combined with employment equity programs to provide equal access to professional and technical jobs.[57]

> The demand for work solidarity is the demand for the requalification of work. . . . [It] specifically attacks the neo-conservative agenda of encouraging the development of a lower-wage economy polarized into many low-skilled, poorly paid jobs and fewer highly skilled, well paid jobs.[58]

The labour movement in Sweden has pioneered work solidarity through negotiating the organization of work as a skilling rather than a de-skilling process by broadening and deepening the range of tasks and the level of responsibility on the job.[59]

Besides solidaristic practices around 'good jobs', unions might also address issues related to the distribution of work. In a period of high structural unemployment that is unlikely to decrease in the near future, access to work remains critical. Louise Dulude has suggested a number of alternatives to lay-offs that some unions have brought to the bargaining table. These include reducing working hours, eliminating overtime, negotiating options for shared or part-time positions without loss of benefits, rotating full-time positions, short-term temporary shut-downs, and voluntary lay-offs or early retirement buy-outs through inverse seniority.[60] These are all strategies that unions might negotiate to share work more equitably in a changing economy.

For work solidarity to bridge the gender gap effectively, attention should also be paid to issues of sharing the work in the household, which continues to affect women's labour force patterns. Negotiating better provisions for family leave, elder care, on-site day care, a shorter workweek, job-sharing, and paid sabbaticals for retraining would all enhance gender equity.[61] As well, the culture of 'greedy work' within unions and their tendency to reproduce the gendered division of labour might also be addressed as part of sharing the work:

> If union women continue to have unequal responsibility for domestic work in the home and administrative work in their union locals, this in turn affects their potential to take on greater responsibilities in the union and the paid labour force. Work solidarity must, therefore, also be a policy in the home and in the unions.[62]

Shorter hours in the workplace, for members as well as union staff, would better accommodate domestic responsibilities while making it more difficult for men to use excessive workplace commitments as an excuse for failing to perform their fair share of unpaid work in the home.[63]

Wage solidarity policies are also critical for ensuring equality among workers. As the gap between 'good jobs' and 'bad jobs' increases, so, too, does the income gap; as we have seen, the income gap coincides with the racialized-gendered hierarchy of work in the office. While modified seniority systems, employment equity policies, and work solidarity promise to restructure fundamentally the organization of work, wage solidarity promises to promote economic equality. Pioneered in Sweden, wage solidarity policies are designed to reduce the wage gap between the top and the bottom of workers' incomes. This involves bargaining higher wage increases in real dollars for jobs at the bottom of the wage hierarchy while flattening the hierarchy of pay scales.[64] Specific bargaining strategies might include across-the-board wage increases (equal dollar value raise in pay), bottom-end loading (higher dollar increases for lower-paid workers), raising base rates, pay increases for targeted groups (such as lower-paid part-time or casual workers), reducing the number of pay increments (or steps to the top rate), and reducing the number of job classifications (or flattening the hierarchy).[65] Indeed, there is growing consensus among feminist union activists that wage solidarity is a preferable strategy to pay equity in the struggle to raise women's wages.[66] Unlike pay equity, a technical process that entrenches job evaluation systems and leaves the hierarchy of work untouched, wage solidarity focuses on substantive issues of equality, that is, outcomes in terms of wages. The OPEIU has not been very successful in winning pay equity measures that will significantly reduce the gendered wage gap, and has already begun to bargain a number of wage solidarity measures, including attempts to eliminate job evaluation, flatten the job hierarchy, reduce the number of pay increments, and raise base rates. Strong membership support for the technical skill hierarchy and the traditional wage gap this entails, as well as a history of percentage wage demands, will make a more concerted approach to wage solidarity challenging, but it promises a good option for reducing the wage gap in the office.

Along with wage solidarity, Margaret Hallock has suggested the need to redefine union ideology to attain popular support for greater social equality.[67] In the early part of this century the ideology of the family wage was crucial for working-class gains for White male breadwinners. Redefining these demands along the lines of a living wage for all workers might aid in the political struggle to attain higher minimum wages, a stronger social safety net, and general support for union organizing. Long-established patterns of the feminization of poverty might serve as a cornerstone for such campaigns, while more closely linking unions with the broader feminist and anti-poverty movements.[68]

As this study illustrates, White masculine privilege is not just a remnant of the distant past, it is part of ongoing organizational structures in the workplace and in collective bargaining that requires more creative strategies to challenge and change. Part of this challenge involves redefining traditional union notions of solidarity, equality, and democracy and generally feminizing union culture and practices. Such rethinking is already under way with attempts to create mechanisms that promote participation among diverse groups of workers and practices that accommodate issues and needs that such groups bring with them to the workplace. In the long run this shift also involves a more politically active brand of social unionism that has the potential to place the labour movement, in alliance with other progressive movements, once again at the centre of struggles for social justice and equality in North America.

Appendix:

Reflections on Methodology

This study developed out of my interest in the history of the labour movement and the possibility of renewed social activism as neoliberalism rolls back gains achieved in the postwar period. My interest in the history of unions was combined with feminist and post-colonial theorizing, in particular questions about how class, gender, and race intersect in our daily lives. From this perspective I wanted to explore how unions might negotiate class, gender, and race as part of negotiating conditions of work; how this might affect diverse groups of workers in different ways; and ultimately, how traditions forged in the past might affect the prospects for social change in the present. More than anything, my attempt to identify the ongoing implications of past practices inscribed in systemic patterns of inequality marks this historical research as sociological.[1]

I decided to explore the intersections of class, gender and race through union negotiations in a single case study. The union I identified for the study, the Office and Professional Employees' International Union (then the Office and Technical Employees' Union) Local 378, proved ideal in several respects. The OPEIU had housed its archives with the University of British Columbia Library Special Collections. This material proved extensive, spanning its origins at BC Electric in 1921 as an association of office employees, through to union certification in 1944 and expansion to a number of other companies during the 1960s and 1970s. These archives contain a virtually complete set of union records from 1944 to 1978, from Executive Board and Council minutes to bargaining files, correspondence, grievance files, committee reports, election results, and membership meetings. The wealth of historical material available for this study was unusually rich. To make it more manageable I decided to focus only on the material related to BC Hydro rather than try to explore negotiations at the other companies more recently organized within the local.

A case study of the OPEIU was ideal in other respects as well. It was one of a very few white-collar office unions in existence in Canada at the end of World War II. Given the changing nature of gender relations in Canada in the postwar decades and the growth of women's labour force participation, the study of union practices from the 1940s through the 1970s provided a long enough time span to examine how early postwar negotiations shaped later union strategies. In addition, OPEIU Local 378 had always had a large female membership. Equally important for the purposes of research on gendered class relations, it also had a large male membership. One of the first things I discovered in perusing the OPEIU archives was the important place job evaluation held in union negotiations: beginning in the first round of bargaining in 1946 and culminating in a new job evaluation system in 1981. Negotiating gender through bargaining over job evaluation quickly became a central theme in the research.

The OPEIU was, in some ways, less than ideal for a study of racialized gender relations. Its membership was essentially homogeneous until the 1970s, reflecting both the nature of racialized labour markets in postwar Canada, when office work was reserved for White men and women, and the increasing diversity of the Canadian population after immigration legislation was liberalized in the late 1960s. On the other hand, the social construction of 'Whiteness' is as central to racialization as is the construction of those deemed non-White or 'others'. Thus I tried to be attentive to ways in which constructing Whiteness was also part of collective bargaining in the postwar decades. This theme became more evident again in the 1990s.

Once I knew something about the union's history I contacted Local 378 to get permission to interview union activists who might have been involved in collective bargaining and negotiating job evaluation. The OPEIU was much more responsive than I could possibly have hoped. With union support I applied for an SSHRC research grant, and in the summer of 1991, with the help of research assistants, began the long task of sifting through archival documents. The OPEIU granted permission to research files in the union's office related to the job evaluation plan they helped to design, and this soon led to permission to research any contemporary union records I might consider useful. The time span for the research expanded from 1978 to 1994 and analysis of contemporary union files proved as extensive as that for the archival records. Needless to say, this added years to the research and pursuit of a second SSHRC research grant. With a team of researchers I consulted Executive Board and Council minutes, bargaining files, grievance files, committee minutes (including the Women's Committee), election material, union reports, newsletters, and job stewards' files housed in the OPEIU office. With the extended time-line I was able to tackle more directly some of the contemporary issues confronting unions. Feminist politics, corporate restructuring, and employment equity brought new issues to the forefront of the local. During the 1980s and 1990s, I soon discovered, intersections of class, gender, and race became more complex and more visible than at any time since the immediate postwar years.

In addition to pouring over union files I conducted 32 interviews in 1992 and 1993. These included interviews with five OPEIU business representatives, 18 union activists (current and former members of the Executive Board, Executive Council, and Women's Committee), and five women members who had never been elected to union office. These women responded to an article in the union's newsletter detailing my research interests in Local 378. Interestingly, no men contacted me as a result of that article. Nor did any women of colour. I contacted BC Hydro to get information about their job evaluation plans and interviewed four managers involved in implementing job evaluation. These interviews, even if not as extensive or representative of OPEIU members as I would have liked, added an important dimension to the research, filling in gaps in the documentary material, providing new and sometimes conflicting readings on issues and events, and adding an experiential dimension to the picture being formed of 'doing gender' through collective bargaining.

Of course, important gaps remain. I would have liked to interview more members who were not union activists, in particular women and men of colour, to learn more about experiences on the job and in the union. Another important gap was the failure to analyse the company's side of these negotiations in the same manner as the union's. Other than material on job evaluation and some employee data, I did not have access to company records. Union records included many company documents, such as bargaining proposals, counter-proposals, minutes of negotiating meetings, company reports, and correspondence. However, I cannot claim that this study paints a full picture of collective bargaining; it is a study of negotiations from the union's perspective. Equivalent company records were simply not available.[2] This is a particular weakness for the later period, the 1980s and 1990s, when tracing equity policies adopted by the company would have been very useful.

This, then, was the research process, or at least is a narrative description of sources consulted. The process of selecting, sifting, and interpreting data is always far less transparent. Indeed, the history I have written here about negotiating class, gender, and race in the OPEIU is only one narrative that can be told from these same sources. I have written a much shorter and more conventional history for the OPEIU, revised here as Chapter 2.[3] In the latter I concentrate on the main provisions won in successive collective agreements, strikes, and other job actions, changing labour relations at the utility company, and the organization of other units into the local. Though gendering can be read through the pages of this more conventional history, it is by no means as central to the text, while processes of racialization remain invisible. This more conventional reading of labour history forms an important document for Local 378 members, but in and of itself it is far from the complete story.

In this study I have backgrounded much of that conventional story, which serves as a sort of scaffolding essential to make sense of the rest, and instead foregrounded a set of interconnecting themes embedded in and central to union practices of collective bargaining. Union negotiations were inscribed in historically contingent notions of masculinity/femininity, technical work/skill, and equality/solidarity, simultaneously constructing preferential breadwinner rights, white-collar working-class masculinities and femininities, and racialized-masculine privilege at the utility company. These themes emerged from a grounded research process where theory and data constantly interacted in the formulation and reformulation of interpretations. In discussions of qualitative sociology, grounded theory, that is, theory that emerges from the research data rather than grand theory superimposed from above, is defined as a hallmark of good qualitative research.[4] What I mean by grounded research extends this concept by acknowledging a fuller, more reflexive process of theorizing and data analysis. Not only is theory grounded in historically contextualized research, but research data are grounded in the theoretical locations of the researcher in a continual process of (conscious and unconscious) recognition and making sense.

I tried to be especially responsive and responsible to what OPEIU members told me about the events they were involved in and what they thought about particular issues. Not surprisingly, union members often disagreed with each other, and with me, about issues and events. As far as possible I relied on other documentary evidence to make sense of these contradictions and engaged in ongoing dialogue over interpretations. I presented earlier versions of papers and, later, copies of publications[5] to some union members and received feedback on my research. In some cases errors were pointed out and corrected. In other cases disagreements were over interpretation and the weighting of arguments, leading me to rethink the complexity of union practices. I have not always been able to resolve contradictions between union activists' interpretations and my own. Feminist methodology often stresses notions of authenticity in an attempt to privilege the voices of subjects of research rather than the researcher. As Beverley Skeggs has argued, however, such a position is both impossible to attain and can undermine the 'epistemic responsibility' to search for the fullest possible explanations that one can find.[6] In the end, then, the researcher does privilege her own voice. One can only try to approach what Donna Haraway calls 'embedded objectivity' in the context of consciously and politically engaged 'situated knowledges'.[7]

Others may read this history in the context of recent debates about women's history versus gender history, a debate immersed in disagreements among feminist historians about the efficacy of post-structuralist theories.[8] For one reading these historical debates, the present work on racialized-gendering would likely be placed on the gender history/post-structuralist side of this debate. Within my own discipline of sociology, however, debates over post-structuralism are drawn differently and do not hinge on the concept of gender or gender identities, which has been central to feminist sociology of all kinds for decades.[9] Debates in sociology focus more on the implications of the partiality, multiplicity, and contingency of knowledges and subjects in terms of how or whether to attempt to ground research and its implications for political practice. Within these debates this research is more likely to be identified, by myself as well as by others, as materialist and post-colonial in orientation rather than as post-structuralist.[10]

What I have tried to do in this study is to make visible, in very material ways, practices buried within traditions and conventions, to tease out contradictory strategies, to reconnect historical practices with present possibilities and constraints, and thereby to uncover systemic processes of racialized-gendering through negotiations over conditions at work. I make no claim that this is the complete story, but it is, I believe, an important and overlooked dimension of labour history. As such it is my hope that this study, with all its imperfections, may be of use to other researchers and to union activists who are seeking to understand more fully their own histories in order to develop contemporary strategies to challenge systemic inequities at work.

Notes

Introduction: Gender, Race, and Clerical Work

1. The term 'women of colour' is a self-defined term among feminists who are racialized as 'non-white' in Canada; the term 'visible minorities' is used for government purposes.

2. For example, see Floya Anthias and Nira Yuval-Davis, *Racialised Boundaries: Race, Nation, Gender, Colour and Class and the Anti-Racist Struggle* (London, 1992); Himani Bannerji, ed., *Returning the Gaze: Essays on Racism, Feminism and Politics* (Toronto, 1993); Patricia Hill Collins, *Black Feminist Thought* (New York, 1990); Chandra Talpade Mohanty, Ann Russo, and Lourdes Torres, eds, *Third World Woman and the Politics of Feminism* (Bloomington, Ind., 1991).

3. See Judith Lorber, *Paradoxes of Gender* (New Haven, 1994); Dorothy Smith, *Texts, Facts, and Femininity: Exploring the Relations of Ruling* (London, 1990).

4. See Anthias and Yuval-Davis, *Racialised Boundaries*; Robert Miles, *Racism* (London, 1989); Edward Said, *Orientalism* (New York, 1978).

5. In the Canadian context the meaning of 'White' has expanded in the post-war period from those of British and northern European origin to all those of European origin.

6. For example, see Ruth Frankenberg, *White Women, Race Matters: The Social Construction of Whiteness* (Minneapolis, 1993). Also see Gillian Creese and Daiva Stasiulis, 'Introduction: Intersections of Gender, Race, Class and Sexuality', *Studies in Political Economy* 51 (Fall 1996): 5–14.

7. For discussions of the importance of place and space, see Audrey Kobayashi, ed., *Women, Work, and Place* (Montreal and Kingston, 1994); Linda McDowell, *Capital Culture: Gender at Work in the City* (Oxford, 1997).

8. Management practices are of course also central to this process, but this study focuses on the often overlooked role that workers and unions play through collective bargaining.

9. Several interviewees mentioned the same woman of colour as an exception to the general lack of diversity in senior management.

10. See, for example, Cynthia Cockburn, *Machinery of Dominance: Women, Men and Technical Know-How* (London, 1985); Sally Hacker, *'Doing It the Hard Way': Investigations of Gender and Technology* (Boston, 1990); Rosemary Pringle, *Secretaries Talk: Sexuality, Power and Work* (London, 1988); Barbara Reskin and Patricia Roos, *Job Queues, Gender Queues: Explaining Women's Inroads into Male Occupations* (Philadelphia, 1990).

11. For the most part individuals are not identified by name, but only by pseudonym, interview number, or relevant descriptive phrases. Exceptions to the use of pseudonyms include the identity of public figures, such as the names of Local 378 presidents. On the whole, however, few individuals are identified in the text. In part this is because all interviewees were guaranteed confidentiality. In part, too, it reflects the fact that few union records recorded who said or did what. Minutes of meetings, committees, bargaining sessions, etc. tended to record summaries of issues discussed and decisions made, not verbatim accounts of activity. This format also reflects theoretical and disciplinary decisions, with the emphasis on collective rather than individual agency tied to a sociological focus on broader social processes.

Chapter 1   Who Gets Ahead at the Office?

1. Interview 4.

2. Michael's family status is unknown.

3. June recounts office gossip that the successful candidate, a woman, and the male supervisor were having an affair. Certainly the promotion of any woman to this Group 6 position was unusual in 1973, let alone one not demonstrably well qualified.

4. Two other women who began in non-traditional areas were interviewed for this study. Of these two, Pamela's experience is even more difficult than Megan's. Pamela, trained as a drafter, was laid off from her drafting job (Group 6) at the start of the lay-offs in 1982. Her only option was to accept the clerical position (Group 3 receptionist) offered to her, although she had no clerical training or experience. After taking repeated refresher and new software application courses for drafting, she finally attained a temporary drafting position for vacation relief a decade later, in 1992. At the time of the interview Pamela was again in her regular

Group 4 clerical position in engineering. She has recently attained a regular position as a drafter (Group 6).

5. 'Employment Equity: Positioning for Success', company memo, 31 Mar. 1991, 3.

6. The average job group used here is the median, calculated from 'Employee Counts', 10 July 1991. Average salaries were calculated from the Collective Agreement, 1991–3. The minimum salary for Group 5 at that time was $2,245 a month, while the maximum was $2,691. The minimum for Group 8 was $2,914 and the maximum salary was $3,491.

7. BC Hydro did not make available any data about the distribution of differently racialized groups so such observations are based on interviews and general company memos about employment equity.

8. See Barbara Reskin and Irene Padavic, *Women and Men at Work* (Thousand Oaks, Calif., 1994); Sheila Rowbotham and Swatsi Mitter, *Dignity and Daily Bread* (London, 1994).

9. See Rosemary Crompton and Kay Sanderson, *Gendered Jobs and Social Change* (London, 1990); Ann Game and Rosemary Pringle, *Gender at Work* (Sydney, 1983); Joy Parr, *The Gender of Breadwinners* (Toronto, 1990); Janet Siltanen, *Locating Gender* (London, 1994).

10. Reskin and Roos, *Job Queues, Gender Queues*, 51.

11. Ibid.

12. Ileen DeVault, *Sons and Daughters of Labor: Class and Clerical Work in Turn-of-the-Century Pittsburgh* (Ithaca, NY, 1990); Lisa Fine, *The Souls of the Skyscraper: Female Clerical Workers in Chicago, 1870–1930* (Philadelphia, 1990); David Lockwood, *The Blackcoated Worker: A Study in Class Consciousness*, 2nd edn (Oxford, 1989); Graham Lowe, *Women in the Administrative Revolution* (Toronto, 1987); Pringle, *Secretaries Talk*.

13. Lowe, *Women in the Administrative Revolution*.

14. Ibid., 2. See also Fine, *The Souls of the Skyscraper*.

15. DeVault, *Sons and Daughters of Labor*.

16. Ibid., 176.

17. Lockwood, *The Blackcoated Worker*; also cited in Angus McLaren, *The Trials of Masculinity: Policing Sexual Boundaries, 1870–1930* (Chicago, 1997), 34.

18. DeVault, *Sons and Daughters of Labor*; Fine, *The Souls of the Skyscraper*.

19. Reskin and Padavic, *Women and Men at Work*, 53.

20. Pringle, *Secretaries Talk*; Catherine Truss, Robert Goffee, and Gareth Jones, 'Segregated Occupations and Gender Stereotyping: A Study of Secretarial Work in Europe', *Human Relations* 48, 1 (1995): 1331–54.

21. Mary King, 'Black Women's Breakthrough into Clerical Work: An Occupational Tipping Model', *Journal of Economic Issues* 27, 4 (1993): 1097–125; Denise Segura, 'Chicanas in White-Collar Jobs: "You Have to Prove Yourself More" ', *Sociological Perspectives* 35, 1 (1992):163–82.

22. In 1994, 26.8 per cent of all women workers were clerical workers, compared to 5.4 per cent of men. In 1991 this broke down as follows: visible minority women (26.0 per cent), non-visible minority women (29.2 per cent) (see Table 3); Aboriginal women (25.4 per cent), non-Aboriginal women (29.0 per cent). Statistics Canada, *Women in Canada: A Statistical Report*, 3rd edn (Ottawa, 1995): 76, 144, 160.

23. Statistics Canada data record self-identification as a 'visible minority', with those who do not identify as such classified as 'other'. The residual category of 'other' approximates the population racialized as White in Canada.

24. See, for example, Pat Armstrong and Hugh Armstrong, *Theorizing Women's Work* (Toronto, 1990); Edna Bonacich, 'A Theory of Ethnic Antagonism: The Split Labor Market', *American Sociological Review* 37 (Oct. 1972): 547–59; Wallace Clement and John Myles, *Relations of Ruling: Class and Gender in Postindustrial Societies* (Montreal and Kingston, 1994); John Hagan and Fiona Kay, *Gender in Practice: A Study of Lawyers' Lives* (New York, 1995); David Gordon, Richard Edwards, and Michael Reich, *Segmented Work, Divided Workers* (Cambridge, 1982); Alice Abel Kemp, *Women's Work: Degraded and Devalued* (Englewood Cliffs, NJ, 1994); Alicja Muszynski, *Cheap Wage Labour: Race and Gender in the Fisheries of British Columbia* (Montreal and Kingston, 1996); Stephen Peitchinis, *Women at Work: Discrimination and Response* (Toronto, 1989); Reskin and Padavic, *Women and Men at Work*; Donald Tomaskovic-Devey, *Gender and Racial Inequality at Work* (Ithaca, NY, 1993).

25. For example, the classic work by E.P. Thompson, *The Making of the English Working Class* (Harmondsworth, 1968), is located within neo-Marxist theories, while the literature cited below on 'doing gender' is drawn from various strands of feminist theory.

26. See Anthony Giddens, *Sociology: A Brief but Critical Introduction*, 2nd edn (San Diego, 1987). For a feminist approach, see Dorothy Smith, *The Everyday World as Problematic* (Toronto, 1987); Smith, *The Conceptual Practices of Power: A Feminist Sociology of Knowledge* (Boston, 1990).

27. Candace West and Don Zimmerman, 'Doing Gender', *Gender and Society* 1 (1987): 125–51.

28. Cockburn, *Machinery of Dominance*, 169.

29. Segura, 'Chicanas in White-Collar Jobs'.

30. Pringle, *Secretaries Talk*, 163.

31. Albert Mills, 'Organization, Gender, and Culture', in Mills and Peta Tancred, eds, *Gendering Organizational Analysis* (Newbury Park, Calif., 1992), 93–111.

32. Joan Acker, 'Hierarchies, Jobs, Bodies: A Theory of Gendered Organizations', *Gender and Society* 4, 2 (June 1990): 139–58; Joan Acker,

'Gendering Organizational Theory', in Mills and Tancred, eds, *Gendering Organizational Analysis*, 248–60.

33. Acker, 'Gendering Organizational Theory', 255.

34. Elaine Hall, 'Smiling, Deferring, and Flirting: Doing Gender by Giving "Good Service"', *Work and Occupations* 20, 4 (Nov. 1993): 425–71.

35. Acker, 'Hierarchies, Jobs, Bodies'; Acker, 'Gendering Organizational Theory'.

36. Donna Haraway, *Simians, Cyborgs, and Women: The Reinvention of Nature* (New York, 1991); Judy Wajcman, *Feminism Confronts Technology* (University Park, Pa., 1991); Wajcman, 'The Masculine Mystique: A Feminist Analysis of Science and Technology', in Belinda Probert, ed., *Pink Collar Blues: Work, Gender and Technology* (Melbourne, 1993), 20–40.

37. Cynthia Cockburn, *Brothers: Male Dominance and Technological Change* (London, 1983); Cockburn, *Machinery of Dominance*; Wajcman, *Feminism Confronts Technology*; Wajcman, 'The Masculine Mystique'.

38. Cockburn, *Machinery of Dominance*, 197.

39. Sally Hacker, *Pleasure, Power, and Technology: Some Tales of Gender, Engineering, and the Cooperative Workplace* (Boston, 1989); Hacker, *'Doing It the Hard Way'*; Judith McIlwee and J. Gregg Robinson, *Women in Engineering: Gender, Power, and Workplace Culture* (Albany, NY, 1992).

40. Quoted in Hacker, *Pleasure, Power, and Technology*, 36.

41. Hacker, *'Doing It the Hard Way'*, 136.

42. Beverly Burris, 'Technocratic Organization and Gender', *Women's Studies International Forum* 12, 4 (1989): 447–62.

43. Jane Gaskell, 'Conceptions of Skill and the Work of Women: Some Historical and Political Issues', in Roberta Hamilton and Michele Barrett, eds, *The Politics of Diversity* (Montreal, 1986); Gaskell, 'What Counts as Skill: Reflections on Pay Equity', in Judy Fudge and Patricia McDermott, eds, *Just Wages: A Feminist Assessment of Pay Equity* (Toronto, 1991), 141–59; Sara Horrell, Jill Rubery, and Brendan Burchell, 'Gender and Skills', *Work, Employment and Society* 4, 2 (June 1990): 189–216; Jane Jenson, 'The Talents of Women, the Skills of Men: Flexible Specialization and Women', in Stephen Wood, ed., *The Transformation of Work: Skill, Flexibility and the Labour Process* (London, 1989).

44. Glenn Morgan and David Knights, 'Gendering Jobs: Corporate Strategy, Managerial Control and the Dynamics of Job Segregation', *Work, Employment and Society* 5, 2 (June 1991): 181–200; Barbara Reskin and Irene Padavic, 'Supervisors as Gatekeepers: Male Supervisors' Response to Women's Integration in Plant Jobs', *Social Problems* 35, 5 (Dec. 1988): 536–50.

45. Cynthia Cockburn, *In the Way of Women: Men's Resistance to Sex Equality in Organizations* (London, 1991); Meg Luxton and June Corman, 'Getting to Work: The Challenge of the Women Back Into Stelco Campaign', *Labour/Le Travail* 28 (Fall 1991): 149–85; Pamela Sugiman, *Labour's Dilemma: The Gender Politics of Auto Workers in Canada, 1937–1979* (Toronto, 1994); Suzanne Tallichet, 'Gendered Relations in the Mines and the Division of Labour Underground', *Gender and Society* 9, 6 (Dec. 1995): 697–711.

46. Cockburn, *Machinery of Dominance*, 230.

47. See, for example, Linda Briskin and Patricia McDermott, eds, *Women Challenging Unions: Feminism, Democracy, and Militancy* (Toronto, 1993); Dorothy Sue Cobble, *Dishing It Out: Waitresses and Their Unions in the Twentieth Century* (Urbana, Ill., 1991); Cockburn, *In the Way of Women*; June Corman, Meg Luxton, D.W. Livingstone, and Wally Seccombe, *Recasting Steel Labour: The Stelco Story* (Halifax, 1993); Gillian Creese, 'Gendering Collective Bargaining: From Men's Rights to Women's Issues', *Canadian Review of Sociology and Anthropology* 33, 4 (1996): 437–56; Sheila Cunnison and June Stageman, *Feminizing the Unions: Challenging the Culture of Masculinity* (Aldershot, 1993); Nancy Gabin, *Feminism in the Labour Movement: Women and the United Auto Workers, 1935–1975* (Ithaca, NY, 1990); David Livingstone and J. Marshall Mangan, eds, *Recast Dreams: Class and Gender Consciousness in Steeltown* (Toronto, 1996); Ruth Milkman, *Gender at Work: The Dynamics of Job Segregation by Sex During World War II* (Urbana, Ill., 1987); Mercedes Steedman, *Angels of the Workplace: Women and the Construction of Gender Relations in the Canadian Clothing Industry, 1890–1940* (Toronto, 1997); Sugiman, *Labour's Dilemma*; Julie White, *Mail and Female: Women and the Canadian Union of Postal Workers* (Toronto, 1990); White, *Sisters and Solidarity: Women and Unions in Canada* (Toronto, 1993).

48. See Gillian Creese, 'Exclusion or Solidarity? Vancouver Workers Confront the "Oriental Problem"', *BC Studies* 80 (Winter 1988–9): 24–51; Cunnison and Stageman, *Feminizing the Unions*; Ruth Frager, *Sweatshop Strife: Class, Ethnicity, and Gender in the Jewish Labour Movement of Toronto, 1900–1939* (Toronto, 1992); Franca Iacovetta, *Such Hardworking People: Italian Immigrants in Postwar Toronto* (Montreal and Kingston, 1992); Ronnie Leah, 'Black Women Speak Out: Racism and Unions', in Briskin and McDermott, eds, *Women Challenging Unions*, 157–71; Leah, 'Linking the Struggles: Racism, Feminism and the Union Movement', in Jesse Vorst, ed., *Race, Class, Gender: Bonds and Barriers* (Toronto, 1989), 166–95; Muszynski, *Cheap Wage Labour*.

49. R.W. Connell, *Masculinities* (Berkeley, 1995); Michael Kaufman, 'The Construction of Masculinity and the Triad of Men's Violence', in

Michael Kaufman, ed., *Beyond Patriarchy: Essays by Men on Pleasure, Power, and Change* (Toronto, 1987), 1–29; Michael Kimmel, 'Masculinity as Homophobia: Fear, Shame, and Silence in the Construction of Gender Identity', in Harry Brod and Michael Kaufman, eds, *Theorizing Masculinities* (Thousand Oaks, Calif., 1994), 119–41; Michael Kaufman, 'Men, Feminism, and Men's Contradictory Experiences of Power', in Brod and Kaufman, eds, *Theorizing Masculinities*, 142–63; McLaren, *The Trials of Masculinity*.

50. For example, see Rosemary Crompton and Gareth Jones, *White Collar Proletariat: Deskilling and Gender in Clerical Work* (London, 1984).

51. Lowe, *Women in the Administrative Revolution*, 163–7.

52. See DeVault, *Sons and Daughters of Labor*. She documents patterns whereby the children of blue-collar workers entered clerical work in the early part of this century not as a form of upward social mobility, but to maintain their positions as conditions of craft work declined.

53. Lockwood, *The Blackcoated Worker*.

54. Connell, *Masculinities*; see also Arthur Brittain, *Masculinity and Power* (Oxford, 1989); Tim Carrigan, Bob Connell, and John Lee, 'Hard and Heavy: Toward a New Sociology of Masculinity', in Kaufman, ed., *Beyond Patriarchy*, 139–92; Steven Maynard, 'Rough Work and Rugged Men: The Social Construction of Masculinity in Working-Class History', *Labour/Le Travail* 23 (Spring 1989): 159–69.

55. Michele Barrett, *Women's Oppression Today* (London, 1980); Gillian Creese, 'The Politics of Dependence: Women, Work and Unemployment in the Vancouver Labour Market Before World War II', *Canadian Journal of Sociology* 13, 1–2 (1988): 121–42; Bryan Palmer, *Working-Class Experience: Rethinking the History of Canadian Labour, 1800–1991* (Toronto, 1992); White, *Sisters and Solidarity*.

56. Thomas Dunk, *It's a Working Man's Town: Male Working-Class Culture in Northwestern Ontario* (Montreal and Kingston, 1991); Kimmel, 'Masculinity as Homophobia'; Paul Willis, *Learning to Labor: How Working Class Kids Get Working Class Jobs* (New York, 1977).

57. Interviews 1 and 10.

58. For a discussion of dreams of suburbia, see Doug Owram, *Born at the Right Time: A History of the Baby Boom Generation* (Toronto, 1996); Ester Reiter, *Making Fast Food* (Montreal and Kingston, 1991); Veronica Strong-Boag, 'Home Dreams: Women and the Suburban Experiment in Canada, 1945–60', *Canadian Historical Review* 72, 4 (1991): 471–504; Strong-Boag, ' "Their Side of the Story": Women's Voices from Ontario Suburbs, 1945–1960', in Joy Parr, ed., *A Diversity of Women, Ontario 1945–1980* (Toronto, 1995), 46–74.

59. See Michael Asch, *Home and Native Land: Aboriginal Rights and the Canadian Constitution* (Toronto, 1984); James Frideres, *Native Peoples*

in Canada: Contemporary Conflicts, 3rd edn (Toronto, 1988); Paul Tennant, *Aboriginal Peoples and Politics* (Vancouver, 1990).

60. See Kay Anderson, *Vancouver's Chinatown: Racial Discourse in Canada, 1875–1980* (Montreal and Kingston, 1991); Freda Hawkins, *Canada and Immigration: Public Policy and Public Concern*, 2nd edn (Montreal and Kingston, 1988); Peter Li, *The Making of Post-War Canada* (Toronto, 1996); Peter Li, ed., *Race and Ethnic Relations in Canada* (Toronto, 1990); John Porter, *The Vertical Mosaic* (Toronto, 1965); Anthony Richmond, *Global Apartheid: Refugees, Racism, and the New World Order* (Toronto, 1994); Daiva Stasiulis and Radha Jhappan, 'The Fractious Politics of a Settler Society: Canada', in Stasiulis and Nira Yuval-Davis, eds, *Unsettling Settler Societies* (London, 1995), 95–131.

61. Peggy McIntosh, 'White Privilege and Male Privilege: A Personal Account of Coming to See Correspondences Through Work in Women's Studies', in Margaret Anderson and Patricia Hill Collins, eds, *Race, Class, Gender: An Anthology*, 2nd edn (Belmont, Calif., 1995), 76–7. See also Frankenberg, *White Women, Race Matters*; Michelle Fine, Lois Weis, Linda Powell, and L. Mun Wong, eds, *Off White: Readings on Race, Power, and Society* (New York, 1997).

62. Michele Barrett and Mary McIntosh, *The Anti-social Family* (London, 1982); Ruth Schwartz Cowan, *More Work for Mother: The Ironies of Household Technology from the Open Hearth to the Microwave* (New York, 1983); Meg Luxton, *More Than a Labour of Love* (Toronto, 1980).

63. Marilyn Waring, *If Women Counted* (New York, 1988).

64. See, for example, Melody Hessing, 'Talking on the Job: Office Conversations and Women's Dual Labour', in Gillian Creese and Veronica Strong-Boag, eds, *British Columbia Reconsidered: Essays on Women* (Vancouver, 1992), 391–415; Audrey Kobayashi, Linda Peake, Hal Benenson, and Katie Pickles, 'Introduction: Placing Women and Work', in Kobayashi, ed., *Women, Work, and Place*, ix–xlv; Carole Pateman, *The Disorder of Women: Democracy, Feminism and Political Theory* (Stanford, Calif., 1989).

65. See DeVault, *Sons and Daughters of Labor*; Fine, *The Souls of the Skyscraper*; Lowe, *The Administrative Revolution*; Pringle, *Secretaries Talk*.

66. Quoted in Pradeep Kumar and Lynn Acri, 'Unions' Collective Bargaining Agenda on Women's Issues: The Ontario Experience', *Industrial Relations* 47, 4 (1992): 625.

67. See, for example, Desmond Morton, *Working People: An Illustrated History of the Canadian Labour Movement*, 3rd edn (Toronto, 1990); Palmer, *Working-Class Experience*; Leo Panitch and Donald Swartz, *The Assault on Trade Union Freedoms: From Wage Controls to Social Contract* (Toronto, 1993); James Rinehart, *The Tyranny of Work: Alienation and the Labour Process*, 3rd edn (Toronto, 1996).

68. Cockburn, Brothers; Cockburn, *Machinery of Dominance*; Cockburn, *In the Way of Women*; Cunnison and Stageman, *Feminizing the Unions*; Gabin, *Feminism in the Labour Movement*; Milkman, *Gender at Work*; Sugiman, *Labour's Dilemma*.

69. Cynthia Cockburn, 'Trade Unions and the Radicalizing of Socialist Feminism', *Feminist Review* 16 (Apr. 1984): 43–6; Cunnison and Stageman, *Feminizing the Unions*; Gabin, *Feminism in the Labour Movement*; Anne Phillips, *Democracy and Difference* (Cambridge, 1993); Sugiman, *Labour's Dilemma*.

70. Sugiman, *Labour's Dilemma*, 199–204.

71. Gabin, *Feminism in the Labour Movement*, 230.

72. Maureen Baker and Mary-Anne Robeson, 'Trade Union Reactions to Women Workers and their Concerns', *Canadian Journal of Sociology* 6, 1 (1981): 19–31; Phillips, *Democracy and Difference*.

73. Louise Dulude, 'Seniority and Employment Equity for Women', Ph.D. thesis (University of Ottawa, 1993).

74. Thirty-nine per cent of all women workers were unionized in 1989; by 1991 this had increased to 41 per cent. White, *Sisters and Solidarity*, 56; Statistics Canada, *Women in Canada*, 3rd edn, 68.

75. White, *Sisters and Solidarity*, 165–6.

76. Ruth Milkman, 'New Research in Women's Labour History', *Signs* 18, 2 (Winter 1993): 377.

77. Santina Bertone and Gerard Griffin, 'Immigrant Female Workers and Australian Trade Unions', *Industrial Relations* 50, 1 (1995): 117–45; Carl Cuneo, 'Trade Union Leadership: Sexism and Affirmative Action', in Briskin and McDermott, eds, *Women Challenging Unions*, 109–36; Cunnison and Stageman, *Feminizing the Unions*; Barbara Pocock, 'Women in Unions: What Progress in South Australia?', *Journal of Industrial Relations* 37, 1 (Mar. 1995): 3–23; Pamela Roby and Lynet Uttal, 'Trade Union Stewards: Handling Union, Family, and Employment Responsibilities', *Women and Work: An Annual Review* 3 (1988): 215–48; Jane Stinson and Penni Richmond, 'Women Working for Unions: Female Staff and the Politics of Transformation', in Briskin and McDermott, eds, *Women Challenging Unions*, 137–56; White, *Sisters and Solidarity*.

78. Cunnison and Stageman, *Feminizing the Unions*, 14.

79. Linda Briskin, 'Union Women and Separate Organizing', in Briskin and McDermott, eds, *Women Challenging Unions*, 89–108; White, *Sisters and Solidarity*.

80. Cockburn, 'Trade Unions and the Radicalizing of Socialist Feminism', 45; see also Briskin, 'Union Women and Separate Organizing'.

81. Briskin, 'Union Women and Separate Organizing'; Gillian Creese, 'Gender Equity or Masculine Privilege? Union Strategies and Economic

Restructuring in a White Collar Union', *Canadian Journal of Sociology* 20, 2 (1995): 143–66; Creese, 'Gendering Collective Bargaining'; Pradeep Kumar, 'Collective Bargaining and Women's Workplace Concerns', in Briskin and McDermott, eds, *Women Challenging Unions*, 207–30; Kumar and Acri, 'Unions' Collective Bargaining Agenda'.
82. Miriam Henry and Suzanne Franzway, 'Gender, Unions and the New Workplace', in Probert, ed., *Pink Collar Blues*, 126–53.
83. Milkman, *Gender at Work*, 96.
84. Patricia Hill Collins, *Black Feminist Thought: Knowledge, Consciousness, and the Politics of Empowerment* (New York, 1990). See also Vijay Agnew, *Resisting Discrimination: Women from Asia, Africa, and the Caribbean and the Women's Movement in Canada* (Toronto, 1996); Himani Bannerji, ed., *Returning the Gaze: Essays on Racism, Feminism and Politics* (Toronto, 1993); bell hooks, *Feminist Theory From Margin to Center* (Boston, 1984).

Chapter 2 Becoming a Union

1. General Minutes, Box 1, File 1: Constitution, 1.
2. *B.C. Electric Employees' Magazine* (Mar. 1926): 8, records 2,770 employees in 1921 and 3,240 in 1925.
3. Patricia Roy, 'The British Columbia Electric Railway Company Ltd., 1897–1928', Ph.D. thesis (University of British Columbia, 1970), 266–92.
4. General Minutes, Box 1, File 1: Constitution, 4.
5. Ibid., 1.
6. Ibid., 3.
7. Ibid., Minutes, 1921–39.
8. Ibid., Jan. 1933.
9. Ibid., Files 1 and 2: Minutes, 1931–9.
10. Ibid.
11. Power Corporation, *Annual Report*, 1948.
12. There is no mention of OEA women leaving their jobs to join the armed forces, but no doubt some did. There is no indication whether such women could also return to their jobs at BC Electric.
13. General Minutes, Box 1, Files 2 and 3A: Minutes, 1939–43.
14. There is no mention of a move to nationalize the electrical system in Victoria.
15. General Minutes, Box 1, Files 2 and 3A: Minutes, 1942–3.
16. Panitch and Swartz, *The Assault on Trade Union Freedoms*, 11.
17. Morton, *Working People*, 175–200; Bryan Palmer, *Working-Class Experience: The Rise and Reconstitution of Canadian Labour, 1800–1980* (Toronto, 1983), 229–45; Panitch and Swartz, *The Assault on Trade Union Freedoms*.

18. Interview 1C.

19. General Minutes, Box 1, File 3A: Minutes, 9, 15 May, 13 June, 10 Oct. 1944. According to these minutes the first contract was signed in 1944, but no record of that contract remains. It is likely that the 1944 agreement was an interim agreement setting out issues the union and the company negotiated over the next two years. The first full contract was signed in 1946.

20. Ibid., 11 Sept. 1945.

21. Ibid., 5 Sept. 1945.

22. Bargaining Files, Box 24, File 31: letter from BC Electric, 9 Nov. 1945, 10–11.

23. The male salary scale referred to 16 job groups and the female salary scale included only nine job groups. In actual fact, women were concentrated in the first four job groups. Collective Agreement, 1946.

24. Ibid.

25. General Minutes, Box 1, Files 1 and 2: Minutes, 1948–9.

26. Ibid., Files 1, 2, 3A, and 4: Minutes, 1949–50.

27. Ibid., File 4: Minutes, 1950–6.

28. According to some members the attitude that a white-collar union, and a union with a large number of women members, was somehow not a serious trade union persists among other BC Hydro unions until the present time. Interviews 1, 10, 15, and 21.

29. General Minutes, Box 1, File 4: Minutes, 1950–3.

30. The Office Employees' International Union (OEIU) was later renamed the Office and Professional Employees' International Union (OPEIU).

31. General Minutes, Box 1, File 4: Minutes, 1 Jan. 1953.

32. Ibid., 29 Apr., 13 Nov. 1953.

33. Ibid., 1955–6.

34. Collective Agreements, 1953, 1956, and 1958.

35. General Minutes, Box 1, Files 5 and 10: Minutes, 1958–60.

36. Ibid., File 11: Minutes, 1960–1.

37. Ibid., Files 5 and 11: Minutes, 1959–61.

38. Ibid., File 11: Minutes, 1960.

39. Ibid., 1961.

40. Ibid., File 12: Minutes, 1962; Interview 1.

41. General Minutes, Box 1, File 13: Minutes, 1963.

42. Elsewhere in Canada members of the OPEIU adopted the name Office and Professional Employees' International Union (OPEIU). At the time labour legislation in British Columbia prevented unionization of professionals, so Local 378 instead opted to include 'technical' in its title to signal its commitment to organizing the broadest range of office work. Local 378 changed its name to OPEIU in January 1996.

43. General Minutes, Box 2, File 1: Minutes, 10 Apr. 1965.

44. For example, IPEC placed employees on unpaid leave of absence during short lay-offs, varied the workweek without paying overtime, and failed to pay premiums for underground work and living-out allowances.

45. General Minutes, Box 2, File 2: Minutes, 29 Nov. 1966; File 3: Minutes, 18 Apr. 1967.

46. Ibid., File 8: Minutes, 1968.

47. Ibid., File 2: Minutes, Jan.-Nov. 1966.

48. Ibid., File 3: Minutes, Aug. 1967.

49. Ibid., File 9: Minutes, Aug. 1969.

50. Collective Agreements, 1960, 1961, 1963, 1965, and 1969.

51. General Minutes, Box 2, File 10: Minutes, 1970.

52. See Morton, *Working People*, 213–25; Palmer, *Working-Class Experience*, 252–5.

53. Not all members were supportive, however, and a dozen OTEU members were fined for crossing the IBEW picket lines. General Minutes, Box 5, File 9: Minutes, 1971.

54. Ibid., Box 2, File 12: Minutes, 26 Apr. 1972.

55. Ibid., *WOFAC News Digest*, 16 Feb. 1972; also BC Hydro, *Intercom* (Sept. 1971): 11.

56. General Minutes, Box 5, File 8: Minutes, 1972.

57. Ibid., Box 3, File 5: Minutes, 1973.

58. Ibid., Box 3, File 6, and Box 5, File 7: Minutes, 1974.

59. Ibid., Box 3, File 7: Minutes, 1975.

60. Bargaining Files, Box 21, Files 15 and 16: Bargaining Files, 1974.

61. General Minutes, Box 3, File 8: Minutes of Regional Meeting, 1976.

62. Ibid.

63. Ibid., Box 5, File 6: BCFL convention policy statements, 1977.

64. At the time of writing Ron Tuckwood remains president of Local 378, having been re-elected in 1993 and again in 1996.

65. In early 1981 a long strike occurred at ICBC that had already stretched the union's resources. Executive Board Minutes, 1981.

66. Collective Agreement, 1981.

67. Bargaining Files, 1983: Memo from OTEU to BC Hydro, Dec. 1982.

68. Ibid., 1989.

69. Ibid., 1991.

Chapter 3 Normalizing Breadwinner Rights

1. Bargaining Files, Box 24, File 19, Summary of Proposals for Revision of the Collective Agreement, 1 Nov. 1947, 2.

2. The process of the feminization of clerical work was well under way before World War II. For a discussion of the feminization of clerical work

in early twentieth-century Canada, see Lowe, *Women in the Administrative Revolution*.

3. It should be noted that accountants and auditors, a predominantly male occupation, were included under clerical occupations in 1941 but not in later census data. In the postwar period, accountants become more differentiated from bookkeepers and, along with many other groups like teachers and nurses, adopted professional certification through formal educational requirements. While accountants continued to work in offices, claims to professional status were likely related to their reclassification independent of lower-status clerical occupations.

4. For a historical overview of gender segregation in the labour force, see Pat Armstrong and Hugh Armstrong, *The Double Ghetto: Canadian Women and Their Segregated Work*, 3rd edn (Toronto, 1994).

5. For the effect of World War II on drawing more women into paid employment, and then legislating women out of paid labour after the war, see Ruth Roach Pierson, *'They're Still Women After All': The Second World War and Canadian Womanhood* (Toronto, 1986).

6. The labour force participation rate of Canadian women increased from 20.7 per cent in 1941 to 33 per cent at the end of the war in 1945, declined to 24 per cent in 1951, and rose to 29.5 per cent in 1961 and 40 per cent in 1971. Armstrong and Armstrong, *The Double Ghetto*, 16–17.

7. *Census of Canada*, 1941, vol. 3, 54–5; 1951, vol. 4, 11–153, 11–154; 1961, vol. 3, 17–5, 17–6.

8. Ibid., 1961, vol 3, 17–5, 17–6, 17–19, 17–20. British Columbia had more married women and older women in the clerical workforce than the national average. In 1951, 61 per cent of these women were single and 32 per cent were married, compared to 70 per cent and 25 per cent nationally. In 1961 only 32 per cent of clerical women in BC were single and 54 per cent were married, compared to 47 per cent each nationally.

9. Pierson argues that ideologies of women's femininity were used to redefine women's paid labouring roles without challenging gender norms during World War II. Pierson, *'They're Still Women After All'*, 215–20.

10. Milkman, *Gender at Work*.

11. As discussed in Chapter 1, racialization refers to the processes by which groups come to be defined as belonging to separate races, often coinciding with assumptions that there are inherent biological differences between groups. Since scientists have rejected the notion that there are any meaningful biological distinctions between groups of human beings, and since definitions of racial categories vary cross-culturally and change over time, social scientists focus on the social processes by which groups come to be thought of as constituting distinct races and the ways in which these change over time.

12. Porter, *The Vertical Mosaic*.

13. Immigrants from India were entirely prohibited by 'continuous journey' legislation in 1908 requiring direct passage from India to Canada (when there were no such shipping routes); immigrants from China were severely curtailed through enactment of progressively higher head taxes, beginning in 1884, and complete exclusion (with a few exceptions, such as merchants and diplomats) in 1923 with the passage of the Chinese Immigration Act; immigrants from Japan were restricted through the 'Gentlemen's Agreement' that severely limited the number of Japanese men who could migrate each year. See Peter Ward, *White Canada Forever: Popular Attitudes and Public Policy Toward Orientals in British Columbia* (Montreal and Kingston, 1978).

14. Ibid., 170–1.

15. For general sources, see ibid.; Edgar Wickberg, *From China to Canada: A History of Chinese Communities in Canada* (Toronto, 1982); Ken Adachi, *The Enemy That Never Was: A History of the Japanese Canadians* (Toronto, 1976). For sources on Asian-Canadian women, see The Women's Book Committee, Chinese Canadian National Council, *Jin Guo: Voices of Chinese Canadian Women* (Toronto, 1992); Tomoko Makabe, *Picture Brides: Japanese Women in Canada* (Toronto, 1995). It should be noted that there were also far fewer Chinese- or Indo-Canadian women than men in the province until the 1960s.

16. Lockwood, *The Blackcoated Worker*, 202–4.

17. Fifty-five per cent of men and 79 per cent of women clerical workers in BC were Canadian-born. *Census of Canada*, 1941, vol. 3, 330–1, 336–7, 436–7, 440–1.

18. Ibid.

19. Ibid. Only two men and one woman were recorded as Native Indian clerical workers in BC in 1941; 70 men and 45 Native Indian women were recorded nationally.

20. The 1951 census did not publish these data by province. In 1961, 2 per cent of clerical men and 2 per cent of clerical women in BC were of Asian origin. Those of British origin had decreased to 71 per cent each, while other Europeans made up 27 per cent each. Nationally, Asian-Canadian men and women each constituted one-half of 1 per cent (0.6) of all clerical workers. The number of First Nations people was even lower: Native Indian men and women each constituted 0.08 of a percentage of all clerical workers. In BC, only 14 men and 65 Native Indian women were recorded as clerical workers in 1961. *Census of Canada*, 1961, vol. 3, 21–3, 21–4, 21–17, 21–18, 22–37, 22–38, 22–39, 22–40.

21. For a discussion of postwar suburban dreams and consumer culture, see Strong-Boag 'Home Dreams'; Strong-Boag, 'Their Side of the Story'; Reiter, *Making Fast Food*; Owram, *Born at the Right Time*.

22. As discussed in Chapter 1, there is a growing literature on masculinity in union culture. See Briskin and McDermott, eds, *Women Challenging Unions*; Cockburn, *Brothers*; Cockburn, *Machinery of Dominance*; Cockburn, *In the Way of Women*; Cunnison and Stageman, *Feminizing the Unions*; Gabin, *Feminism in the Labour Movement*; Livingstone and Mangan, eds, *Recast Dreams*; Milkman, *Gender at Work*; Pamela Sugiman, ' "That Wall's Comin' Down": Gendered Strategies of Worker Resistance in the UAW Canadian Region', *Canadian Journal of Sociology* 17, 1 (1992): 1–27; Sugiman, *Labour's Dilemma*; White, *Mail and Female; White, Sisters and Solidarity*.

23. Bargaining Files, Box 24, File 11, copy of certificate for bargaining representatives, 9 June 1944.

24. General Minutes, Box 1, File 3: list of executive and councillors, 1949.

25. Councillors were designated so as to ensure wide representation of members. So, for example, one councillor represented the first floor, home office; another the gas division. By the early 1950s some positions were further identified by gender: for example, women in general sales on the main, first, and second floors of home office; or men of the seventh, eighth, or ninth floors of home office. See ibid.; also Box 1, File 4: list of executive and councillors, 1957.

26. The number of councillors specified by gender dropped from 18 (nine men and nine women) in 1957 to eight (four men and four women) in 1958, to six (three men and three women) in 1967, and to none in 1975. See ibid., File 5, File 6: list of executive and councillors, 1957, 1958, and 1975.

27. Ibid., File 3B: Minutes, 11 Oct. 1949.

28. The gender order did not only apply to jobs, but also to use of the union's club room. In September 1948 the union sent the following notice to female union councillors: 'The Business committee has decided to extend an invitation to the lady members to have the opportunity of enjoying lunches at the social club. . . . The girls can be served meals with a minimum of confusion at the following times: 11.30 and before noon and between 1 and 2 p.m. Could you stress as well as point out to the girls not to infringe on the men in the Billiard Room or in the Lounge.' Bargaining Files, Box 24, File 18: memo from union president to female councillors, 27 Sept. 1948.

29. One former union activist remembered the first hiring of workers of colour in the late 1950s when the company 'started bringing minorities in'. Although the racialized division of labour began to give way slightly in some areas of the company during the 1950s, it did not change so quickly in the office, perhaps, he suggests, because people of colour 'probably didn't have the education to go into the office'. Interview 1B.

30. Bargaining Files, Box 24, File 31: negotiation proposal, 12 Oct. 1945: 3.

31. Ibid., company response to union proposal, 9 Nov. 1945.

32. Ibid., File 19: executive council minutes, 8 July 1947; File 20: letter from management to union, 29 Jan. 1947.

33. *Census of Canada*, 1961, vol. 3, 17–5, 17–6, 17–19, 17–20.

34. Bargaining File, Box 24, File 31: letter from company to union, 9 Nov. 1945, 10–11.

35. Company job evaluation manuals.

36. For a detailed assessment of gender bias in job evaluation schemes, many of which are still based on a point factor system, see Fudge and McDermott, eds, *Just Wages*; Debra Lewis, *Just Give Us the Money* (Vancouver, 1988).

37. Bargaining Files, Box 24, File 20: internal union memo, 13 May 1946; Executive Minutes, Box 1, File 3: Minutes, 14 May, 11 June 1946.

38. Collective Agreement, 1946, 4.

39. Executive Minutes, Box 1, File 3: Minutes, 30 Sept. 1947.

40. Bargaining Files, Box 21, File 8: letter to management, 7 Nov. 1947.

41. Ibid., Box 24, File 19: summary of union proposals and revisions of the collective agreement, 7 Jan. 1948, 2.

42. Ibid., File 15: memo from management to union on employment policy, 5 Feb. 1948.

43. Ibid., File 19: summary of proposals for revision of the collective agreement, 7 Jan. 1948, 2.

44. Ibid.

45. The OEA's role in shaping job evaluation supports feminist arguments that 'skill' is socially constructed, and men's work is often defined as more skilled than women's because men have greater political resources to press their demands to be recognized as skilled. See Gaskell, 'Conceptions of Skill and the Work of Women'; Jenson, 'The Talents of Women, the Skills of Men'; Fudge and McDermott, eds, *Just Wages*; Cockburn, *Brothers*; Cockburn, *Machinery of Dominance*.

46. Collective Agreement, 1949, 7.

47. See Josie Bannerman, Kathy Chopik, and Ann Zurbrigg, 'Cheap at Half the Price: The History of the Fight for Equal Pay in B.C.', in Barbara Latham and Roberta Pazdro, eds, *Not Just Pin Money* (Victoria, 1984).

48. Collective Agreement, 1953, 7–8; emphasis added.

49. Ibid.

50. Bargaining Files, Box 21, File 7: Salary Scales, 1 Nov. 1949.

51. Ibid., Box 24, File 19: summary of union proposals and revisions of the collective agreement, 7 Jan. 1948, 2.

52. Ibid., File 20: internal union memo, 13 May 1946; Executive Minutes, Box 1, File 3: Minutes, 14 May, 11 June 1946.

53. Ibid., File 19: Minutes, 13 Aug., 30 Sept. 1947.
54. In the union movement generally, demands for equal pay for women surfaced during both World War I and World War II but then subsided
quickly. In the context of war mobilization equal pay was most often
advocated as insurance that wages would not decline while women performed traditionally male jobs. See, for example, Pierson, *'They're Still
Women After All'*; Bannerman, Chopik, and Zurbigg, 'Cheap at Half the
Price'. On the other hand, Ruth Milkman found that the gender composition of the union affected equal pay strategies. During World War II the
UE (electrical workers), a union with a large female membership,
advanced an early demand for equal pay for equal value. See Milkman,
Gender at Work.
55. General Minutes, Box 1, File 3: 26 Oct. 1949.
56. Interviews 1A, 1B, 1C, and 1D.
57. Reading the union records makes it clear that, prior to the 1980s, at any
given time a handful of men were the key players in the union. This
impression is also substantiated in interviews with union activists. Thus,
while women were present on Council, they played a marginal role in
directing union affairs. Other research points to a number of reasons why
women have tended to find it difficult to be union activists, including a
male-dominated union culture, greater domestic responsibilities, such as
child care, and, for most of these women in the 1940s and 1950s, the
short-term nature of their paid careers, which were usually interrupted by
marriage and motherhood. See Linda Briskin and Linda Yanz, eds, *Union
Sisters: Women in the Labour Movement* (Toronto, 1983); Briskin and
McDermott, eds, *Women Challenging Unions*.
58. This view tends to be substantiated by some women who started with the
company in the early 1960s when the explicit female differential was still
in place (interviews 2, 3, 18, and 19). For these women, the wage gap
was not something they thought much about since lower pay for women
was a common feature of the labour market.
59. Bargaining Files, Box 20, File 13: company response to union proposals,
Nov. 1959. Some variation of these arguments was provided by the
company each time a new collective agreement was negotiated.
60. Ibid., Box 21, File 2: Minutes, 21 Jan. 1958.
61. One former union activist (interview 1B) remembers thinking that, as the
only large clerical union in the province until the mid-1960s, every time
they went into negotiations they were, in a sense, negotiating on behalf of
all office workers to try to raise the community standard.
62. Bargaining Files, Box 24, File 19: Minutes, 9 Dec. 1947.
63. Ibid., Box 21, File 2: bargaining proposals, Jan. 1958.
64. Ibid., File 4: proposals for negotiations, 1957.

65. These proposals were made at various times between 1953 and 1965 in an effort to get some movement on this issue.
66. Bargaining Files, Box 21, File 1: Jan. 1958.
67. Ibid., Box 20, File 12: 'Equal Pay for Equal Work', May 1961, 14–15.
68. Ibid., File 5: Minutes, 8 Feb. 1963.
69. Ibid., File 7: Minutes, 20 Feb. 1962.
70. Ibid., minutes of negotiating committee, 19 Dec. 1961; Minutes, Feb. 1962.
71. Ibid., File 5: letter from member to union, 23 Aug. 1962.
72. Ibid., Minutes, 8, 21 Feb. 1963; Collective Agreement, 1963.
73. Bargaining Files, Box 20, File 2: employee distribution charts, 18 Jan. 1965, Collective Agreement, 1965.
74. Bargaining Files, Box 20, File 1, Box 19, Files 12, 13; Status of Women File, Box 14, File 4: 'Brief on the Status of Women Employed as Office Workers', 21 Mar. 1968; Collective Agreement, 1967.
75. Correspondence Files 1962–73, Box 6, File 15: letter from woman councillor to union president, 4 Dec. 1967.
76. Collective Agreement, 1967–9, 7.
77. In the 1969 collective agreement, for example, the maximum salary for a Group 4 office job was $514. In comparison, Group 4 non-office jobs had a maximum salary of $552. Collective Agreement, 1969, pay scales.
78. Executive Council Minutes, Box 2, File 9: charts of salary scales and increases, 30 Sept. 1969; Bargaining File 790378A: letters from union president to company president, 2, 9 Dec. 1969; Collective Agreements, 1967, 1969.
79. Unfortunately, the main bargaining files for 1969 are missing; information about negotiations contained in the minutes of Executive Council are less detailed than those in the bargaining files. Moreover, none of those interviewed were able to recall more details of these events. Therefore, a more detailed rationale for union acceptance of this contract is unknown, but agreement was reached without job action, though after a strike vote, and without recourse to conciliation or arbitration.
80. Bargaining Files, Box 21, File 5: notes on salary comparisons, 1955; emphasis added.
81. Ibid., File 6: narrative outline of reasoning behind 20 per cent wage demand, 1953, 1; emphasis added.
82. Ibid., 4.
83. Ibid., 2.
84. Ibid., Box 20, File 11, wage brief for Conciliation Board, Jan. 1960.
85. Ibid., Box 19, File 12: quote from union brief to Conciliation Board, cited in the company's rebuttal to Conciliation Board, Sept. 1967, 8.
86. Ibid., company's rebuttal to Conciliation Board, Sept. 1967.

87. There were also a handful of women in non-office jobs, all of whom worked in the cafeteria. However, the wages of these women were lower rather than higher than comparable female clerical workers. See, for example, ibid., Box 20, File 1: employee distribution and salary scales, 12 Dec. 1966.
88. Ibid., Box 21, File 6: narrative outline of reasoning behind 20 per cent wage demand, 1953, 3.
89. If we add 70 per cent to the male Group 1 rate, for example, in 1953 the utility man made more money than 93 per cent of female union members and about the same as men in Group 4. For 1953 salaries, see ibid., salary scales, 1 Nov. 1953.
90. *Census of Canada*, 1961, vol. 3, 17–5, 17–6, 17–19, 17–20.
91. See Creese, 'Exclusion or Solidarity?', 24–51.

Chapter 4 Transforming Clerical Work

1. Interview 17.
2. See Pierre Bourdieu, *Distinction: A Social Critique of the Judgement of Taste* (Cambridge, Mass., 1984), for discussion of habitus and cultural capital. Bourdieu considers habitus in the context of class-based ways of living and knowing and consequent social networks and esteem, but it is also applicable to gendered and racialized relations in contemporary societies.
3. For the culture of engineering, see Hacker, *Pleasure, Power and Technology*; Hacker, *'Doing It the Hard Way'*.
4. These percentages exclude those in non-office jobs. The only women's jobs designated as non-office were in Groups 1 through 4, and almost all of them worked in the cafeteria, making slightly lower wages than their office counterparts. Men's non-office jobs were somewhat more varied, though most were in Group 4. In contrast to women, men in non-office jobs earned higher salaries than their office counterparts. As a total proportion of union members, only 8 per cent of women were in non-office jobs, compared to 23 per cent of men in 1960 (Table 7). These numbers had declined to 3 per cent and 19 per cent respectively by 1966 (Table 8).
5. Average salaries are based on the entire union membership and include those in non-office designations. When non-office jobs are excluded, average monthly salaries remain virtually the same for women ($274.63) and increase marginally for men ($447.13). Bargaining Files, Box 20, File 14: distribution of office employees, Dec. 1960; Collective Agreement, 1960, salary scales in effect 1 Oct. 1960. The gap between full-time earnings of men and women in British Columbia has fluctuated around one-third throughout this century. See Creese, 'The Politics of Dependence', 123–4.

6. Bargaining Files, Box 20, File 14: distribution of office employees, Dec. 1960.

7. General Minutes, Box 14, File 14: Brief on the Status of Women as Office Workers, 21 Mar. 1968, 12.

8. Ibid.; Collective Agreement, 1965–7.

9. General Minutes, Box 14, File 14: Brief on the Status of Women, 9–10.

10. Ibid.

11. Interview 2.

12. For a discussion of the feminine heterosexual behaviour expected of female office workers and the construction of learned skills as innate talents, see Pringle, *Secretaries Talk*; Jane Gaskell, *Gender Matters From School to Work* (Toronto, 1992).

13. For similar processes of equating male work with technical skills and female work with non-technical clerical tasks, as well as the role of men and unions in this process, see Cockburn, *Machinery of Dominance*.

14. Bargaining Files, Box 20, File 12: Equal Pay for Equal Work, joint union-management report on equal pay, May 1961, 12–13.

15. General Minutes, Box 14, File 14: Brief on the Status of Women, 9–10.

16. Interview 2.

17. Interview 8.

18. Interview 3.

19. Interview 16.

20. Excluding the non-office designations. When men in non-office jobs are included, 38 per cent of all men were in Groups 7 and 8 in 1960, and 31 per cent in 1966 (Tables 7 and 8).

21. Interview 8.

22. Interview 13.

23. Interview 16.

24. Interview 6.

25. Interview 10.

26. Interview 14.

27. Interview 11.

28. In these two tables (7 and 9) we are comparing the distribution of numbers of employees in 1960 with job titles in 1967. Unfortunately, the distribution of female employees in 1966 (in Table 8) was not detailed enough for comparison with the job titles in 1967 (Table 9). While 1960 and 1967 are not directly comparable, evidence of the stability of the patterns of job segregation none the less makes this comparison worthwhile.

29. Only 26 men were listed in Groups 3 and 4 in 1960 (Table 7), plus an additional 148 men in non-office jobs. The distribution of employees in the non-office jobs in 1960 was not available. However, as can be seen from Table 10, the majority of men's non-office jobs were in Group 4,

including meter readers, the single largest non-office job for men, and there were no non-office jobs higher than Group 4. I would estimate, then, that there may have been as many as 150 men in Groups 3 and 4 in 1960.

30. General Minutes, Box 14, File 14: Brief on the Status of Women, 7.
31. Interview 21.
32. Interview 8.
33. Interview 17.
34. Interview 3.
35. Interview 14.
36. Interview 3.
37. Ibid.
38. Interview 19.
39. Interview 17.
40. Interview 8.
41. Interview 3.
42. Interview 17.
43. Interview 3.
44. Ibid.
45. Interview 8.
46. Interview 21.
47. Grievance Files, Box 25, File 11: grievance correspondence, June 1951.
48. Ibid., Aug.-Oct. 1951.
49. Ibid., Box 24, File 33: grievance correspondence, Feb. 1949.
50. Industrial/Labour Relations Files, Box 7, File 22: correspondence between labour relations manager and business representative, 11 Feb. 1957.
51. Ibid., business representative's summary of a meeting with the industrial relations manager, 23 May 1957.
52. Ibid., correspondence between labour relations manager and business representative, 11 Feb. 1957.
53. Labour Relations Manager Files, Box 10, File 6: memo from company to union, 6 July 1960
54. Ibid., Final Draft of Seniority Agreement, 11 Oct. 1960.
55. Ibid., memo from company to union, 12 June 1958; memo from union to company, 27 June 1958.
56. Collective Agreement, 1965–7.
57. Maternity Leave Files, Box 10, File 17, 1977–8.
58. Grievance Files, Box 25, File 11: grievance correspondence, Aug.-Oct. 1951.
59. For example, ibid., Dec. 1950.
60. Ibid., Aug.-Sept. 1951.
61. Ibid., May 1954-Sept. 1955.

62. Labour Relations Manager Files, Box 10, File 6: diary of meeting with the labour relations manager, 19 June 1957.

63. Ibid., 28 Oct. 1957.

64. Collective Agreement, 1967–9; Labour Management Files, Box 10, File 4: correspondence between business representative and labour relations manager, 8 Apr. 1968, 1, 8, 21 May 1969.

65. General Minutes, Box 14, File 14: Brief on the Status of Women, 11–12.

66. Some women worked their way up to senior office jobs by taking accounting courses at night school. According to a former manager of the computer systems department, in its early years gender-neutral tests were used to assess computer aptitude and all interested employees were encouraged to take the test. The result was that in the early 1970s this department employed many of the senior women in the office union. However, post-secondary degrees in computer science soon shifted this department towards men. Interview 9.

67. General Minutes, Box 1, File 4: Minutes, 29 Apr., 13 Nov. 1953; Minutes 1955–6; Interviews 1B, 1C, 1D.

68. For example, Labour Management Files, Box 10, File 4: correspondence between the labour relations manager and the president of the union, 15, 16 June 1966.

69. For example, ibid., correspondence between the business representative and the labour relations manager, 21 Jan. 1972; Technologists-in-Training File, Box 14, File 20: correspondence, 1967–76.

70. Technologists-in-Training File, Box 14, File 20: correspondence, 1967–76.

71. General Minutes, Box 14, File 14: Brief on the Status of Women, 11–12.

72. Collective Agreement, 1958–60.

73. General Minutes, Box 14, File 14: Brief on the Status of Women, 11.

74. This is, in fact, the basis for human capital explanations for gender and other differences in the labour market, based on how much investment people choose to make in the development of their human capital. For a critique of this theoretical school, see John Hagan and Fiona Kay, *Gender in Practice* (Toronto, 1995).

75. The New Democratic Party, a social democratic party with close links to organized labour, was elected in British Columbia in 1972, replacing the business-oriented Social Credit Party, which had held power for 20 years.

76. Board of Directors File, Box 4, File 12: union brief to the Advisory Committee to the Minister of Labour, June 1973, 4; emphasis added.

77. For the first time unionization among engineers was possible under the new BC labour code. Engineers were already organized in their own association, the Management and Professional Employees' Society (MAPES), and were divided over the advisability of becoming a legal trade

union, especially since so many were recruited into management. It is highly unlikely that MAPES would ever have sought inclusion in the OTEU. In the end MAPES did not unionize, and it ceased to be a force at BC Hydro in the mid-1980s. Thanks to Don Black for sharing unpublished research on engineers in BC.

78. Board of Directors Files, Box 4, File 12: union brief to the Advisory Committee to the Minister of Labour, June 1973, 6–8.

79. Job Evaluation Files, Box 8, File 14: job evaluation grievances, 1969–72.

80. On this issue, see Cockburn, *Brothers*; Cockburn, *Machinery of Dominance*.

81. Job Evaluation Files, Box 8, File 14: correspondence between business representative and labour relations manager, 3, 24 Mar., 11, 21 Apr., 6, 16, 19 June, 18 Aug. 1972.

82. Interviews 5, 9.

83. Collective Agreement, 1974–6.

84. The OTEU engaged in its first (illegal) walk-out over threatened office reorganization and time management in 1972. The next contract, in 1974, witnessed a 93 per cent strike vote and a strong contract, including the joint job evaluation task force, without the need to withdraw labour. The following contract, in 1976, produced the first strike among office workers. General Minutes, Box 2, File 12: *WOFAC News Digest*, 16 Feb. 1972; Bargaining Files, Box 21, Files 15 and 16: 1974 negotiations; Regional Meeting Files, Box 3, File 8: general minutes of regional meetings, 1976. Also see Chapter 2.

85. At least one manager involved in bargaining, however, referred to this whole set of negotiations as the '74 give-aways'. It was his view that the chairperson of the company, appointed by the social democratic NDP government then in power, was determined to grant the union major concessions. Whether or not this was true, union negotiators do not remember events this way. The 1974 collective agreement was arguably the best agreement the union ever accomplished, with large wage increases, a dental plan, a 35-hour week, and a joint job evaluation plan. Interviews 1, 6, 10; Collective Agreement, 1974–6.

86. Job Evaluation Files, Box 8, File 13: memo from job evaluation manager to staff services manager, 'Job Upgroupings resulting from union agreement', 7 Oct. 1974; Box 9, File 3: letter from union president to job evaluation manager, 6 Jan. 1975.

87. Job Evaluation Task Force Files, Box 9, File 4: letter to union and company presidents, 5 Dec. 1974.

88. Ibid., Minutes of the Steering Committee meeting, 16 Dec. 1974; letter from union president to member, 17 Dec. 1974.

89. Ibid., petition to union president, 26 Feb. 1975.

90. Ibid., letter from union president to member, re petition, 18 Mar. 1975.
91. Ibid.
92. Ibid., letters to union president, 26 Mar., 2 Apr. 1975.
93. Interview 16.
94. Interview 9.
95. Interview 5.
96. When these data were produced by the Job Evaluation Task Force in 1981 there were most likely a few women meter readers, though it is impossible to know how many. A handful of women were crossing into traditional men's jobs, including meter reading, in the late 1970s and early 1980s. As Table 14 shows, 71 women were in non-office jobs in 1981, but nearly one-quarter of these women were temporary employees. Women comprised 17 per cent of all non-office employees in 1981, only 4 per cent of female union members.
97. Job Evaluation Task Force Files, Box 9, File 4: memo from Job Evaluation Task Force, 26 Jan. 1978.
98. Interviews 5, 7, 9.
99. Interview 5.
100. *Report of the Job Evaluation Task Force*, 31 Mar. 1981, Table 3, Summary of Movement by Incumbent.
101. Interview 12.
102. Interviews with members of the Job Evaluation Task Force from both union and management more than a decade after its implementation revealed that some members of the task force still believed it to be a gender-neutral system. Most, however, had developed more sophisticated understandings of job evaluation in the intervening time and expressed considerable insight about the ways in which it continued to undervalue women's work.
103. Interview 10.
104. Interviews 9, 12, 16.
105. Bargaining Files 800378: Minutes, 20 Aug. 1981; Newsletter, 18 Sept. 1981; president's memo to members, 2 Oct. 1981.
106. Ibid., members' petition to the Executive Board, 2 Oct. 1981.
107. Interviews 6, 9.
108. The union ostensibly agreed to abandon the job evaluation system it had helped to create in order to save money. A change in union administration, with the new administration lacking the decade-long history of this project, and union preoccupation with massive corporate downsizing in the mid-1980s no doubt contributed to the decision to accept the shift to job families in 1986.
109. The job families were clerical, computer operations, computer systems, corporate services, customer service, drafting, economic-statistical-

technical studies, equipment operation, financial administration, property management, purchasing, research, survey, technical design, technical inspection, technical maintenance, training and information services, and word processing. Classification system for office union jobs, Feb. 1987.

110. Acker, 'Hierarchies, Jobs, Bodies', 139–58; Acker, 'Gendering Organizational Behavior', 248–60.

111. Interview 24.

112. Interviews 11, 13, 14, 21.

Chapter 5   Can Feminism Be Union Made?

1. Interview 20.

2. Phillips, *Democracy and Difference*, 95.

3. Cockburn, *In the Way of Women*, 10–11.

4. There are, of course, many types of feminism, including liberal feminist traditions that share the individualist orientation and definitions of equality found in liberal theory. Other feminist traditions offer more radical critiques of gender relations and its connection with family and kinship structures (radical feminism), class (socialist feminism), colonialism and race/ethnicity (post-colonial feminism), and sexuality and identity (post-structuralist feminism). For an overview of feminist theories, see Patricia Ticineto Clough, *Feminist Thought* (Oxford, 1994). Feminists politics in Canada has been strongly influenced by feminist traditions critical of liberal feminism; radical and socialist feminist traditions predominated in the 1970s, with post-colonial and post-structuralist critiques prominent during the 1980s and 1990s. For histories of the women's movement in Canada, see Nancy Adamson, Linda Briskin, and Margaret McPhail, *Feminist Organizing for Change: The Contemporary Women's Movement in Canada* (Toronto, 1988); Agnew, *Resisting Discrimination*.

5. General Minutes, Box 14, File 14: Brief on the Status of Women as Office Workers, 21 Mar. 1968.

6. For example, see Briskin and McDermott, eds, *Women Challenging Unions*.

7. Interview 11.

8. For a fuller discussion of gendered strategies in the labour movement, see Sugiman, ' "That Wall's Comin' Down" ', 1–27; and Sugiman, *Labour's Dilemma*.

9. Armstrong and Armstrong, *The Double Ghetto*, 16.

10. Statistics Canada, *Women in Canada: A Statistical Report*, 71.

11. Ibid., 72.
12. Ibid., 73, 83, 95. Three-quarters of women in the Canadian labour force work full time. Moreover, the increasing number of women who are single parents increases the trend towards the double day for women. However, a 1992 Statistics Canada survey shows that this trend also remains strong among those in two-parent, two-income households: for those with children under five, women performed 5.3 hours per day of domestic labour, while men performed 3.4 hours; for those with children aged five and over, women performed 4.4 hours per day of domestic work, while men performed 2.8 hours. Domestic work includes house-keeping, child care, shopping, and personal care, and was performed in addition to the paid work of each partner.
13. Armstrong and Armstrong, *The Double Ghetto*, 34–6.
14. Executive Council Files, Box 1, File 4: Executive Council list, 1957–8; Box 1, File 5: Executive Council list, 1958–9; Box 2, File 3: Executive Council list, 1967; Box 5, File 6: Executive Council list, Sept. 1976.
15. There were 1,879 members of the OTEU at BC Hydro in 1966 (see Table 8). In the 1960s new bargaining units of Local 378 were organized at Caseco, CBA Engineering, Inland Natural Gas, Dominion Glass, Federal Pacific Electric, and Hertz and Avis Rent-a-Car. All of the new units were much smaller than that at BC Hydro. In 1974 the Insurance Corporation of British Columbia joined the OTEU, adding 1,800 new members at one time, and from then on the local was shaped by two large bargaining units. See Chapter 2 and Gillian Creese, 'The OPEIU at B.C. Hydro: The First Half Century, 1944–1994', 1996, 43–57 (unpublished manuscript written for the OPEIU).
16. Union newsletter (*Article 378*), 1, 1 (Aug. 1977).
17. Interview 11.
18. Complaints File, Box 4, File 22: letter from member to union, 16 Sept. 1977; notation from business representative dated 19 Sept. 1977.
19. Interview 11.
20. There were a series of grievances from female clerical workers on con-struction sites in the 1970s, for example. These women were denied liv-ing-out allowances, a separate recreation hall, and proper security for their rooms. The union pursued all of these grievances to gain parity with men on the sites. Columbia Hydro Correspondence Files, Box 5, Files 15 and 16, 1975–7.
21. Union Correspondence Files, Box 6, File 15: conference call from the BC Federation of Labour, 30 June 1972.
22. Ibid., List of union committees, 21 Apr. 1972; letter from president to Women's Committee, 24 June 1972.
23. Ibid., File 14: letter from member to Executive Board, 4 Apr. 1976.

24. Industrial/Labour Relations Files, Box 10, File 8: letter from company CEO to union president, 12 July 1977.
25. Ibid., letter from union president to company CEO, 4 Aug. 1977.
26. Women's Committee Files: Women's Committee Policy Paper, 1980, 2.
27. Ibid., Minutes, 30 Aug. 1978; membership list, 27 Nov. 1979.
28. The OTEU grew dramatically in the 1970s but BC Hydro remained at the centre of the union and continued to dominate leadership positions. Though this changed somewhat by the 1990s (such that the Insurance Corporation of British Columbia now vies for leadership) it remains the case, at the time of writing in 1998, that there has never been a president from outside BC Hydro.
29. By the early 1980s the mailing lists were quite long. For example, there were 138 names on the mailing list in December 1981 and 174 in February 1984. Women's Committee Files: Women's Committee lists, 4 Dec. 1981, 9 Feb. 1984.
30. Ibid., Minutes, 16 Oct. 1980; Women's Committee Policy Paper, 1980.
31. Ibid., Minutes, 28 Feb., 6 Sept., 23 Oct. 1979.
32. Interview 16a.
33. Some of these women were also very innovative during the election, introducing real campaigns with brochures distributed to members. Interviews 16a, 16b.
34. Executive Board Files: Minutes, 14 Aug. 1979, 9 Sept. 1982.
35. Union newsletter, Executive Board list, June 1985.
36. Women's Committee Files: Minutes, 6 Sept. 1979.
37. Ibid., Women's Committee Review, Nov. 1983, 4; Bargaining Files, Minutes, 1981.
38. Interview 15.
39. Interview 16a.
40. Interview 20.
41. Interview 15.
42. Interview 16a.
43. Interview 20.
44. Women's Committee Files: Minutes, 8 Jan. 1981.
45. Interview 15.
46. Interview 16a.
47. Ibid.
48. Interview 20.
49. Women's Committee Files: Minutes, 11 Apr., 9 May 1983.
50. Ibid., 30 Apr. 1981; Policy Paper on Personal and Sexual Harassment, 1981; Women's Committee Review, Nov. 1983, 5.
51. Interview 22.
52. Women's Committee Files: Women's Committee Review, Nov. 1983, 5; Minutes, 8 Nov. 1982, 13 June 1983, 9 Jan., 13 Feb. 1984.

53. Ibid., Minutes, 13 Feb. 1984. The surveys were never returned to the Women's Committee. When the union election installed a new president a few months later, the former president reported that the survey had been thrown away. Minutes, 11 June 1984.

54. Interview 16b.

55. In all, 1,249 women replied to the survey, 37 per cent of all women in the local; of these, 628 women were employed at BC Hydro (a 35 per cent response rate). Women's Committee Files: Summary of Women Members Survey, 1980.

56. Ibid.

57. Ibid.

58. Ibid.

59. The meeting following the distribution of the questionnaire saw six men in attendance, the president plus five business representatives, there to reprimand the Women's Committee. Women's Committee Files: Minutes, 13 May 1980; Women's Committee Review, 1983, 3.

60. This was the first competitive election the OTEU had ever experienced. When the incumbent president was challenged (something unheard of in the past) he withdrew from the race. Another business representative and close associate stood in his stead but was defeated.

61. In November 1983, as part of Operation Solidarity protests against the provincial government in British Columbia, office and electrical workers struck BC Hydro. The strike lasted three months, until February 1984, and ended with union members accepting concessions for the first time in over 20 years (see Chapter 6). Needless to say, it was a very unpopular strike, and member dissatisfaction with the existing executive was a key factor in the election of the first woman president. Bargaining Files: Minutes, 1983–4; Collective Agreement, 1983; Interviews 11, 15, 16a, 16b, 20, 23, 25.

62. Interview 17.

63. Interview 21.

64. Women's Committee Files: mailing and membership lists, 1978–87.

65. In the 1987 election the incumbent president was unopposed.

66. For a fuller discussion of these events, see Creese, 'Gender Equity or Masculine Privilege?', 143–66.

67. In fact, the extent of the Women's Committee's activities during this period is still not fully appreciated by many union activists. Thus, there is a tendency to understate its role in mobilizing women activists in the 1980s. For example, interviews 23, 24, 25.

68. Interviews 16a, 16b.

69. Interview 16b.

70. In the mid-1980s BC Hydro laid off one-third of its entire labour force, including over 1,000 members of the OTEU. These lay-offs began months

after the 1984 elections and resulted in prioritizing language on lay-offs, bumping and recall, job security, and the like, further sidelining many women's issues. These events are discussed in Chapter 6. Also see Creese, 'Gender Equity or Masculine Privilege?'

71. The committee was unable to publish the results of the sexual harassment questionnaire confiscated by the previous president because this material had been destroyed. Women's Committee Files: Minutes, 11 June, 14 Nov. 1984.

72. Ibid., 11 Mar., 15 Apr., 19 Aug. 1985.

73. The union negotiating team believed that management had agreed to a letter of understanding and printed the 1986 collective agreement as such. Management disagreed that this had been the intention, and the letter of understanding on sexual harassment disappeared from the next contract (signed in 1989). It was renegotiated in 1991. Bargaining Files: letters from company to union, 29 Oct., 20 Nov. 1986; letter from union to company, 17 Nov. 1986; Collective Agreements, 1986, 1989, 1991.

74. Bargaining Files: Minutes, 7 Nov. 1985.

75. Women's Committee Files: Minutes, 6 Apr. 1987.

76. Ibid., 2 Feb., 6 Apr., 4 May, 10 Aug., 26 Oct. 1987, 13 Apr., 11 May, 16 Nov. 1989.

77. Ibid.; Executive Board Files: Minutes, 11 Apr. 1988.

78. Union newsletter, June-July 1989, 10.

79. Bargaining Files, 1989.

80. When two members share a job only one of those members has any claim to a regular full-time job at the company. Some feminist activists have suggested that failure of the Executive Board to support job-sharing in principle has resulted in discouraging its use and no attempt to improve this contract language. Interviews 11, 24, 28.

81. Women's Committee Files, 1990–4; interviews 15, 22.

82. Interviews 22, 27.

83. Bargaining Files, 1991; Collective Agreement, 1991.

84. Interview 22.

85. No women of colour could be identified among members of the Women's Committee, though there may be some of which I remain unaware.

Chapter 6 Restructuring, Resistance, and the Politics of Equity

1. Interview 3.

2. The Employment Equity Act was passed by the federal government in 1986. It applies to employers with over 100 employees included under federal labour jurisdiction (including federal civil servants, transportation,

communications, fisheries, etc.) and companies that serve as federal contractors. Targets to improve employment opportunities for the four designated groups are voluntary, requiring only that employers file an annual report. It should be noted that most workers are covered under provincial labour legislation, and are not covered by the Employment Equity Act. There is no similar legislation in British Columbia or in most provincial jurisdictions. See Canadian Advisory Council on the Status of Women, *Re-evaluating Employment Equity: A Brief to the Special House of Commons Committee on the Review of the Employment Act*, publication number 92–E–184 (Ottawa, 1992).

3. In 1991, 9 per cent of the population of BC were of visible minority background; in greater Vancouver the figure was 24 per cent. The Aboriginal population was 5 per cent in the province and just under 3 per cent in Vancouver. *Census of Canada*, 1991; Statistics Canada, *Women in Canada*, 133–5, 148.

4. Stan Persky and Lanny Beckman, 'Downsizing the Unemployment Problem', in Warren Magnusson et al., eds, *The New Reality: The Politics of Restraint in British Columbia*, (Vancouver, 1984), 192–208.

5. Magnusson et al., eds, *The New Reality*; Bryan Palmer, *Solidarity: The Rise and Fall of an Opposition in British Columbia* (Vancouver, 1987); Panitch and Swartz, *The Assault on Trade Union Freedoms*, 35–9.

6. Interview 5.

7. Interview 24.

8. Union newsletters: *Article 378*, 1978–82; *Steward 378*, 1982, 10; *Vancouver Sun*, 14 Sept. 1982, B6; ibid., 8 June 1983, F14; Bargaining Files, 1983–4: memo from union to company, 10 Dec. 1982; company news release, 17 Feb. 1983.

9. See Palmer, *Solidarity*.

10. Some of those involved in negotiations in 1983–4 suggest they were pressured to strike by Operation Solidarity and by the IBEW, which had reached a contract stalemate over contracting out. In contrast, negotiations with the OTEU had not broken down. Once the strike began, however, the company became more intransigent. Interviews 11, 23, 25.

11. Bargaining Files, 1983–4, 3 Feb. 1984.

12. Executive Board Minutes: 8 Aug. 1984; *Vancouver Sun*, 18 Jan. 1985, C5; 1 March 1985, C6; June 26, 1985, A9; 19 Oct. 1985, A1; 11 Jan. 1986, D7.

13. *Vancouver Sun*, 20 Sept. 1984, A5; 2 Oct. 1984, A3; interviews 6, 12, 23, 25.

14. Privatization began in 1987 under the auspices of the same neo-conservative provincial government (under the Social Credit Party) that had initiated restraint legislation sparking the Solidarity protests. The gas division was the first to be privatized, followed by the rail division,

research and development, computing, and management information systems. Those divisions for which buyers could not be found immediately were made wholly owned subsidiaries of BC Hydro. *Vancouver Sun*, 31 Aug. 1987, B6; 12 Sept. 1987, E1; 12 Oct. 1987, E12; 24 Mar. 1988, B2; 9 June 1988, A1; Bargaining Files, 1990–2: union 'Report to the Minister of Labour', 9 Dec. 1991, 3.

15. The reduction to a 35-hour workweek was won in 1974 in the form of 17 additional days off, called reduced workweek leave. When added to statutory holidays, union members worked nine 7.5-hour days every two-week period, or the 'nine-day fortnight'. In 1983 the company for the first time tried to take away this popular union provision; thereafter it would be a recurring bargaining demand.

16. Collective Agreement, 1983–6; Bargaining Files, 1982–4.

17. Bargaining Files, 1983–4: Minutes of ratification meeting, 3 Feb. 1984.

18. These jobs included: industrial liaison committee, electrical lighting technician, industrial advisory technician, energy plan clerk, agricultural clerk, energy use specialist, divisional advisory representative, service technician, service planner, customer representative, customer advisory representative. Bargaining Files, 1985–6: Minutes, 21 May 1986, company bargaining proposals.

19. The union estimated a saving of about $20,000 a year, its cost for joint management of the appeals process, thus eliminating the need for the small monthly surcharge on members. Some union activists were opposed to this decision, arguing that the union was giving back to management complete control over job evaluation—and after such a long struggle to win union input. Bargaining Files, 1985–6; interviews 16a, 16b, 24, 25.

20. Bargaining Files, 1987–9.

21. This job action was characterized as a 'user-friendly strike', with selective action to impair the company's operations without a full-out strike inconveniencing hydro consumers. For example, accounts payable was shut down and generators used to produce power for American customers were shut down. Bargaining Files, 1988–9: clipping, *Pacific Tribune*, 28 Aug. 1989.

22. Collective Agreement, 1989–91.

23. Bargaining Files, 1990–2: Negotiation minutes and management proposal, 11 Mar. 1991.

24. Ibid., Understanding the New Collective Agreement, 18 Feb. 1992.

25. In April 1996 the existing contract was essentially rolled over for one year, prior to the expiration of the existing contract. It included a 0.8 per cent compensation increase, to be determined later whether it should be applied as wages or benefits, and 'a form of cross-divisional bumping'

rights in response to more lay-offs the previous year. Union newsletter, Apr.-May 1996, 1.

26. Bargaining Files, 1993–4: Management Agenda, Sept. 1993; *Bargaining Update* (union newsletter), 28 Sept. 1993.

27. The BC government never did legislate in the area of employment equity (at least not as of the time of writing in 1998), although it had been an election promise of the New Democratic Party government.

28. Bargaining Files, 1993–4, 'Analysis of Proposed Contract "Offer of Settlement' "; union *Bulletin*, 17 Oct. 1994.

29. Interview 22.

30. Interview 23.

31. Interview 4.

32. Interviews 22, 23, 24.

33. Women in non-office jobs decreased from 4 to 2 per cent.

34. The rest of the male members (18 per cent in 1981 and 13 per cent in 1991) were in non-office jobs generally spanning salary equivalents from Groups 4 through 7.

35. The median job group for women was Group 5, with a maximum salary of $2,691 per month; for men the median job group was Group 8, with a maximum monthly salary of $3,491. Employee counts, 10 July 1991 (supplied by BC Hydro); Collective Agreement 1991–3.

36. For example, one former drafter (Group 6) accepted a Group 3 clerical position in spite of a complete lack of clerical experience in order to hang onto anything in the company. Ten years later she was still in a clerical position, Group 4. She had moved to a clerical job in engineering and, after several years of taking recommended refresher courses for computer drafting, had just completed a brief stint as a summer replacement drafter. At the time of the interview she was again performing her regular position as a clerical Group 4. In 1997 she finally got a regular position as a drafter.

37. Since neither the union nor the company collected data by ethnicity/race, observations about the differential impacts on women of colour are drawn from general hiring patterns, with women of colour concentrated among the most recent employees.

38. Interview 22.

39. Employee counts, 10 July 1991 and 31 Mar. 1981. Supplied by BC Hydro.

40. Interview 22.

41. Union newsletter, *Steward 378*, 1982, 10–11; Collective Agreement, 1981–3.

42. Bargaining Files, 1983–4: Minutes of ratification meeting, 3 Feb. 1984.

43. Ibid., 1985–6, 'Union Agenda 1986': 10 June 1986, article 8.

44. Collective Agreement, 1986–9.
45. Bargaining Files, 1987–9.
46. Ibid., 1990–2: 'Report to the Minister of Labour', 9 Dec. 1991, 4; Collective Agreement, 1989–91; emphasis added.
47. Interviews 3, 11, 22.
48. Bargaining Files, 1990–2: bargaining proposals, 6 Mar. 1991.
49. In 1991 the company reported that two-thirds of its employees were over the age of 40. *Building Team 2000: Human Resources Strategy for the 90s*, Company publication, Mar. 1991, 10.
50. Bargaining Files, 1990–2: union *Bulletin*, 23 May 1991.
51. Ibid., 17 Dec. 1991; Collective Agreement, 1991–3, 119.
52. Collective Agreement, 1991–3, 52.
53. Bargaining Files, 1990–2: union *Bulletin*, 20 Aug. 1990; union newsletter, Sept.-Oct. 1990, 10.
54. Bargaining Files, 1990–2: 'Understanding the New Collective Agreement', 18 Feb. 1992, 1; Collective Agreement: 7.
55. Interview 11.
56. Bargaining Files, 1993–4.
57. Union newsletter, Nov.-Dec. 1994, 9.
58. *Building Team 2000*.
59. 'Employment Equity: Positioning for Success', company memo, 31 Mar. 1991, 1.
60. *Building Team 2000*, 12.
61. *1990 Annual Report*, 31 Mar. 1990, 44. There were 4,904 regular and 857 temporary employees of BC Hydro in 1990, following the sale of its rail and gas divisions (with a loss of 1,000 employees) and the creation of six subsidiaries (with several hundred additional employees). See Table 1 for total employees in 1991.
62. The failure to note a total of Aboriginal employees is conspicuous, suggesting that there were indeed no Aboriginal employees prior to these six 'native hires' and that the latter were probably only temporary placements. 'Employment Equity: Positioning for Success', 3.
63. Ibid.
64. Interview 5.
65. 'Employment Equity: Positioning for Success', 2.
66. Interview 27.
67. Several people mentioned this woman as the only example they had known of a union member with a disability. These union activists all believed that adequate support for her to perform her job was not forthcoming, resulting in lay-off at the end of the year. Interviews 11, 16b, 24, 27.
68. Interview 17.

69. Interview 21.
70. Ibid.
71. Interview 3.
72. Interview 4.
73. *Building Team 2000*, 16.
74. Interview 8.
75. Interview 9.
76. Interview 8.
77. Interview 21.
78. Interview 23.
79. Interview 3.
80. Interview 2.
81. Ibid.
82. Interview 17.
83. Interview 2.
84. Interview 24.
85. Union newspaper, *OTEU News*, Apr.-May 1994, 1. This article focused on concerns about employment equity at the local's other large unit, the Insurance Corporation of British Columbia. The issues raised and the language used are the same as those expressed during bargaining at BC Hydro.
86. Ibid., 2.
87. Ibid., 3.
88. Ibid., Oct.-Nov. 1993, 4
89. Bargaining Files, 1993–4: letter from business representative to employment equity co-ordinator, 18 June 1993.
90. Ibid., Management Agenda, 1993, 2.
91. Ibid., Bargaining Update, 28 Sept. 1993.
92. Ibid., *Collective Bargaining News* 1, 2 (10 Aug. 1994), memo from the President, 5.
93. Ibid., Collective Bargaining Update, 22 July 1994, memo regarding mediation impasse.
94. Although the joint union-management job evaluation system was abandoned in favour of streamlined 'job families' that ended union involvement in 1986, the joint job evaluation plan was the foundation for the job families plan. Interview 12.
95. Bargaining Files, 1990–2; interviews 17, 22.
96. Interview 28.
97. The company agreed to a joint subcommittee to investigate pay equity. However, it met rarely and did not seem to accomplish anything. Collective Agreement, 1991–3; Bargaining Files, 1993–4: 'What's Missing in Company Pay Equity Proposal?', 1; interview 28.
98. Interviews 27, 28.

99. Bargaining Files, 1992–4; interview 28.
100. Interview 12.
101. Bargaining Files, 1993–4: union *Bulletin*: 'Summary of Key Collective Bargaining Issues', 17 Jan. 1994.
102. Bargaining Files, 1993–4: 'Report on Bargaining 93', June 1993, 3.
103. Interview 25.
104. Bargaining Files, 1993–4: 'Report on Bargaining 93', 3.
105. Interview 28.
106. For feminist critiques of job evaluation, see Joan Acker, *Doing Comparable Worth: Gender, Class and Pay Equity* (Philadelphia, 1990); Carl Cuneo, *Pay Equity: The Labour-Feminist Challenge* (Toronto, 1990); Margaret Hallock, *Unions and the Gender Wage Gap: An Analysis of Pay Equity and Other Strategies*, Labor Education Research Center, University of Oregon, Working Paper No. 8, Feb. 1991.
107. Interview 28.
108. Union newspaper, *OTEU News*, Feb.-Mar. 1993, 10.
109. *Collective Bargaining News* 1, 2 (10 Aug. 1994): 3.
110. Bargaining Files, 1993–4; interviews 17, 22, 23, 24, 28.
111. Interview 22.
112. Interview 25.
113. Interview 26.
114. Four hundred nine women were in Groups 2 to 4 (92 per cent in Group 4); 57 men were in Groups 3 and 4. Bargaining Files, 1993–4: 'Report on Bargaining 93', 2–3.
115. Interview 22.
116. Bargaining Files, 1993–4: letter from female member to negotiating committee, 29 Apr. 1993. Dozens of such letters, from both men and women, opposed the union's pay equity initiative on similar grounds.
117. Interview 23.
118. Interview 26.
119. Interview 24.
120. Interview 22.
121. Interview 23.
122. Interview 17.
123. Bargaining Files, 1993–4: letter from female member to negotiating committee, 29 Apr. 1993.
124. Ibid., letter from member to business representative, 15 Apr. 1993.
125. Ibid., company memo to employees, 31 Aug. 1994; 'Analysis of Company Proposed Contract "Offer of Settlement"', union memo, 28 Sept. 1994.
126. Interview 28.
127. Interviews 17, 27, 28.

128. Interview 17.
129. Interview 23.
130. Bargaining Files, 1993–4: letter from union member to negotiating committee, 29 Apr. 1993.
131. Union newspaper, *OTEU News*, Apr.-May 1996, 4.
132. See Chapter 1 for a discussion of the concept of unearned advantages and the social construction of 'Whiteness' as a form of social power and entitlement in North America. See also McIntosh, 'White Privilege and Male Privilege', 76–7; Frankenberg, *White Women, Race Matters*; Fine, Weis, Powell, and Wong, eds, *Off White*.

Chapter 7 Learning from the Past

1. Anne Forrest, 'A View from Outside the Whale: The Treatment of Women and Unions in Industrial Relations', in Briskin and McDermott, eds, *Women Challenging Unions*, 325.
2. See Linda Briskin and Patricia McDermott, 'The Feminist Challenge to the Unions', in Briskin and McDermott, eds, *Women Challenging Unions*, 3–19; Carl Cuneo, 'Trade Union Leadership: Sexism and Affirmative Action', ibid., 109–36; Jane Stinson and Penni Richmond, 'Women Working for Unions: Female Staff and the Politics of Transformation', ibid., 137–56; Rosemary Warskett, 'Can a Disappearing Pie Be Shared Equally?: Unions, Women and Wage "Fairness"', ibid., 249–65; Cunnison and Stageman, *Feminizing the Unions*.
3. Cunnison and Stageman, *Feminizing the Unions*, 219, make a similar point, arguing that the 'culture of femininity directs women both forward and backward' at the same time.
4. See also Briskin and McDermott, eds, *Women Challenging Unions*; Cunnison and Stageman, *Feminizing the Unions*.
5. Cunnison and Stageman, *Feminizing the Unions*, 43–5; Pradeep Kumar and Lynn Acri, 'Union's Collective Bargaining Agenda on Women's Issues', *Industrial Relations* 47, 4 (1992): 623–53; Pradeep Kumar, 'Collective Bargaining and Women's Workplace Concerns', in Briskin and McDermott, eds, *Women Challenging Unions*, 207–30.
6. That definitions of skill and the value of work are tied to whether men or women perform the work is well documented in the literature on pay equity. See, for example, Acker, *Doing Comparable Worth*; Cuneo, *Pay Equity*; Fudge and McDermott, eds, *Just Wages*.
7. Hallock, *Unions and the Gender Wage Gap*, 14–15, points out that reliance on job evaluation in pay equity initiatives results in a 'technical reform' that enhances management control over personnel issues.
8. Interview 28.

9. Wage increases were as follows: 1981–3, 15 per cent (applied to a realigned pay grid that produced higher increases in Groups 1–4) and 13 per cent; 1983–6, 4.5 per cent; 1986–9, 1 per cent, 1 per cent, and 1 per cent; 1989–91, 4 per cent, 2 per cent, and 6 per cent; 1991–3, 6 per cent and 5 per cent; and 1993–6, 2 per cent, 0, and 2 per cent. See Collective Agreements.

10. Rosemary Warskett has argued that simultaneously negotiating percentage wage increases and demands for pay equity is common in public-sector unions in Canada. See Warskett, 'Can a Disappearing Pie Be Shared Equally?', 255.

11. For example, see Luxton and Corman, 'Getting to Work', 149–85.

12. See also Hallock, *Unions and the Gender Wage Gap*; Warskett, 'Can a Disappearing Pie Be Shared Equally?'; Judy Fudge, 'The Gendered Dimension of Labour Law: Why Women Need Inclusive Unionism and Broader-Based Bargaining', and Julie White, 'Patterns of Unionization', both in Briskin and McDermott, eds, *Women Challenging Unions*, 231–48, 191–206.

13. For example, see Dulude, 'Seniority and Employment Equity for Women'; Pateman, *The Disorder of Women*; Phillips, *Democracy and Difference*.

14. Cockburn, *In the Way of Women*, 110.

15. Phillips, *Democracy and Difference*, 161.

16. In 1994, 45 per cent of the Canadian labour force was female. In 1992, 41 per cent of all union members were women. Among employed men, 38 per cent were unionized compared to 31 per cent of employed women. Statistics Canada, *Women in Canada: A Statistical Report*, 64, 68.

17. Briskin and McDermott, 'The Feminist Challenge'; White, 'Patterns of Unionization'.

18. White, *Sisters and Solidarity*, 204.

19. Cuneo, 'Trade Union Leadership', 134.

20. Briskin and McDermott, 'The Feminist Challenge', 6.

21. There have been a few other members of colour on the larger Executive Council, but the election of the secretary-treasurer in 1996 was the first person of colour elected to the 12-member Executive Board. In addition, I am only aware of one previous business representative who was a man of colour. I do not know whether there have been any gay or lesbian activists on Council or Executive Board. Union memo: '1996 Tri-ennial Election Results', 3 May 1996.

22. Interview 11.

23. Interview 17.

24. Stinson and Richmond, 'Women Working for Unions', 146.

25. Cunnison and Stageman, *Feminizing the Unions*, 14.

26. Ibid., 229.
27. Interviews 11, 16b, 22.
28. Cuneo, 'Trade Union Leadership'.
29. Interviews 11, 15, 16a, 16b, 21.
30. Stinson and Richmond, 'Women Working for Unions'; Cunnison and Stageman, *Feminizing the Unions*; Edmond Henry and John Kelly, 'Do Female Representatives Make a Difference? Women Full-Time Officials and Trade Union Work', *Work, Employment and Society* 2, 4 (1988): 487–505.
31. Stinson and Richmond, 'Women Working for Unions', 150.
32. Cunnison and Stageman, *Feminizing the Unions*, 17.
33. Interviews 22, 27.
34. Rosemary Warskett, 'Defining Who We Are: Solidarity Through Diversity in the Ontario Labour Movement', in Colin Leys and Marguerite Mendell, eds, *Culture and Social Change: Social Movements in Quebec and Ontario* (Montreal, 1992), 109–27.
35. Panitch and Swartz, *The Assault on Trade Union Freedoms*, 20.
36. Warskett, 'Defining Who We Are', 111.
37. Stinson and Richmond, 'Women Working for Unions'; Warskett, 'Defining Who We Are'.
38. Dulude, 'Seniority and Employment Equity for Women'; Pateman, *The Disorder of Women*; Phillips, *Democracy and Difference*.
39. Dulude, 'Seniority and Employment', 48.
40. Cunnison and Stageman, *Feminizing the Unions*, 150–68.
41. Cynthia Cockburn, 'Strengthening the Representation of Trade Union Women in the European Social Dialogue,' *European Journal of Women's Studies* (1996): 7–26.
42. Linda Briskin, 'Union Women and Separate Organizing', in Briskin and McDermott, eds, *Women Challenging Unions*, 89–108.
43. Leah, 'Black Women Speak Out', 157–71.
44. Warskett, 'Defining Who We Are'.
45. J.G. Gelman and J.D. Blackburn, *Labor Relations: Law, Practice and Policy*, 2nd edn (Mineola, 1983), 236, cited in Dulude, 'Seniority and Employment', 43.
46. White, *Sisters and Solidarity*, 76.
47. Ibid., 77.
48. Dulude, 'Seniority and Employment', 2.
49. Ibid., 39–42.
50. Fred Gaboury, *Labour Today* (July-Aug. 1977): 1, 6, cited ibid., 92.
51. Ibid.; Corman and Luxton, 'Getting to Work'.
52. White, *Sisters and Solidarity*, 76–85.
53. Dulude, 'Seniority and Employment', 199–204.

54. Ibid., 218. The Canadian Auto Workers' union attempted to bargain similar affirmative action measures with less success. See White, *Sisters and Solidarity*, 77–9.
55. Wallace Clement and John Myles, *Relations of Ruling: Class and Gender in Postindustrial Societies* (Montreal and Kingston, 1994).
56. Judy Fudge has suggested that unions need to embrace broader-based bargaining units that expand beyond individual workplaces in order to organize contingent workers. She argues that women and other marginalized workers have been ill-served by the fragmentation of bargaining units and rivalry between unions. Fudge, 'The Gendered Dimension of Labour Law', 231–48.
57. Hallock, *Unions and the Gender Wage Gap*, 25.
58. Warskett, 'Can a Disappearing Pie Be Shared Equally?', 261.
59. Ibid.
60. Dulude, 'Seniority and Employment', 219–24.
61. Hallock, *Unions and the Gender Wage Gap*, 25–6.
62. Warskett, 'Can a Disappearing Pie Be Shared Equally?', 262.
63. Ibid.
64. Hallock, *Unions and the Gender Wage Gap*; Warskett, 'Can a Disappearing Pie Be Shared Equally?'; Joan Acker, 'Pay Equity in Sweden and Other Nordic Countries', in Fudge and McDermott, eds, *Just Wages*, 247–53.
65. White, *Sisters and Solidarity*, 70–1.
66. For example, see Fudge and McDermott, eds, *Just Wages*.
67. Hallock, *Unions and the Gender Wage Gap*, 23–4.
68. This strategy was successful in the campaign for pay equity in Oregon. See Acker, *Doing Comparable Worth*; Hallock, *Unions and the Gender Wage Gap*.

Appendix

1. For discussions of historical research in sociology, see Philip Abrams, *Historical Sociology* (Ithaca, NY, 1982); Theda Skocpol, *Vision and Method in Historical Sociology* (Cambridge, 1984); Dennis Smith, *The Rise of Historical Sociology* (Philadelphia, 1991).
2. Archival material relating to the company's bargaining strategies, job evaluation, and personnel policies is not available in collections deposited by BC Electric or in the BC Hydro library. Nor did I request access to any current company files. The confidential nature of this material made company permission to view such files highly unlikely. Moreover, the focus of this research was clearly on union rather than management practices in negotiating racialized-gender relations at work.

Thus, the only material requested from BC Hydro, which the company did provide, was information about job evaluation systems and the distribution of employees in the company.

3. Creese, 'The OPEIU at B.C. Hydro'.

4. On qualitative research, see Anselm Strauss and Juliet Corbin, *Basics of Qualitative Research: Grounded Theory Procedures and Techniques* (Newbury Park, Calif., 1990); Jim Thomas, *Doing Critical Ethnography* (Newbury Park, Calif., 1993).

5. Gillian Creese, 'Power and Pay: The Union and Equal Pay at B.C. Electric/Hydro', *Labour/Le Travail* 32 (Fall 1993): 225–45; Creese, 'Gender Equity or Masculine Privilege?'; Creese, 'Gendering Collective Bargaining'.

6. Beverley Skeggs, *Formations of Class and Gender* (London, 1997), 30–3.

7. Haraway, *Simians, Cyborgs, and Women*, 188.

8. For recent reviews of Canadian contributions to this debate, see Joy Parr, 'Gender History and Historical Practice', *Canadian Historical Review* (Sept. 1995): 354–76; Joan Sangster, 'Beyond Dichotomies: Re-Assessing Gender History and Women's History in Canada', *Left History* 3, 1 (Spring-Summer 1995): 109–21.

9. To give one example, debates in Marxist feminism in the 1970s often included theoretical discussions of gender identities. See, for example, the classic text by Michele Barrett, *Women's Oppression Today: Problems in Marxist Feminist Analysis* (London, 1980).

10. For other examples of materialist and post-colonial analyses by sociologists that focus on connections between gender, race, and class, see Anthias and Yuval-Davis, *Racialised Boundaries*; Bannerji, ed., *Returning the Gaze*; Collins, *Black Feminist Thought*; Stasiulis and Yuval-Davis, eds, *Unsettling Settler Societies*.

Index

Aboriginal peoples, 27, 59, 163, 164, 168, 179, 200, 212, 215, 217, 239 n.19, 239 n.20, 258 n.62; cultural genocide, 27; marginalization, 27, 58; population, 255 n.3, 258 n.62; resistance, 27; women, 22

Absenteeism, 72

Accounting department, 9, 92, 104, 112, 170

Acker, Joan, 22

Activists, 32, 134, 146, 154–5, 158, 160, 162, 204 208, 220–2, 224, 242 n.57

Administrative revolution, 17

Affirmative action, 30, 157, 161, 177, 179, 187, 188, 199

Allied Hydro Council of British Columbia, 46

Anti-racist caucuses, 31, 32

Appearance. *See* Women, appearance of

Arnott, Fred, 38

Asia, 58–9, 85, 184, 239 n.20

Australia, 18, 21, 31

Authority, 26, 27

Automation, 54, 86

Automobile industry, 30

Avis Rent-a-Car, 47, 48, 251 n.15

Bargaining. *See* Union, bargaining

Bargaining certificate, 39

Benefits, 35, 36, 37, 40

Blue-collar workers. *See* Workers, blue-collar

Bone, Ron, 46, 51

Bourdieu, Pierre, 244 n.2

Breadwinner rights, 56–85. *See also* Masculine, breadwinner

Briskin, Linda, 210

Britain, 31, 58

British colonialism, 58

British colonization, 27

British Columbia: fiscal restraint, 53; government of, 255 n.3, 257 n.27; labour force, 84, 238 n.8, 239 n.17, 244 n.5; Labour legislation, 40, 44, 190; Ministry of Labour, 114; nationalization of BC Electric, 45; public-sector downsizing, 53

British Columbia Electric Island, 45

British Columbia Electric Office Employees' Association. *See* Office Employees' Association

British Columbia Electric Railway Company, 5, 8, 34, 35, 36, 37, 40, 42, 44, 89, 102, 107, 108, 110; administration, 45; control, 38; customer service, 45; discriminatory hiring, 61, 64–5, 67, 69, 72, 85; discriminatory pay practice, 40, 63; gendered division of labour, 70; general

secretary, 40; job reclassification, 41, 68, 81–2, 85; masculine privilege, 84–5; president, 34, 39, 40; restructuring, 44–5; supervisory staff, 41. *See also* British Columbia Hydro and Power Authority
British Columbia Engineering, 44, 50
British Columbia Federation of Labour, 49, 50, 141–2, 166; Women's Rights Conference, 141
British Columbia Government Employees' Union (BCGEU), 51
British Columbia Hydro and Power Authority, 5, 14, 15, 32, 45, 47, 48, 74, 76, 90, 111, 112, 113, 114, 116, 119, 127, 128, 132, 137, 139, 142, 145, 163, 174, 186, 187, 202, 206–7, 217–18, 222, 228 n.7, 236 n.28, 248 n.77, 251 n.15, 252 n.28, 253 n.61, 256 n.14, 258 n.61, 265 n.2; Local 378, 51; bargaining committee, 236; Board of Directors, 190; Committee on Women's Rights, 141; control of job evaluation, 128; discriminatory wages, 40, 63, 78; discriminatory hiring, 61, 64–5, 67, 69, 72; employees, 258 n.61; 'gender discrimination', 136, 149, 154, 157, 162; gendered division of labour, 70; jurisdictional conflicts, 116; Manpower Development Committee, 48; technocratic organization, 23, 160
British Columbia Power Commission, 45, 46
British Columbia Trades and Labour Congress, 42
Business representatives. *See* Union organization
Business unionism, 38, 212–13

Cafeteria work. *See* Work, cafeteria
Canadian Auto Workers, 264 n.54

Canadian Congress of Labour (CCL), 41, 49
Canadian Labour Congress, 29, 49
Canadian labour laws, 14
Canadian Union of Public Employees (CUPE), 51
Canadian unions, 31, 47, 215
Career ladder. *See* Job ladder
Career mobility, 163, 198, 199; for men, 92, 93, 107, 164, 165, 175, 185, 205; for women, 10, 18, 53, 90, 170
Caseco, 47, 251 n.15
CBA Engineering, 47
Child care. *See* Day care
China, 58–9, 239 n.13
Chinese Immigration Act, 239 n.13
CIO unions, 32, 41
Civil rights movement, 135
Class, 2, 3, 33, 202, 221; differences, 25; location of jobs, 25; middle class, 4, 18, 22, 26, 27, 29, 203; working class (blue-collar), 2, 22, 25, 29, 59
Class consciousness, 6, 18, 25, 130
Class divisions; blue-collar/white-collar, 18; management/clerical, 18; mental/manual, 25. *See also* Racialized-gendering
Clerical men, technical, 87–9, 91–5, 98, 101–33. *See* Masculine, office workers; Work, clerical, male
Cockburn, Cynthia, 21, 31, 209
Collective agreements, 30, 40, 41, 45, 46, 50–5, 67, 109, 112, 113, 117, 118, 202, 224, 236 n.19, 243 n.77, 248 n.85, 254 n.73, 256 n.25
Collective bargaining, 7, 29, 30, 34, 36, 38, 39, 50–5, 79, 82, 85, 88, 129, 144, 147, 160, 172, 208, 210, 227; and gendering, 24, 33, 47, 67, 70, 162, 202, 203; and politics, 49. *See also* Union, bargaining
Collins, Patricia Hill, 33

THE CANADIAN SOCIAL HISTORY SERIES

Terry Copp,
The Anatomy of Poverty:
The Condition of the Working Class
in Montreal, 1897–1929, 1974.
ISBN 0–7710–2252–2

Alison Prentice,
The School Promoters:
Education and Social Class in
Mid-Nineteenth Century
Upper Canada, 1977.
ISBN 0–7710–7181–7

John Herd Thompson,
The Harvests of War:
The Prairie West, 1914–1918, 1978.
ISBN 0–19–541402–0

Joy Parr, Editor,
Childhood and Family in Canadian
History, 1982.
ISBN 0–7710–6938–3

Alison Prentice and
Susan Mann Trofimenkoff, Editors,
The Neglected Majority:
Essays in Canadian Women's History,
Volume 2, 1985.
ISBN 0–7710–8583–4

Ruth Roach Pierson,
'They're Still Women After All':
The Second World War and
Canadian Womanhood, 1986.
ISBN 0–7710–6958–8

Bryan D. Palmer,
The Character of Class Struggle:
Essays in Canadian Working-Class
History, 1850–1985, 1986.
ISBN 0–7710–6946–4

Alan Metcalfe,
Canada Learns to Play:
The Emergence of Organized Sport,
1807–1914, 1987.
ISBN 0–19–541304–0

Marta Danylewycz,
Taking the Veil:
An Alternative to Marriage,
Motherhood, and Spinsterhood in
Quebec, 1840–1920, 1987.
ISBN 0–7710–2550–5

Craig Heron,
Working in Steel: The Early Years in
Canada, 1883–1935, 1988.
ISBN 0–7710–4086–5

Wendy Mitchinson and
Janice Dickin McGinnis, Editors,
Essays in the History of
Canadian Medicine, 1988.
ISBN 0–7710–6063–7

Joan Sangster,
Dreams of Equality: Women on the
Canadian Left, 1920–1950, 1989.
ISBN 0–7710–7946–X

Angus McLaren,
Our Own Master Race: Eugenics in
Canada, 1885–1945, 1990.
ISBN 0–19–541365–2

Bruno Ramirez,
On the Move:
French-Canadian and Italian Migrants
in the North Atlantic Economy,
1860–1914, 1991.
ISBN 0–19–541419–5

Mariana Valverde,
The Age of Light, Soap, and Water:
Moral Reform in English Canada,
1885–1925, 1991.
ISBN 0–7710–8689–X

Bettina Bradbury,
Working Families:
Age, Gender, and Daily Survival in
Industrializing Montreal, 1993.
ISBN 0–19–541211–7

Andrée Lévesque,
*Making and Breaking the Rules:
Women in Quebec, 1919–1939*, 1994.
ISBN 0–7710–5283–9

Cecilia Danysk,
*Hired Hands: Labour and the
Development of Prairie Agriculture,
1880–1930*, 1995.
ISBN 0–7710–2552–1

Kathryn McPherson,
*Bedside Matters: The Transformation
of Canadian Nursing, 1900–1990*, 1996.
ISBN 0–19–541219–2

Edith Burley,
*Servants of the Honourable Company:
Work, Discipline, and Conflict in the
Hudson's Bay Company, 1770–1870*,
1997.
ISBN 0–19–541296–6

Mercedes Steedman,
*Angels of the Workplace: Women and
the Construction of Gender Relations in
the Canadian Clothing Industry,
1890–1940*, 1997.
ISBN 0–19–541308–3

**Angus McLaren and
Arlene Tigar McLaren,**
*The Bedroom and the State: The
Changing Practices and Politics of
Contraception and Abortion in Canada,
1880–1997*, 1997.
ISBN 0–19–541318–0

**Kathryn McPherson, Cecilia
Morgan, and Nancy M. Forestell,
Editors,**
*Gendered Pasts: Historical Essays in
Femininity and Masculinity in Canada,*
1999.
ISBN 0–19–541449–7

Gillian Creese,
*Contracting Masculinity: Gender,
Class, and Race in a White-Collar
Union, 1944–1994*, 1999.
ISBN 0–19–541454–3